F2892

Leaders' Personalities and the Outcomes of Democratic Elections

EDITED BY

ANTHONY KING

OXFORD
UNIVERSITY PRESS

OXFORD

UNIVERSITY PRESS

Great Clarendon Street, Oxford OX2 6DP

Oxford University Press is a department of the University of Oxford.
It furthers the University's objective of excellence in research, scholarship,
and education by publishing worldwide in

Oxford New York

Auckland Bangkok Buenos Aires Cape Town Chennai
Dar es Salaam Delhi Hong Kong Istanbul Karachi Kolkata
Kuala Lumpur Madrid Melbourne Mexico City Mumbai Nairobi
São Paulo Shanghai Singapore Taipei Tokyo Toronto

with an associated company in Berlin

Published in the United States
by Oxford University Press Inc., New York

© Anthony King 2002

First published 2002

British Library Cataloguing in Publication Data

Data available

Library of Congress Cataloging in Publication Data
Leaders' personalities and the outcomes of democratic elections/edited by Anthony King.
p. cm.
1. Elections. 2. Personality and politics. 3. Presidential candidates.
4. Political parties. 5. Political science. I. King, Anthony Stephen.
JF1001.L38 2002   324.9—dc21   2001059144
ISBN 0–19–829791–2
ISBN 0–19–925313–7 (Pbk.)

1 3 5 7 9 10 8 6 4 2

Typeset by Hope Services (Abingdon) Ltd.
Printed in Great Britain
on acid-free paper by
T. J. International Ltd.,
Padstow, Cornwall

CONTENTS

LIST OF TABLES

LIST OF FIGURES

NOTES ON CONTRIBUTORS

Larry M. Bartels is Donald E. Stokes Professor of Public and International Affairs, Princeton University

John Bartle is Lecturer in Government, University of Essex

Frank Brettschneider is Professor of Political Communication, University of Augsburg

Timothy J. Colton is Director of the Davis Center for Russian Studies, Harvard University

Ivor Crewe is Vice-Chancellor and Professor of Government, University of Essex

Oscar W. Gabriel is Professor of Political Science, Institute for Social Research, University of Stuttgart

Richard Johnston is Professor of Political Science, University of British Columbia, and research associate of the Annenberg Public Policy Center, University of Pennsylvania

Anthony King is Essex County Council Millennium Professor of British Government, University of Essex

Roy Pierce is Professor of Political Science, University of Michigan

1

Do Leaders' Personalities
Really Matter?

ANTHONY KING

Almost every casual conversation during a national election campaign contains references to the personal characteristics of major party leaders and candidates. In the United States in 2000, George W. Bush was said to be affable and relaxed but at the same time ruthless and not desperately bright, while Al Gore was described as arrogant, wooden, and verbose but, at the same time, oddly unsure of himself. On the other side of the Atlantic in 2001, the British prime minister, Tony Blair, was said to be youthful, vigorous, and dynamic—or, alternatively, smarmy, smug and unctuous—while the then Conservative leader, William Hague, was usually dismissed as a political lightweight—in British parlance, as "a bit of a wally." French commentators in the 1990s uniformly paid tribute to Lionel Jospin's doggedness and evident sincerity. To many Germans during the 1998 federal election Helmut Kohl seemed old and tired (as well as fat) while Gerhard Schröder seemed more vigorous and "charismatic" (as well as possibly somewhat glib and superficial). Comments along these lines are the small change of electoral politics in every country at all times.

Moreover, leaders' and candidates' personal characteristics are thought to be important; they are thought to matter. Those who earnestly contemplated Pierre Trudeau's sex life in the Canada of the 1970s, or Boris Yeltsin's drinking habits when he ran for the presidency of Russia in 1996, did not imagine that they were engaging in idle gossip. They took it for granted that the personalities and personal behavior of these leaders, especially as compared with those of their opponents, were likely to sway the votes of individual electors and thereby, quite possibly, the outcomes of whole elections. This belief in the importance of leaders' personal characteristics underlies much of the talk of the "presidentialization" of modern election campaigns, even in countries with parliamentary systems of government.[1]

---

[1] On whether or not presidentialization is actually occurring, see, among other things, Ivor Crewe and Anthony King, "Are British Elections Becoming More 'Presidential'?" in M. Kent Jennings and Thomas E. Mann, eds., *Elections at Home and Abroad: Essays in Honor of Warren*

In view of some of the things to be said later in this volume, we need to emphasize the ubiquity and centrality of this kind of political discourse. For example, newspaper headlines during the 1997 election campaign in Great Britain frequently focused on the two main party leaders. "Never mind the policies," one of them read, "just feel the leaders." Others read: "Why women don't trust Tony Blair," "Do you know anyone who actually *likes* Tony Blair?" "Major is just not up to the job," "More than ever, Major is Tories' prime asset" and "Leaders in trial of strength."[2] And there was more—much more—of the same. Similarly, following John Major's defeat in the 1997 election and his replacement as Conservative leader by William Hague, media comment and saloon-bar conversation alike concentrated on Hague's premature baldness and his efforts to portray himself as even younger than he was.

As though that were not enough, one British newspaper pointed to one of the challenges allegedly facing the new leader under the headline: "We need a Hague baby, say Tories." The accompanying report claimed that:

For the Tory party still struggling to come to terms with its crushing election defeat, help may be at hand.

Research has uncovered the secret to a revival in electoral fortunes. New policies? A new image? No, something far more fundamental is needed.

William Hague and his bride-to-be Ffion must have a baby as soon as possible if they are to have any chance of resurrecting the Tories' appeal, the research shows.

Voters believe Mr Hague's abysmal ratings will increase considerably if he sports the family image cultivated by Tony Blair.[3]

Similarly, in the United States three years later a political scientist attributed a sudden drop in support for the Democratic candidate, Al Gore, to his "smart-alecky" performance in the first of the presidential debates: "Voters found his demeanor snide, rude and offensive, characteristics they don't like in a president." He added that Gore "just came across as not very likeable" while his Republican opponent, George W. Bush, "verbal stumbles and all, just seemed more human."[4] Reporting on the second of the debates, *USA Today* commented on Gore's efforts to compensate for his earlier shortcomings:

E. Miller (Ann Arbor: University of Michigan Press, 1994) and Max Kaase, "Is There Personalization in Politics? Candidates and Voting Behavior in Germany," *International Political Science Review*, 15 (1994), 211–30.

  [2] *Observer*, August 28, 1996, p. 13; *Daily Mail*, April 29, 1997, p. 8; *Daily Telegraph*, March 25, 1997, p. 24; *The Times*, April 22, 1997, p. 22; *Mail on Sunday*, April 13, 1997, p. 7; *Guardian*, April 22, 1997, p. 13.

  [3] *Express*, December 4, 1997, p. 17.

  [4] Mark Rozell of the Catholic University of America, quoted in *USA Today*, October 10, 2000, p. A1.

His makeup was far more natural than last week's slathered-on paste. He was conversational rather than confrontational. He cautiously added qualifiers to his statements and apologized for being careless about details . . . Gore even mocked his aggressiveness last week. "May I respond? I don't want to jump in," Gore said during a discussion of hate crimes.

Bush meanwhile was anxiously appearing "knowledgeable and presidential."[5]

There was even serious discussion of which make of automobile each of the two candidates most resembled. According to the *New York Times*, a political advisor to the governor of California asked voters in focus groups: "If Al Gore and George W. Bush were cars, what would they be?" The responses were thought to be significant:

"Among men, Gore is viewed as a Ford Taurus, a Chevy station wagon, a Volvo, safe and kind of boxy," said Garry South, the chief political aide for Mr. [Gray] Davis, a Democrat. "With Bush, you get things like Maserati and Mustang convertible, and by no means all of the men who say that are doing it pejoratively. They're saying: 'Wait a minute; that guy's like who I'd like to be.' "[6]

As in the British case, there was more—much more—of the same.[7]

These examples relate, of course, to only two countries during only two election campaigns; but most readers will recognize that reports and comments like these could be replicated in almost every country during almost all campaigns. The concentration on leaders' personalities and other personal characteristics—sometimes trivial, as in most of the above instances, sometimes more serious—often borders on the obsessional.

But is it justified? Are the personas of leaders and candidates as important in determining the outcomes of democratic elections as is usually supposed? This book's purpose is to ask this central question and to provide at least tentative answers to it.

The issue of whether or not leaders' and candidates' personalities and personal characteristics are important is one that clearly deserves to be taken seriously and seriously addressed. It is, therefore, surprising to discover that political scientists and other social scientists, especially outside the United States, have had relatively little to say on the subject. Published writings are relatively sparse and sustained empirical research even more so, with the result that an assiduous student could absorb the entire relevant academic literature in less than a week. This is, in fact, the first comparative volume ever devoted to the subject.

---

[5] *USA Today*, October 12, 2000, p. A5.   [6] *New York Times*, October 8, 2000, p. 1.

[7] Autotrader.com, a website for would-be purchasers of used cars, also asked people—this time in an online poll—what kind of car they thought Bush and Gore most resembled. Bush came out as a Porsche 911, Gore, again, as a Volvo. In a commentary on the poll, Marjorie Williams noted: "The Volvo, you see, is a Mom Car. It's safe. It's boxy. It has the power of incumbency." By contrast, she added: "The Porsche Carrera 911 . . . is a Male Menopause Car." Williams seemed to be at least half serious. *New York Times*, October 6, 2000, p. A31.

This lack of interest on the part of political scientists is all the more surprising because the subject is important on a number of different levels. Most obviously, it is important for the reasons already alluded to: namely, that leaders' personalities and personal characteristics may (or may not) play a large part in determining how individuals vote in democratic elections and thereby in determining the outcomes of those elections. In other words, leadership effects are, or ought to be, central to the academic study of voting behavior and elections.

But the importance of the topic goes much wider than that. In the first place, the belief among politicians that leaders' and candidates' personalities determine the outcomes of elections—whether accurate or not—has a profound influence on the way they campaign; election campaigns in most democratic countries today are leader-centered rather than ideology-centered or policy-centered. Second, political leaders' influence and power, including their influence and power in government, are partly determined by their fellow politicians' beliefs about their personal election-winning capacity or their lack of it; for instance, whether or not a U.S. presidential candidate is thought to have "coattails" plays a considerable part in determining the extent of his influence on other politicians, including after he becomes president. Finally, and perhaps most signficantly, politicians' beliefs about the importance of leaders' personalities and other personal characteristics—and about which specific traits and characteristics are especially important—have a profound bearing on who they actually choose as leaders and candidates; John F. Kennedy spent much of 1960 persuading fellow Democrats that a Roman Catholic was, after all, capable of being elected president of the United States, and the first woman to mount a serious challenge for the U.S. presidency will inevitably be engaged in much the same activity.

The chapters that follow explore the importance of leadership effects in the modern electoral politics of the United States, Great Britain, France, Germany, Canada, and Russia. Before we proceed to consider each of these countries in turn, however, there are a number of preliminary points that need to be made. The subject, it turns out, is not only important: it is also very complicated—more complicated than may at first appear.

Indirect and Direct Effects

The first point that needs to be made is perhaps the most important, because it explains what this book is *not* about as well as what it is.

A few moments' reflection suggests that a political leader could have an influence on individual voters and on the outcome of a national election in either or both of two quite distinct ways. The first we can label "indirect." Indirect influence is exerted when a leader influences voters, not as a result of anything he or she *is*, but as a result of things that he or she *does*. Influence of this type is exerted indirectly via the leader's influence on, typically, either his political party or his government or administration. The leader who succeeds in changing his party's ideology or modernizing its image is exercising influence in this indirect sense.

Such indirect influence can be, and often is, enormously important. To say that it is indirect is not in any way to diminish its significance. On the contrary, a leader's indirect influence over his party or government may constitute by far his greatest contribution to his or his party's electoral success. François Mitterrand almost certainly won the 1981 French presidential election and led his Socialist and radical alliance to victory in the subsequent parliamentary elections, not because he was François Mitterrand (he had been François Mitterrand for a very long time and, as such, had lost two previous presidential elections), but because he had succeeded in transforming the ideology and image, and even the name, of the French Socialist Party.[8] Margaret Thatcher was never particularly popular as a person, but, largely because of the way in which she led her party and government, the Conservatives under her leadership dominated British electoral politics for the best part of a generation between 1979 and 1990.[9]

Furthermore, it is not denied here—on the contrary, it is robustly asserted—that indirect electoral influence of this kind may owe a great deal to the personality of the leader in question. Indeed the leader's personality, in the first instance, is likely to bear most forcefully of all on his or her immediate party colleagues and thus on his or her party or government. It was François Mitterrand's political cunning and guile—and his innate secretiveness—that enabled him to turn around the French Socialist Party.[10] It was Margaret Thatcher's tenacity and refusal to see both sides of any question that enabled her during the 1980s to dominate first the Conservative Party and then her Conservative administration.[11] More recently, Tony Blair transformed the

---

[8] For brief accounts of the transformation of the French Socialist Party, see Vincent Wright, *The Government and Politics of France*, 3rd edn. (London: Unwin Hyman, 1989), chap. 10, and Jack Hayward, "Ideological Change: The Exhaustion of the Revolutionary Impetus," in Peter A. Hall, Jack Hayward, and Howard Machin, eds., *Developments in French Politics* (Basingstoke, Hants.: Macmillan, 1990).

[9] On Thatcher's relative unpopularity, see Ivor Crewe, "Has the Electorate Become Thatcherite?" in Robert Skidelsky, ed., *Thatcherism* (London: Chatto & Windus, 1988); and Anthony King, ed., *British Political Opinion 1937–2000: The Gallup Polls* (London: Politico's, 2001), chap. 7.

[10] Vincent Wright attributes a large part of the French Socialist Party's success in the 1980s to Mitterrand's brilliant leadership: "Helped by his 'court' (composed of close friends), he dominated his party to such an extent that he earned for himself the nickname[s] of 'the Prince' and 'the Pope'. Mitterrand was an indefatigable organizer, a shrewd and tough negotiator and an ambitious politician. He managed to out-manoeuvre all his party opponents first to grasp and then to retain his leadership of the party." *Government and Politics of France*, p. 224.

[11] On the role that Thatcher's personality played in her career as Conservative leader and prime minister, see Hugo Young, *One of Us: A Biography of Margaret Thatcher*, 2nd edn. (London: Macmillan, 1991); and Anthony King, "Margaret Thatcher as a Political Leader," in Skidelsky, ed., *Thatcherism*.

British Labour Party in a way that his predecessor, John Smith, would never have done. Smith had been relaxed and comfortable; by contrast, Blair was hungry.[12]

But indirect effects of the type just described, however important they often are in the internal affairs of parties and governments, and however important they may be in influencing individual voters and election outcomes, are not what this book is about. This book is, rather, about the direct effects of leaders' personalities and personal characteristics on the voters they seek to woo and the elections they seek to win. And by "direct" effects is meant the influence that a leader or candidate exerts on voters by virtue of who he or she is, how he or she appears and how he or she publicly comports him or herself. The distinction is set out schematically in Figure 1.1. To take a somewhat far-fetched example, the distinction is that between the influence that Karl Marx exerted on future generations via his writings and the influence that he exerted on his immediate contemporaries via his acid tongue, forceful physical presence and dominating intellect.[13] The first type of influence was indirect, the second direct. A dead man can wield indirect influence; he cannot wield direct influence. A living man or woman can wield both.

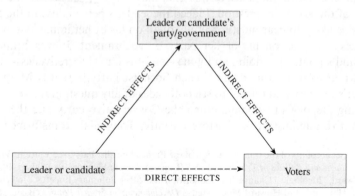

Fig. 1.1. Paths of potential leader or candidate influence

---

[12] On John Smith's lack of interest in transforming the Labour Party, and Tony Blair's passionate insistence on doing so, see John Rentoul, *Tony Blair: Prime Minister* (London: Little, Brown, 2001), esp. chaps. 8–14; Jon Sopel, *Tony Blair: The Moderniser* (London: Michael Joseph, 1995); Patrick Seyd, "Tony Blair and New Labour," in Anthony King, ed., *New Labour Triumphs: Britain at the Polls* (Chatham, N.J.: Chatham House, 1997); and Philip Gould, *The Unfinished Revolution: How the Modernisers Saved the Labour Party* (London: Little, Brown, 1998).

[13] A recent biography of Marx (Francis Wheen, *Karl Marx* (London: Fourth Estate, 1999)) contains numerous examples of Marx's capacity to influence directly—by the sheer force of his personality—those around him. A contemporary described him as "a born leader of the people," adding: "His speech was brief, convincing and compelling in its logic. He never said a superfluous word . . . Marx had nothing of the dreamer about him" (p. 117).

The case for focusing narrowly and exclusively on direct rather than indirect effects is a straightforward one: they are the ones that almost everyone has in mind when they talk about leaders' and candidates' electoral importance, and they are also the ones that political scientists have to a considerable extent neglected. It is worth noting that all the examples cited at the beginning of this chapter refer exclusively to leaders' personal qualities and to the (alleged) relationship between these qualities and the voting decisions of individuals. If Al Gore were less like a Chevy wagon or Volvo, he would win more votes; if Ffion Hague had a baby, her husband would look more like a family man and would therefore attract more votes to the Conservative Party. *Tout court.*

This point about the (alleged) importance of direct personality effects is worth emphasizing because of course it is precisely direct effects of this type that politicians—and, even more, their image-makers and media advisors—have in mind when they try to present their leader or candidate in the best possible light. If it turned out that direct effects were not desperately important, or were important only on rare occasions, then it would also turn out that a great deal of campaign consultants' time and money would have been wasted. It is because they believe in the importance of direct personality effects that image-makers subject their clients to elocution lessons, hair transplants, face-lifts, heavy make-up, and all manner of undignified photo-opportunities.

These effects, if they exist, have been described as "direct," but it goes without saying that in the modern world they are not strictly direct but are, rather, mediated by television, radio, the press, and, increasingly, the internet. No one who was not physically in his presence ever saw or heard Abraham Lincoln, William Gladstone, Adolphe Thiers, Otto von Bismarck, or Sir Wilfrid Laurier. Television is now so pervasive that voters think they know people they have never met. As a result, whereas in the nineteenth century, even in democracies, leaders' and candidates' direct influence could be exerted, if at all, only by word of mouth and through the press, in the twentieth and twenty-first centuries the possibilities for direct influence have been enormously increased.

There is no doubt that the possibilities for direct influence *have* increased, but how great, as a matter of fact, is that influence in determining the outcomes of elections in the modern world? That is the question that needs to be explored.

Personality and Personal Characteristics

So far we have used the phrase "personality and personal characteristics" rather vaguely and in a generic sense. What do we mean by the phrase in the present context?

Broadly, the reference is to four attributes of party leaders or presidential candidates: their physical appearance, their native intelligence, their character or temperament, and their political style. With the exception of intelligence, about which not a great deal can be done, each of these elements is to some extent manipulable. A woman cannot become a man, a short person cannot become a tall one, an ugly person cannot easily be transmogrified into a handsome or beautiful one; but within those broad bands a fair amount can be achieved, by means of careful grooming, the judicious choice of clothes, and the careful modulation of the voice. Likewise, although a person's underlying personality or character may not be open to manipulation, his or her "presentation of self"—his or her persona—certainly is. The leader or candidate's political style—the way in which he or she operates in the political world—is also to a considerable extent a matter of choice.

This is not the place to catalog all of the personal attributes that might conceivably have a bearing on individual voters' decisions and hence on overall election outcomes, but a full list would undoubtedly include the ones set out—in the form of a list of adjectives and adjectival phrases—in Table 1.1. The list in the table is set out in strictly alphabetical order, certainly not in any order of presumed or actual importance. Whether or not someone is, in fact, "effective" or "honest" is obviously highly relevant to the likelihood of that person's performing well in high office, and for that reason voters' perceptions of competing candidates' effectiveness and honesty might be expected to influence their vote. By contrast, whether or not a leader or candidate is "good-looking" or "likeable" might be thought to be less relevant to that person's probable performance in office; voters may nevertheless be influenced by touchy-feely, seemingly non-political, characteristics of this type. What, if anything, does influence them is a matter for empirical investigation.[14]

However, it must be emphasized that these kinds of considerations—concerning which attributes might be thought most likely to influence voters' decisions—are largely irrelevant for our purposes. The reason is that, before determining *which* attributes of leaders and candidates have a direct effect on the vote, we need first to determine whether *any* of them do. There is no point in discovering, for example, that voters evaluate most favorably leaders and candidates who are "effective," "strong," and "tough" if it turns out that their evaluations of leaders seldom, if ever, affect what they actually do in the

---

[14] More investigative effort has gone into identifying the personal characteristics of leaders that most impress voters than into ascertaining whether leaders' characteristics actually influence voters in the way they cast their ballots. In other words, much of the research (see the Select Bibliography at the end of this volume) takes as its major premise an assumption that may, or may not, be true. For what it is worth, most of the research suggests that, in evaluating leaders and candidates, most voters are more interested in leaders' actual and potential effectiveness in office than they are in whether or not the individuals in question are likeable human beings. In other words, most voters appear to distinguish between the qualities they would like to see in their president, prime minister, or chancellor and the qualities they would like to see in the man or woman next door.

Table 1.1. Personal attributes that might have a bearing on vote decisions

Bold	Intelligent
Caring	Likeable
Competent	Principled
Decisive	Self-disciplined
Determined	Shrewd
Effective	Sincere
Experienced	Strong
Fair-minded	Tough
Friendly	Trustworthy
Goodhumored	Vigorous
Good-looking	Warm
Honest	Willing to listen to reason
Inspiring	Youthful

privacy of the polling place—or that, even if they do affect them, they seldom go on to affect overall election outcomes. To us, what goes on in an individual voter's psyche is of interest only if it influences his or her behavior. Putting it bluntly, people's mental states are politically irrelevant unless they influence actual votes—and do so in substantial numbers.

One final point needs to be made about "personality and personal characteristics"—a point about what the phrase does *not* encompass. It does not encompass, specifically, leaders' and candidates' ideologies or views on policy issues. It does not do so for two reasons. The first is that when most people, including most political scientists, speak of a leader or candidate's personality or other personal characteristics they do not have in mind his or her views on inflation, unemployment, or the war on terrorism; they have in mind his or her intelligence, honesty, human warmth, or whatever. It would, to say the least of it, be a very strange use of language to include a person's views on highway tolls as part of his or her personality. The second reason is the obvious one that a person's views may change without his or her personality in any way changing. Harold Wilson, Britain's prime minister in the 1960s and mid 1970s, radically changed his views on British membership of the Common Market (as it then was, the forerunner of the European Union) and on the desirability of reforming Britain's trade unions; but his personality, all observers agree, remained the same.

Why Leaders' Attributes Might be Thought to Matter

Leaders' and candidates' personalities and other personal attributes are widely supposed to influence votes. If such a view were not widespread, there would be no need for anyone to write this book. But what is this widespread supposition based on? Saloon-bar gossip apart, are there solid grounds for supposing that a leader or candidate with one set of personal characteristics is likely to triumph over a leader or candidate with a different set of characteristics?

It has to be said at the outset that the evidence that leaders' personalities influence voters is largely anecdotal. Anthony believes it because Barbara believes it, Barbara believes it because Carol believes it, Carol believes it because Donald believes it—and so on. The belief in the importance of personality and other personal characteristics has become part of the culture, seldom questioned, completely taken for granted. The mass media focus on personalities. So, much of the time, do politicians (most of whom in any case are inveterate gossips). In recent years, the belief in the political importance of personality has undoubtedly owed much, too, to the star system that exists in other spheres of life: in the movies, on the catwalk, and on television. If superstars are undoubtedly big box office, it is hard to imagine that super-politicians are not also big box office.[15] The result is that, although most of the evidence that politicians' personalities influence voters is anecdotal, the weight of such evidence is so great that it is oddly difficult to challenge the notion that they do, indeed, have this effect. Any suggestion that politicians' personalities may not be desperately important—or may not be as important as is often supposed—is liable to be greeted with incredulity, even derision.

Luckily, anecdotal evidence apart, there exist more solid theoretical grounds for the belief that leaders' and candidates' personalities stand a good chance of influencing voters and determining election outcomes. They were laid out a generation ago by David Butler and Donald Stokes in *Political Change in Britain*.[16] Butler and Stokes began by noting that, if any political issue or object is to influence the vote of any individual elector, it has to pass a series of three tests. In the first place, the elector has to have some awareness of the issue or object. In the second place, he or she has to have some strength of feeling about the object—a "genuine attitude" toward it. In the third place, the elector has to identify the issue or object with one or other of the political parties. Failure to pass any one of these tests means that the issue or object in question cannot, in simple logic, influence the vote decision of the elector in question. An elector can hardly be said to have been influenced by a party's pesticides policy if he or she knows nothing about pesticides, or knows something about them but has no views about them, or knows something about them and has views about them but does not think that any one party has a better policy on pesticides than any other. Butler and Stokes also pointed out

---

[15] A good book could be written on the recent expansion of what might be called the "celebrity industry" and on the extent to which top political leaders have become celebrities in the Hollywood style. Few political leaders before World War II were celebrities in the modern sense. Now even the dullest of political leaders is treated as though he or she were a celebrity—or, alternatively, is chastised for not being one. It is a peculiarly modern indictment to say of a political leader that he or she "lacks charisma."

[16] David Butler and Donald Stokes, *Political Change in Britain: The Evolution of Electoral Choice*, 2nd edn. (London: Macmillan, 1974), chap. 17.

that, if an issue or object is to influence the overall outcome of an election, as distinct from the votes of discrete individuals, opinion toward that issue or object needs to be skewed in favor of one or other of the political parties. Large numbers of individual voters may be influenced by an issue, but their individual votes will not affect an overall election outcome if, in effect, they cancel each other out.

The bearing of all this on the potential for major party leaders and candidates to influence individual vote decisions and the outcomes of elections is obvious. National-level leaders and candidates are highly visible; the great majority of voters are aware of them. They usually arouse some strength of feeling. And the great majority of voters, however ignorant on other matters, do actually know which leaders lead which parties. In presidential elections, it may not even be necessary for voters to link presidential candidates with parties: it may be enough for them simply to know that they prefer one candidate—for whom they can vote directly—to another. All that does matter, in both parliamentary and presidential elections, is that the distribution of voters' preferences is sufficiently skewed to affect the outcome.

For the reasons given by Butler and Stokes, and by others who think along the same lines, the idea that leaders' and candidates' personal characteristics influence the outcomes of democratic elections obviously has to be taken seriously. Any suggestion that the opposite was the case—that they have little or no influence—would strike most people as bizarre. Nevertheless, it is possible to make out a strong case pointing in that unexpected direction.

Why Leaders' Attributes Might be Thought Not to Matter

There is, of course, no denying the validity of Butler and Stokes's contentions, first, that major party leaders and candidates are salient to most voters—the great majority of voters do know who they are—and, second, that most voters have views about them, have, in Butler and Stokes's terms, "genuine attitudes" toward them. Very few German voters in 1998 did not know who Helmut Kohl and Gerhard Schröder were and did not have at least some thoughts and feelings about them.

It is, however, a good deal less clear how often such thoughts and feelings are heavily skewed in favor of one leader and against others. Every voter in the land may have views about every leader or candidate running in a given election, but those views will have little or no effect on either individuals' vote decisions or the outcome of the election unless one leader happens to be preferred, and probably strongly preferred, to the others; and a balance of preference that tilts that sharply in favor of one leader or candidate probably occurs less commonly than is often supposed. There are three reasons why leader and candidate preferences are likely, more often than not, to neutralize one another to a considerable extent.

The first is that the political parties, in choosing their leaders and candidates, are likely to confine their choices to people who are reasonably presentable on a personal level. They have a vested interest in *not* choosing as their standard-bearers people who manifestly lack the human qualities needed to appeal to a mass electorate. They are most unlikely, in other words, to choose the aged and infirm, the clinically insane, the obviously stupid, or people with pre-senile dementia, horrendous acne, or a serious speech impediment. In declining to elect or nominate such people, the parties are collectively acting so as to limit the range of persons, personalities, and personal characteristics on offer to the electorate; and, in doing that, they are also acting—though not deliberately—to reduce the chances that leaders' and candidates' personalities will have a significant electoral impact. The choice facing voters at most democratic elections is thus, in personal terms, relatively narrow. It is not between geniuses and dunces or between honest citizens and convicted criminals; it is between a number of individuals all of whom are tolerably personable and tolerably well equipped to appeal to voters and hold public office. Only in the United States, where presidential candidates are chosen by primary electorates rather than party machines, is it at all likely that candidates will be chosen who fall outside this minimal "presentability" range.

The second reason why views of leaders and candidates are seldom likely to be skewed heavily in one direction rather than another relates to the internal mental and emotional life of voters as individuals. Most voters most of the time have somewhat mixed views about the leaders and candidates of most parties. The voter who reckons that one party leader is a cross between Attila the Hun and Adolf Hitler while another contrives to marry the virtues of Charles the Bold, Philip the Good, and Saint Louis of France is likely to be relatively rare, especially in the television age when voters can see for themselves the good and bad points of every one of any country's leading politicians. No survey evidence exists bearing directly on the point, but it seems inconceivable that in 1945 millions of British voters who backed the Labour Party, the party of Clement Attlee, were not also aware of Winston Churchill's claims on their affection and respect. The same was undoubtedly true in the United States in 1996 when Bill Clinton defeated Bob Dole; each candidate's supporters could see defects in their own preferred candidate and at least some redeeming features in his opponent. To the extent that this lack of skewing exists in the minds of individual voters, it must tend to damp down the probability that their own individual vote will be swayed, let alone determined, by the leaders' and candidates' personalities.

The third reason for doubting whether electors' views of leaders and candidates are as heavily skewed as is often supposed is an extension of the second. Just as there is likely to be a rough balance of opinion about leaders and candidates in the minds of individual voters, so there is likely to be a similar balance—or something approaching a balance—among the electorate as a whole. Few people are universally loved and respected; few are universally execrated and held in contempt. Most people do not succeed in arousing passionate feelings in others, and the relatively small number who do are likely to have both admirers and detractors, sometimes in roughly equal numbers. Franklin D. Roosevelt and Margaret Thatcher were hated as well as loved; Richard Nixon and Pierre Trudeau were loved as well as hated. (Thomas E. Dewey, to name but one, was neither.) This tendency for there to be a rough balance of opinion among the electorate as a whole is, of course, reinforced by the parties' tendency to choose leaders and candidates who can be counted upon—they hope—not to alienate voters. Candidates who are not intended to be divisive are unlikely to elicit a divided response.

There are, moreover, other reasons to be suspicious of the idea that leaders' personalities are desperately important in determining election outcomes, reasons suggested as much by ordinary conversation as by the academic literature. One of them has to do with most people's need to simplify. The world of politics is a complicated world, one that most voters are not frightfully interested in and do not know a great deal about. The kinds of abstract expressions that politicians and political commentators typically use—"reinventing government," "downsizing the state," "the third way"—mean little or nothing to most of them. Nor do most voters have in their own vocabularies and modes of thought elaborate means of articulating their own political preferences and the reasons underlying them. Ask someone on an airplane to explain why he or she intends to vote Democratic or Republican at the next presidential election and the response is apt to take the form "Because times are good," or, even more vaguely, "Because the country's lost its way."

Under these circumstances, it is hardly surprising that many voters, pressed by pollsters, television interviewers, and others to expound their political views, fall back on references to leaders, candidates, and their personalities. The complexities of politics are hard; people are (or seem) easy. At the very least, references to people and their personalities constitute a convenient shorthand, a way of avoiding a protracted and possibly difficult discussion. It also, of course, makes a difference that the voters have probably seen the individuals in question on television and formed views about them; and the views they have formed are likely to be real enough. But giving expression to them may simply be a convenient way of summarizing a far more complex array of dispositions and attitudes. At the verbal level, (expressed) responses to persons are likely to be merely surrogates for (unexpressed) responses to more subtle political phenomena—phenomena that may actually be far more important in determining individual vote decisions.

An example from British politics illustrates the point. In the summer of 1999 it was widely reported—with some derision—that the members of focus groups organized by the Conservative Party were no longer to be asked the question, "What single thing could the Conservatives do that would make you more likely to vote for them?" The reason the question was dropped was that the answer invariably came back, "Sack William Hague," Hague at that time being the party's leader—and this response was too embarrassing to report back, especially to Hague.[17] But when a conventional opinion poll subsequently offered respondents a battery of possible reasons for not voting Conservative—such as "The Conservatives did not do a good job when they were in power" and "They are not really interested in public services like health and education"—Hague as an individual turned out to be relatively insignificant, with only 17 percent of respondents (compared with the focus groups' 100 percent) singling him out.[18]

Voters not only simplify, citing leaders, candidates and their personalities when they have other and possibly more important things in mind; they also rationalize—and they may simultaneously both simplify and rationalize. Political commentators are apt to assume (more than do academic political scientists) that, if a survey respondent cites a leader or candidate as a reason for voting for a party, then the causal arrow points straightforwardly from leader-preference to party-preference; but of course the causal arrow may just as easily point the other way, from party-preference to leader-preference. And the same kind of rationalization may take place in the respondent's or voter's own mind; he or she may not realize, or may only half realize, that his or her preference for, say, Schröder over Kohl, owes more to his or her preference for the Social Democratic Party than to any particular liking for Schröder (or dislike of Kohl). Ask a voter who claims she is voting for party A because she likes leader X whether she would still vote for the same party if it were led by leader Y or leader Z and the answer, much more often than not, will be "Yes" (always assuming that leaders Y and Z are, like X, reasonably personally presentable).

All of the above is important as well as true; but it goes without saying that the overriding single reason for questioning the electoral importance of leaders' and candidates' personalities is simply that, as factors in determining voters' decisions and the outcomes of elections, they face so much, and such serious, competition from a wide variety of other factors. Voters do not approach each national election in an intellectual and emotional near-vacuum, one occupied solely by the major parties' leaders and candidates. On the contrary, the great majority of voters bring to each election their own class and other group loyalties, their long-standing partisan likes and dislikes, their personal values, their ideological preferences and, not least, their memories of how well or badly the competing parties have performed in office in the recent or distant past. In addition, each national election presents the voters at that election with specific sets of economic, social, and other circumstances and

---

[17] *Guardian*, August 18, 1999, p. 1.

[18] *Daily Telegraph*, September 3, 1999, p. 8. Many more people chose as reasons for not voting Conservative: "They did not do a good job when they were in power" (24 percent), "They are not really interested in public services like health and education" (21 percent), and "The Conservatives are too weak and divided" (20 percent).

with specific sets of party policies and platforms. In other words, leaders—
who they are, what they look like, and how they present themselves—
represent only a single term in the decision-equations of most individual voters, decision-equations that are often extremely complex. The rest of this book
is devoted to enquiring into just how important this single personality term
actually is.

Analytic Strategies

There is no problem in determining which leaders and candidates are more
popular than others. There is likewise little problem in determining which
particular attributes of leaders and candidates are most esteemed by mass
electorates. The problem lies, rather, in disentangling the effects of leaders'
and candidates' personalities and other personal attributes from the effects of
all the other factors, such as those mentioned in the previous paragraph, that
bear on individuals' vote decisions and overall election outcomes. It may be
that the difficulty of disentangling these factors helps account for the paucity
of political scientists' writings on the subject.

   Three broad analytic strategies for achieving such a disentangling—and for
isolating "pure" leadership effects—suggest themselves. The first is the
experimental strategy. Employing this strategy, a considerable number of
national elections would be run in one or more countries, and in each of these
elections most of the factors that might be thought to determine individuals'
votes and the overall outcome of the election—group loyalties, party identification, ideological preferences, memories of the parties' past performance,
party policies, current economic and other circumstances, etc.—would be
held constant, i.e. controlled for. The only factor that would vary would be
the personalities and other personal characteristics of one or more of the parties' leaders or candidates. The 1996 American presidential election would be
rerun with Bill Clinton chaste instead of wanton and perhaps also aged 73
(Bob Dole's age in 1996) instead of 50; the 1997 general election in Britain
would be rerun with John Smith instead of Tony Blair as Labour leader; the
1998 elections to the German Bundestag would be rerun with an energetic
young woman instead of Helmut Kohl as the Christian Democrats' leader;
and so on. As these examples suggest, the number of personalities and personal characteristics that could, in principle, be varied is almost infinite.

   The only trouble with the experimental strategy is that it is impossible to
execute. Millions of people, including some very famous people (and some
dead ones) would have to be involved, the expense would be prodigious, and
in any case there is no way in which the unique circumstances of a national
election in any country could be reproduced after the event. An additional
complicating factor, though not a fatal one, is that, in any experimental
design, decisions would have to be taken concerning the point at which, and

the circumstances under which, one or more of the leaders' attributes were to be varied. Many leaders and candidates have a considerable influence on their own parties and administrations, and in that way—"indirectly," to repeat the language used earlier—they also affect their own parties' or administrations' prospects of election or reelection. Should these indirect effects be included in any experimental research design, or should they be factored out? Strictly, they should be factored out, but that would only emphasize the artificiality, as well as the impossibility, of the whole exercise.

Despite these difficulties, there exists one study of leadership effects using an experimental design, albeit on a considerably more modest scale than would be required to study a real election, let alone a real national election.

Shawn W. Rosenberg and his colleagues at the University of California, Irvine, invited a number of undergraduate students at the university, and then a number of adults shopping at a local department store, to "vote" for "candidates" on the basis of flyers containing information about the candidates' partisanship, their personal backgrounds, their issue positions, and their photographs.[19] Some of the photographs were of individuals who had previously been identified by other students, also on the basis of photographs, as possessing positive personal qualities and as therefore being fit to hold public office; the other photographs were of individuals who, on the same basis, had been rated less positively and as therefore being less fit to hold office. The aim was to discover whether, controlling for the other variables, individual candidates' faces and facial expressions affected voters' decisions. The election was not a real election, and the candidates were not real candidates, but the students and shoppers taking part in the experiment were led to believe that they were. They appear to have taken the task of "voting" quite seriously.

The experiment's results were striking. Candidates whose physical appearance was rated favorably consistently outperformed candidates whose physical appearance was rated unfavorably. If, for example, one of the experimenters' notional candidates was assigned Democratic partisanship and liberal issue positions, but at the same time an unattractive photograph, he consistently failed to secure as many votes as a candidate who had been assigned the same Democratic partisanship and identical liberal issue positions but at the same time a more attractive photograph. These findings were replicated for conservative Democrats, liberal Republicans and conservative Republicans. Faces and facial expressions clearly mattered, at least in this experimental setting. Rosenberg and his colleagues conclude: "The results of our research indicate that, other things being equal, a candidate's appearance does have a powerful impact on voters' preferences. Even when clear and substantial information on candidates' party affiliations and positions on major campaign

---

[19] Shawn W. Rosenberg, Lisa Bohan, Patrick McCafferty, and Kevin Harris, "The Image and the Vote: The Effect of Candidate Presentation on Voter Preference," *American Journal of Political Science*, 30 (1986), 108–27.

issues were presented, the photographs of the candidates exercised a strong and consistent influence on the vote."[20]

The California experiment and its results are suggestive and will be borne in mind in the chapters that follow; but, as the authors of the experiment freely acknowledge, the number of participating students and shoppers was small and, "even if we accept that the subjects believed the candidates to be legitimate, the fact remains that their votes were cast in the laboratory and not in the election booth."[21] Moreover, "the 'campaign' to which they were exposed was a balanced one which lasted for one-half hour rather than an uneven contest which lasted for several weeks or months."[22] Perhaps even more important is another factor that the authors do not mention: namely that their elections were unreal also in the sense that their experimental "voters" had no conceivable stake in the outcome. It did not matter to them who won. Indeed they would probably never find out who won. Whatever happened, they personally would remain unaffected. The perceived stakes in real elections are usually considerably higher, especially for those who bother to turn out.

For the reasons just given, the strictly experimental strategy has relatively little part to play in exploring leadership effects in real-world elections. More promising is what might be termed the *improved-prediction* strategy.

The improved-prediction strategy proceeds along the following lines. Suppose we already know quite a lot about a voter's personal values, ideological inclinations, group loyalties, and partisan preferences, and suppose we also know quite a lot about his or her perceptions of current economic and other conditions and about his or her evaluations of the political parties' and candidates' recent performance in office and their current platforms and policies. The improved-prediction strategy asks, in effect: What does it add to our ability to predict how an individual will vote to know, in addition, quite a lot about his or her personal judgments of the leaders and candidates who happen to be contesting the election? To take a simple example, to know in the United States in 1996 that someone was a black liberal Democrat, and also an economic optimist, was to be able to predict, with considerable confidence, that he or she would vote for Bill Clinton for president—irrespective of his or her views about Clinton as a human being. Indeed, in the specific circumstances of 1996 (with Clinton's fidelity and veracity both already in doubt), to have known this particular individual's views about Clinton, in isolation from these other considerations, might have made one's prediction of his or her behavior worse rather than better. At the same time, it is not hard to envisage elections in which the personalities of one or other of the leaders might make all the difference.

---

[20] Rosenberg *et al.*, "Image and the Vote," p. 119.
[21] Rosenberg *et al.*, "Image and the Vote," p. 120.   [22] Ibid.

Warren E. Miller and J. Merrill Shanks employ the improved-prediction strategy (though they do not call it that) in their writings on the U.S. presidential elections of the 1980s and 1990s, notably in a series of articles published in the *British Journal of Political Science* and in their major work, *The New American Voter*.[23] Their method, essentially, is to suggest that the choices of individual voters are best understood as the cumulative consequences of six temporally ordered sets of factors: (1) their stable social and economic characteristics, (2) their party identification and their stable policy-related predispositions, (3) their preferences concerning current policy issues and their perceptions of current economic and other conditions, (4) their explicit evaluations of the incumbent president's performance, (5) their evaluations of the competing candidates' personal qualities, and (6) their "prospective evaluations" of the parties and candidates—that is, their present assessments of the parties' and candidates' probable future performance.[24] Each of these sets of factors, in ascending numerical order, is assumed to be nearer in time to the individual's final vote decision. Earlier and more stable factors (party identification, for instance) are commonly found to influence later and less stable ones (such as prospective evaluations of the parties and candidates). The converse, though possible, is less likely to occur.[25]

In *The New American Voter*, Miller and Shanks focus primarily on the 1992 presidential election, which pitted the incumbent president, George Bush (perceived by voters as being moral and honest but also uninspiring), against the governor of Arkansas, Bill Clinton (perceived by voters as being immoral and dishonest but also compassionate and as someone who "cares about people like me").[26] The authors conclude, cautiously, that three of the nine perceived personality traits they explored—honesty, the capacity to inspire, and "caring about people like me"—did make a small contribution, controlling for all other factors, to individuals' vote decisions; the influence of these specific personal qualities appears to have been, in the authors'

[23] Warren E. Miller and J. Merrill Shanks, "Policy Directions and Presidential Leadership: Alternative Explanations of the 1980 Presidential Election," *British Journal of Political Science*, 12 (1982), 299–356; J. Merrill Shanks and Warren E. Miller, "Policy Direction and Performance Evaluation: Complementary Explanations of the Reagan Elections," *British Journal of Political Science*, 20 (1990), 143–235; J. Merrill Shanks and Warren E. Miller, "Partisanship, Policy and Performance: The Reagan Legacy in the 1988 Election," *British Journal of Political Science*, 21 (1991) 129–97; Warren E. Miller and J. Merrill Shanks, *The New American Voter* (Cambridge, Mass.: Harvard University Press, 1996), chap. 15.

[24] A brief summary and outline of the Miller/Shanks approach can be found on p. 15 of *The New American Voter*.

[25] The converse *is* possible. For example, although a voter's assessment of the incumbent president's performance in office is taken by Miller and Shanks to be likely to be prior to his or her evaluations of the currently competing candidates' personalities, it is possible that current candidate evaluations could color the voter's assessment of the incumbent candidate's performance. In connection with the location in the model of "personal qualities of the candidates," see Miller and Shanks, *New American Voter*, pp. 420–2.

[26] For the authors' findings on Clinton, see *The New American Voter*, pp. 422–5.

words, "visible—but limited."[27] However, the distribution of voters' positive and negative perceptions of the two candidates' personality traits does not appear, controlling for all other factors, to have been sufficiently skewed in favor of either Bush or Clinton to have made a significant difference to the overall election outcome; the net effect of the candidates' personal qualities was, also in the authors' words, "close to invisible."[28]

The improved-prediction strategy clearly does have a part to play in exploring the effects of party leaders' and candidates' personal characteristics on individuals' vote decisions and overall election outcomes, and it is a strategy that will be employed in several of the chapters of this book. A third strategy is also potentially useful, and it also will be referred to below. It might be called the *counterfactual* strategy.

The counterfactual strategy is akin to the experimental strategy, except that, whereas the experimental strategy relies on conducting actual psycho-political experiments, like the one with candidates' photographs in California, the counterfactual strategy relies on a technique akin to Einstein's famous "thought-experiments."[29] This strategy emphasizes the asking and answering of explicit "What if?" questions, exploiting what the historians call "counterfactuals." What if the leaders or candidates in a given election had no perceived personal characteristics at all (they were just blanks)? What if in the United States in 1996 the Democratic presidential candidate had been a Bob Dole clone while the Republican candidate's personal characteristics, as distinct from his partisan coloration and policy views, had been identical to Bill Clinton's? What if, to revert to an earlier example, John Smith instead of Tony Blair had led the Labour Party at the time of the 1997 British election? The number of thought-experiments that can be carried out based on this type of counterfactual proposition is, of course, infinite in principle. In practice, the few researchers who have adopted this strategy have chosen to run their thought-experiments on the basis of counterfactuals for which real-world data are actually available.

A good example is an article by Clive Bean and Anthony Mughan published in the *American Political Science Review* in 1989.[30] Bean and Mughan asked a pair of intriguing "What if?" questions. First, what if someone with Margaret Thatcher's personal characteristics, as seen by the voters, had led the British Labour Party instead of the British Conservative Party at the time of the 1983 general election while someone with Michael Foot's personal characteristics, as seen by the voters, had led the Conservative Party instead

---

[27] *The New American Voter*, p. 428.   [28] *The New American Voter*, p. 480.

[29] For one of the classic instances of a thought experiment in physics, see Ronald W. Clark, *Einstein: The Life and Times* (London: Hodder and Stoughton, 1973), pp. 100–1. It goes without saying that the improved-prediction strategy also involves thinking in terms of counterfactuals, even if the counterfactuals are not usually specified explicitly.

[30] Clive Bean and Anthony Mughan, "Leadership Effects in Parliamentary Elections in Australia and Britain," *American Political Science Review*, 83 (1989), 1165–79.

of the Labour Party? Second, what if, in Australia in 1987, someone like Bob Hawke, the Labor Party leader, had instead been leader of the Liberal and National conservative coalition while someone like John Howard, the leader of the conservative coalition, had instead been leader of the Labor Party? In short: Swap the personalities and other personal attributes of the two main parties' leaders, and what happens?

In answering their questions, Bean and Mughan were able to draw on data from the 1983 British Election Study and the 1987 Australian Election Study. Both studies asked respondents to say whether they believed each of a number of adjectives and adjectival phrases—caring, determined, shrewd, likeable as a person, tough, listens to reason, decisive, and sticks to principles—did or did not apply to the two main party leaders in their country. Respondents were also asked to rate the leaders in terms of effectiveness. Having observed that certain leadership qualities—listening to reason, sticking to principles, caring, and, above all, effectiveness—appeared to be highly valued by individual voters in both Britain and Australia, and also to be liable to influence their votes, Bean and Mughan went on to ask whether the distribution of voters' perceptions of Thatcher, Foot, Hawke, and Howard was skewed to such an extent in 1983 and 1987 that it might have made a difference to the outcomes of the two elections. To answer this question, they undertook "a hypothetical projection of how the 1987 Australian and 1983 British elections would have turned out had the unsuccessful leaders (Howard and Foot respectively) been perceived to possess the range of leadership qualities in the same proportions as their more succcessful counterparts, Hawke and Thatcher."[31] For example, "what would have happened in the Australian election had Howard been seen as caring, determined and so on by the same proportion of voters as was Hawke?"[32]

The authors' conclusions, based on this hypothetical projection, are striking. Their data indicate quite clearly, they say, "that both Hawke and Thatcher were a substantial electoral asset for their party:"

If Foot had possessed Thatcher's personality profile, Labour's vote in the 1983 general election would, other things being equal, have been some six to seven percentage points higher than it was. The difference is less stark in the Australian case, but the contrast in Hawke's and Howard's personality profiles was still worth some four percentage points to the ALP [Australian Labor Party].[33]

In those two cases, at least, leaders' personalities would appear to have made a substantial difference to the way in which individuals voted and, while in Great Britain Thatcher and the Conservatives would almost certainly have won in any case, in Australia the election was more closely fought and the difference between voters' perceptions of Hawke and their perceptions of

---

[31] Bean and Mughan, "Leadership Effects in Parliamentary Elections," p. 1174.   [32] Ibid.
[33] Bean and Mughan, "Leadership Effects in Parliamentary Elections," p. 1175.

Howard, may have been, Bean and Mughan suggest, "sufficient on its own to tilt the outcome of the . . . election in the ALP's favor."[34]

Previous Findings

Reference has already been made to the findings of Rosenberg and his colleagues, Miller and Shanks, and Bean and Mughan. Rosenberg *et al.* found that "candidates'" photographic images did make a difference to the way in which individuals "voted" in a controlled experimental situation. Miller and Shanks concluded, however, that the personalities of Bush and Clinton made little difference either to individuals' votes or to the outcome of the presidential election in the United States in 1992. By contrast, Bean and Mughan concluded that leaders' personal characteristics did make a substantial difference both to individuals' vote choices in Great Britain in 1983 and Australia in 1987 and also, quite possibly, to the actual outcome of the 1987 election in Australia.

Against that diverse and seemingly discrepant background, it is clearly worth attempting a more general conspectus of political scientists' views concerning the importance—or unimportance—of direct leadership effects on individual vote choices and overall election outcomes. Does there exist a conventional wisdom on the subject? If so, what does it amount to? The question is worth asking because, although hitherto the quantum of research and writing focusing directly on leadership effects has been quite small, most researchers have had something to say, if only in passing, on the subject. There may not be a large corpus of relevant research, but there are lots of bits and pieces.

United States

In the case of the United States, there has, historically, been nothing approaching a conventional wisdom, let alone a consensus. On the contrary, existing scholarly writing in the field forms a virtual bimodal distribution, with some political scientists insisting on the importance of presidential candidates' personal characteristics but with others producing evidence suggesting that candidates' personal characteristics matter scarcely at all.

A 1966 article by Donald E. Stokes can be made to stand for the school that holds candidates' characteristics to be important—in many cases crucial—in determining the outcomes of elections.[35] The article is entitled "Some Dynamic Elements of Contests for the Presidency," and Stokes is clear that among the most dynamic of those elements are the persons and personalities

---

[34] Ibid.
[35] Donald E. Stokes, "Some Dynamic Elements of Contests for the Presidency," *American Political Science Review*, 60 (1966), 19–28.

of the Democratic and Republican nominees, which, he argues, frequently constitute a principal component of short-term electoral change. He seems inclined to attribute Dwight D. Eisenhower's victories in 1952 and 1956 in large part to Eisenhower's personal ascendancy over his Democratic opponent, Adlai Stevenson, and he notes, in connection with all four presidential elections between 1952 and 1964, that the "evidence of the changing personal impact of the candidates is especially impressive" (as compared with, for example, the impact of changes in attitudes toward the parties).[36] "The fluctuations of electoral attitudes over these four elections," he concludes, "have to a remarkable degree focused on the candidates themselves."[37]

Stokes is by no means alone in holding these views. Stanley Kelley, Jr., in his article "The Simple Act of Voting," written with Thad W. Mirer, and later in his book *Interpreting Elections*, surmises that "the voter's decision rule," as he calls it, is based on his or her assessments of the two major political parties at the time of any presidential election and—more or less equally—on his or her assessments of the two major parties' nominees.[38] Voters' attitudes toward the candidates thus form a central part of Kelley's analysis (though he and Mirer note in passing that issues of policy "may be implicated in such attitudes").[39] More specifically, Kelley attributes Lyndon Johnson's landslide victory in 1964 in large part to voters' doubts about Barry Goldwater's competence.[40] He also attributes the scale of Richard Nixon's victory over George McGovern in 1972 to voters' belief that Nixon was more competent than McGovern. "Collectively," he says, "voters did not see Nixon simply as the all-round better man. It was issues related to the competence of the two candidates—experience, record in public life, strength of leadership, realism—that gave him such a decisive advantage."[41]

Moreover, although Stokes, Kelley, and Mirer were writing about the elections of the 1950s, 1960s, and 1970s, the notion that presidential candidates matter, and may even be decisive in determining overall election outcomes, continues to dominate much of the academic literature. Arthur H. Miller and his colleagues take for granted "the unquestioned importance of candidate evaluations."[42] Going further, they claim that "candidate evaluations are one of the most important . . . facets of American voting behavior."[43] Shawn W. Rosenberg and his colleagues, the results of whose experimental research were cited above, begin their report by maintaining that "how a political candidate

[36] Stokes, "Some Dynamic Elements," p. 26.

[37] Stokes, "Some Dynamic Elements," p. 27.

[38] Stanley Kelley, Jr., and Thad W. Mirer, "The Simple Act of Voting," *American Political Science Review*, 68 (1974), 572–91; Stanley Kelley, Jr., *Interpreting Elections* (Princeton, N.J.: Princeton University Press, 1983).

[39] Kelley and Mirer, "Simple Act of Voting," p. 573.

[40] Kelley, *Interpreting Elections*, p. 98.   [41] Kelley, *Interpreting Elections*, p. 107.

[42] Arthur H. Miller, Martin P. Wattenberg, and Oksana Malanchuk, "Schematic Assessment of Presidential Candidates," *American Political Science Review*, 80 (1986), p. 521.

[43] Ibid.

looks and speaks has a significant impact on the candidate's chances of being elected—style shapes image and image affects the vote."[44] Similarly, Wendy M. Rahn and her colleagues, in the course of laying out a "social-cognitive model of candidate appraisal," comment that in presidential elections "the process of forming assessments of the professional and personal qualities of candidates plays a central role in determining the vote decision."[45] Such statements more closely resemble assumptions than solid research-based conclusions, but they are none the less significant for that.

Whatever they may be, they are more or less flatly contradicted by the findings of other scholars in the field, who, explicitly or implicitly, refute the idea that American voters' assessments of candidates' personal and professional qualities play a central role in determining how they cast their ballots.

Martin P. Wattenberg in *The Rise of Candidate-Centered Politics* draws attention to the fact that since the 1970s U.S. presidential hopefuls have increasingly conducted their campaigns independently of the political parties and also to the fact that media coverage of U.S. elections has increasingly been candidate-centered rather than party-centered; but he himself, despite the title of his book, does not subscribe to the view that voters' responses to the campaigns and the media coverage have also become increasingly candidate-centered.[46] In particular, he insists that the victories of Ronald Reagan in 1980 and 1984, and the victory of George Bush in 1988, owed far more to Jimmy Carter's failures as the incumbent president between 1977 and 1980, and to Reagan's relative success in office during the ensuing eight years, than they did either to Reagan's and Bush's personal qualities or to those of the three Democrats who ran against them. Reagan, contrary to widespread belief, was not personally popular; Bush, similarly, "did not have strong personal appeal to the voters."[47] Voting during the Reagan–Bush era, Wattenberg maintains, was far more performance-based than personality-based.[48]

Even more telling are the findings of Warren E. Miller and J. Merrill Shanks, who, unusually in the field, deliberately set out to identify and isolate any specific contribution that the personal characteristics of the two main candidates made to their success or failure in each of the post-1980 presidential elections. Reference has already been made to the largely null conclusions they reached in connection with the 1992 Bush–Clinton race. What they have to say about the 1980, 1984, and 1988 races is broadly similar.

[44] Shawn W. Rosenberg *et al.*, "The Image and the Vote," p. 108.
[45] Wendy M. Rahn, John H. Aldrich, Eugene Borgida, and John L. Sullivan, "A Social-Cognitive Model of Candidate Appraisal," in John A. Ferejohn and James H. Kuklinski, eds., *Information and Democratic Processes* (Urbana: University of Illinois Press, 1990), p. 154.
[46] Martin P. Wattenberg, *The Rise of Candidate-Centered Politics: Presidential Elections of the 1980s* (Cambridge, Mass.: Harvard University Press, 1991).
[47] Wattenberg, *Rise of Candidate-Centered Politics*, chap. 14, esp. pp. 82–3, 89.
[48] Wattenberg, *Rise of Candidate-Centered Politics*, chap. 16, esp. pp. 134–6.

Ronald Reagan won in 1980 and Jimmy Carter lost, but, according to Miller and Shanks, the two men's "candidate-related characteristics" had little bearing on the outcome, which was determined far more by voters' "preferences for policy changes in a conservative direction and the public's low assessment of Carter's (and the economy's) performance."[49] Insofar as voters' assessments of the two men did have a bearing on the outcome, they favored Carter rather than Reagan—that is, the loser rather than the winner.[50] Four years later the picture was somewhat different, but only somewhat. On that occasion voters' more favorable assessments of Reagan's personality traits compared with those of his Democratic rival, Walter Mondale, did make a modest contribution to the decision of many individual voters to vote for Reagan rather than Mondale. The contribution that Reagan's personal advantage over Mondale made to securing his overall victory, however, was marginal and in no way decisive.[51]

Four years further on, in 1988, the elder George Bush easily defeated the Democratic candidate, Michael Dukakis. As in 1980, however, it was the loser rather than the winner who enjoyed a small advantage in personal terms. To quote Miller and Shanks directly:

The conventional post-election wisdom held that Dukakis confounded pre-election expectations by proving to be a much less attractive candidate than Bush. In fact, the [National Election Study] evidence suggests that voters evaluated the presumed "cold-fish" Democrat loser of the presidential debates about as positively as candidate Bush where personal traits or leadership-characteristics were concerned.[52]

And they continue:

Moreover, despite the critical evaluations of media experts and political pundits, Dukakis appears to have been relatively well received on his own personal terms as a candidate, so that comparative evaluations of personal traits slightly reduced Bush's margin of victory.[53]

So far as the Bush–Clinton election of 1992 is concerned, we have already seen that Miller and Shanks conclude that the net effect of the two candidates' personal qualities on the final result was "close to invisible."[54]

It may be helpful at this point to provide a summary of Miller and Shanks's findings concerning each of the four presidential elections they studied in detail. Such a summary is set out in Table 1.2. The entries in the table would appear, on the face of it, to give the lie to any simple notion that in the United States candidates' personal traits play a large part in influencing either individuals' vote choices or overall election outcomes. Note, in particular, that in

[49] Miller and Shanks, "Policy Directions and Presidential Leadership," p. 348.
[50] Miller and Shanks, "Policy Directions and Presidential Leadership," p. 352.
[51] Shanks and Miller, "Policy Direction and Performance Evaluation," pp. 203, 212, 213–15.
[52] Shanks and Miller, "Partisanship, Policy and Performance," p. 131.
[53] Shanks and Miller, "Partisanship, Policy and Performance," p. 132.
[54] See above, p. 19.

two of the four elections, according to Miller and Shanks, the candidate whom voters assessed more favorably in personal terms was nevertheless defeated by his rival and that in none of the elections were voters' assessments of the candidates remotely decisive in determining the overall outcome. Clearly, the views of Miller and Shanks and the views of those, like Arthur H. Miller, Shawn W. Rosenberg, and Wendy M. Rahn, who were quoted earlier, are not at all easy to reconcile.

Table 1.2. Influence of candidate assessments on election outcomes, United States, 1980–92

	Who won?	How much influence did assessments of candidates' personal characteristics have on individuals' vote decisions?	How much influence did the balance of individuals' assessments have on the overall election outcome?	Which candidate benefited from any balance of individuals' assessments in his favor?	Did individuals' assessments of candidates determine the election outcome?
1980	**Reagan**	Limited	Negligible	**Carter**	No
1984	**Reagan**	Limited	Limited	**Reagan**	No
1988	**Bush**	Limited	Limited	**Dukakis**	No
1992	**Clinton**	Limited	Negligible	**Clinton**	No

Sources: Warren E. Miller and J. Merrill Shanks, "Policy Directions and Presidential Leadership," *British Journal of Policial Science*, 12 (1982), 348–52; J. Merrill Shanks and Warren E. Miller, "Policy Direction and Performance Evaluation: Complementary Explanations of the Reagan Elections," *British Journal of Political Science*, 20 (1990), 203–18; J. Merrill Shanks and Warren E. Miller, "Partisanship, Policy and Performance: The Reagan Legacy in the 1988 Election," *British Journal of Political Science*, 21 (1991), 180–93; Warren E. Miller and J. Merrill Shanks, *The New American Voter* (Cambridge, Mass.; Harvard University Press, 1996), esp. chaps. 15 and 17.

Great Britain

Like students of American politics, students of British politics have devoted relatively little attention to the importance, or lack of it, of leadership effects in national elections. Even so, political scientists in Britain have managed to arrive at conclusions that are at least as discrepant as those of their American counterparts. On neither side of the Atlantic is there anything approaching a consensus of view.

Butler and Stokes, whose pioneering work on elections and voting in Great Britain was quoted earlier, were cautious on the subject.[55] On the one hand, they were clear that there were theoretical grounds for supposing that the major party leaders' personal characteristics *might* influence both individual voters and overall election outcomes; and their empirical researches in the 1960s led them to conclude "that the party leaders have enough hold on the public's consciousness and are, by the nature of their office, sharply enough

[55] See above, pp. 10–11.

set apart by party for popular feeling towards them to have demonstrable effects on the party balance when it becomes predominantly positive or negative."[56] But, on the other hand, Butler and Stokes noted, and gave weight to, the fact that the Conservative upsurge of the late 1960s was not linked to any improvement in the personal standing of the Conservative leader—a fact that, they added, "should remind us that the pull of the leaders remains but one among the factors that determine the transient shifts of party strength," one "easily outweighed by other issues and events of concern to the public."[57]

Butler and Stokes's successors—in Britain as in the United States—have tended to array themselves into two camps, at least as regards the capacity of party leaders' personal qualities to affect the decisions of individual voters. Brian Graetz and Ian McAllister studied three British general elections—those of October 1974 (there were two general elections in 1974), 1979 and 1983—and concluded that "party leaders are important determinants of voting defection [from individual voters' prior party identifications], and remain so even after a wide range of other influences has been taken into account."[58] On the basis of their study of the 1987 British election, Marianne C. Stewart and Harold D. Clarke were still more emphatic, concluding that "public reactions to the leaders had sizable effects on electoral choice:"[59]

The analyses show[ed] that all coefficients for leader images are statistically significant and correctly signed . . . Favorable perceptions of Thatcher as competent and responsive enhanced, and similar perceptions of other leaders reduced, the likelihood of Tory voting. Favorable views of the Labour leader increased, and sanguine perspectives on other party leaders decreased, the probability of Labour voting.[60]

Moreover, Stewart and Clarke went on to maintain that positive and negative leader images explained more of the variance in individual voting in 1987 than either economic evaluations or issue concerns.[61]

Anthony Mughan in a monograph entitled *Media and the Presidentialization of Parliamentary Elections* reached broadly similar conclusions with regard to both the 1987 and 1992 elections in Britain.[62] He argued that negative evaluations of Labour's leader, Neil Kinnock, probably cost the Labour Party votes in 1987 but concluded that, even so, because the result of that election was so lopsided, "neither party leader [neither Margaret Thatcher nor Neil Kinnock]

---

[56] Butler and Stokes, *Political Change in Britain*, pp. 367–8.

[57] Butler and Stokes, *Political Change in Britain*, p. 368.

[58] Brian Graetz and Ian McAllister, "Popular Evaluations of Party Leaders in the Anglo-American Democracies," in Harold D. Clarke and Moshe M. Czudnowski, eds., *Political Elites in Anglo-American Democracies* (DeKalb, Ill.: Northern Illinois University Press, 1987), p. 500.

[59] Marianne C. Stewart and Harold D. Clarke, "The (Un)Importance of Party Leaders: Leader Images and Party Choice in the 1987 British Election," *Journal of Politics*, 54 (1992), 447–70.

[60] Stewart and Clarke, "The (Un)Importance of Party Leaders," p. 460.

[61] Stewart and Clarke, "The (Un)Importance of Party Leaders," pp. 460–1.

[62] Anthony Mughan, *Media and the Presidentialization of Parliamentary Elections* (Basingstoke, Hants.: Palgrave, 2000).

contributed decisively to the . . . election outcome."[63] However, in his view, the 1992 election told an "altogether different story."[64] The result was extremely close, the Conservatives won only narrowly (a swing of only 0.5 percent to Labour would have deprived them of their parliamentary majority), and the deciding factor, according to Mughan, was undoubtedly voters' positive evaluations of the man who by this time had succeeded Thatcher as prime minister, John Major. The Conservatives, Mughan argues, would have lost if Major had possessed the same personal attributes that Thatcher, his Conservative predecessor, possessed in 1987 and or that Kinnock, still his opponent as Labour leader, possessed in 1992: "Popular goodwill towards [Major] may not have been sufficient to allow his party to maintain the triple-digit majorities that it had won in 1983 and 1987, but the cumulative evidence is that he was the difference between the formation of a majority Conservative government and a hung Parliament in 1992."[65]

Ivor Crewe and Anthony King, in their study of the 1992 general election, similarly reported that large numbers of party identifiers—especially Liberal Democrats but including large numbers of Conservatives and Labour supporters as well—appeared to desert their own party for some other party either when they had a positive preference for the leaders of one or more of the other parties or when they rated their own party's leader equally with the leader or leaders of other parties. Deviant leader preferences, in other words, were associated with deviant voting.[66] Crewe and King, however, qualified their conclusion in one important respect, noting that, on the basis of the evidence available to them, they were "not in a position to distinguish between genuine leader effects and [other] effects that manifest themselves through the leaders but are in fact rooted in voters' prior dispositions and attitudes."[67] All that they could do was establish outer limits to the scale of any such genuine effects. The scale of such effects, they noted, was most unlikely to be greater than their estimates, but it could well be smaller.[68] Unlike Mughan, Crewe and King felt unable to come to any definite conclusions about the rival British leaders' relative pulling power in 1992. Different analytic strategies pointed to disconcertingly discrepant conclusions.[69]

---

[63] Mughan, *Presidentialization of Parliamentary Elections*, p. 111.　　[64] Ibid.

[65] Mughan, *Presidentialization of Parliamentary Elections*, pp. 113–14.

[66] Ivor Crewe and Anthony King, "Did Major Win? Did Kinnock Lose? Leadership Effects in the 1992 Election," in Anthony Heath, Roger Jowell, and John Curtice, eds., *Labour's Last Chance? The 1992 Election and Beyond* (Aldershot, Hants.: Dartmouth, 1994).

[67] Crewe and King, "Did Major Win? Did Kinnock Lose?" p. 136.　　[68] Ibid.

[69] Comparing rates of defection among party identifiers, and noting the absolute number of party identifiers who were available to defect from each party, Crewe and King concluded, against the grain of the conventional wisdom, "that in 1992 . . . net leader effects actually helped the Labour Party marginally and harmed the Conservatives"—that is, that Neil Kinnock was, on balance, an asset to the Labour Party and that John Major, on balance, harmed the Conservative Party. However, when, following the example of Bean and Mughan (see n. 30 above), Crewe and King imagined how the 1992 election would have turned out if the Labour Party had been led by John Major and the Conservative Party by Neil Kinnock, they were forced to the conclusion—in

Four years later, following the 1997 general election, which had been widely portrayed as a personal contest between Tony Blair, the Labour leader of the opposition, and John Major, still the incumbent Conservative prime minister, John Bartle, Ivor Crewe, and Anthony King made a preliminary attempt to disentangle genuine (or "pure") leader effects from the prior dispositions and attitudes that Crewe and King referred to.[70] They concluded, contrary to Crewe and King's 1992 analysis, that, given a knowledge of voters' stable partisan and ideological predispositions and a knowledge also of their retrospective evaluations of the Conservative government's performance, "the addition of further information about voters' evaluations of specific leadership traits adds little to our ability to predict how any given individual will vote."[71] The same held true even when the leadership evaluations in question included assessments of who would make the best prime minister.

These differences of opinion concerning the amount of importance that individual voters attach to leaders' personal characteristics extend to the efforts that have been made, more in Britain than in the United States, to model—month by month and quarter by quarter—the sources of voters' support, or lack of it, for the incumbent prime minister and his or her political party. This is not the place to review what is by now an extensive academic literature, because most of it deals not with individuals' actual voting decisions but with their much more casual expressions of preference between elections; but substantial differences of opinion, although sometimes partially hidden, can nevertheless be detected in the various publications. David Sanders and his colleagues incline to the view that, when one of the major parties changes its leader, the effects on its electoral fortunes are likely to be short-lived and to constitute no more than a temporary blip.[72] By contrast, Harold D. Clarke, Marianne C. Stewart, and their colleagues, on the basis of not dissimilar research, incline to the view that leader evaluations are among the more important—perhaps among the *most* important—determinants of party choice.[73]

There is thus nothing like a consensus in Britain with regard to the role of leaders in motivating the voting choices of individual electors. Interestingly,

line with the conventional wisdom—"that Major's net pulling power in 1992 was in fact greater than Kinnock's." See Crewe and King, "Did Major Win? Did Kinnock Lose?" esp. pp. 139–41.

[70] John Bartle, Ivor Crewe, and Anthony King, "Was It Blair Who Won It? Leadership Effects in the 1997 British General Election." Paper presented to the Annual Meeting of the American Political Science Association, Washington, D.C., 1997.

[71] Bartle, Crewe, and King, "Was It Blair Who Won It?", p. 15.

[72] See, in particular, David Sanders, "Forecasting the 1992 British General Election Outcome: The Performance of an 'Economic' Model," in David Denver, Pippa Norris, David Broughton and Colin Rallings, eds., *British Elections and Parties Yearbook, 1993* (Hemel Hempstead, Herts.: Harvester Wheatsheaf, 1993).

[73] Clarke and Stewart, "The (Un)Importance of Party Leaders" and Harold D. Clarke, Karl Ho, and Marianne C. Stewart, "Major's Lesser (Not Minor) Effects: Prime Ministerial Approval and Governing Party Support in Britain since 1979," *Electoral Studies*, 19 (2000), 255–73.

however, there *is* a substantial measure of agreement on the broader—and, it might be thought, politically more germane—question of the net effect of individuals' leadership preferences on overall election outcomes. The view is almost universally held that, whatever effects party leaders' characteristics may or may not have on individuals, those effects, at least in Britain, are only very seldom *both* on such a large scale *and* so skewed in their direction as to determine which party actually wins.

For example, Graetz and McAllister, in their study of the October 1974, 1979, and 1983 elections, conclude that, although the personalities of the party leaders made some difference to individual voters' decisions in 1983, they made no net difference to the overall outcome of any of the elections.[74] The contribution of leaders to election outcomes, they say, is typically 'more marginal than decisive.'[75] Stewart and Clarke do not dispute the same point as regards 1987.[76] As regards the 1992 election, Mughan, as we have seen, is clear that voters' positive evaluations of Major tipped the balance in the Conservatives' favor; Crewe and King, by contrast, are more doubtful.[77] With respect to the 1997 general election, Bartle, Crewe, and King claim that Blair's personal ascendancy over Major (which undoubtedly existed) made only a modest net contribution to Labour's victory, which was on a prodigious scale.[78]

Only three of the eleven British general elections fought since 1964 (and for which survey data are therefore available) stand out—but they do stand out. One was 1964 itself, when the outcome was extremely close (only 0.7 percentage points separated the two main parties and Labour secured a majority in parliament of only four seats) and when the Labour leader, Harold Wilson, was vastly

---

[74] Graetz and McAllister, "Popular Evaluations of Party Leaders," pp. 499–500.

[75] Graetz and McAllister, "Popular Evaluations of Party Leaders," p. 499.

[76] Stewart and Clarke, "The (Un)Importance of Party Leaders." The authors maintain that the perceived personal characteristics of Thatcher and Kinnock, the two main party leaders, affected voting at the individual level, but they do not suggest that, absent their personal characteristics, the Conservatives would have lost and Labour would have won. Mughan, as we have seen (pp. 26–7 above), asserted that voters' judgments of the leaders did not, in fact, tip the 1987 outcome.

[77] Crewe and King, "Did Major Win? Did Kinnock Lose?" See fn. 69 above.

[78] Bartle, Crewe, and King, "Was It Blair Who Won It?" The authors made use of a somewhat stripped-down version of the Miller/Stokes model (in the absence of some of the data that would have been required to enable them to make use of the full version). They concluded (p. 17) that in 1997 "evaluations of Tony Blair and John Major played a relatively small part in determining both individual vote decisions and the aggregate election outcome. If we were to rewind the film of the election back to the day the election was called, extract both party leaders from the scene and play the film again, the outcome would be very little different." They also conclude, albeit more speculatively, that Labour would have done just about as well under Gordon Brown, another Labour "modernizer," as under Tony Blair and might possibly have done just about as well under John Smith if Smith had chosen—which he had not—to modernize the party. See the discussion above (pp. 4–7) of the difference between the direct and the indirect effects of leaders' personalities.

preferred by voters to the Conservative leader, Sir Alec Douglas-Home.[79] Another was the election of February 1974 when, again, the outcome was extremely close (a mere 0.8 percentage points separated the two main parties and neither secured a parliamentary majority) and when, again, the Labour leader, still Harold Wilson, was preferred by a wide margin to the Conservative leader, Edward Heath.[80] Ivor Crewe and Anthony King are not alone in suggesting that, at those two elections, leadership preferences on their own may well have tipped the balance; but they are also not alone in concluding, more broadly, that, "while leadership effects exist and may on occasion be electorally decisive, they are seldom on a large scale and are not decisive very often."[81] On the outcome of the 1992 election, the jury, despite the passage of time, is still out.

France

The task of assessing the importance of leadership effects in French elections is complicated by the fact that there are two types of elections to be considered, potentially at least: parliamentary elections, in which the various political parties are led by their national leaders as in Britain and most other parliamentary democracies, and presidential elections, in which the parties nominate individual candidates to run, more or less in the style of American presidential candidates, for France's highest—or at least most highly visible—political office. Under France's arrangements, the president is thus directly elected; the prime minister is not. It follows that the names of candidates for the presidency appear on the ballot paper throughout the country whereas the party leaders' names appear only in the parliamentary districts that they, personally, happen to be contesting.

There is a further element of complexity in French politics, which makes France a particularly interesting country from our point of view. In the United States and Great Britain, the party systems are remarkably stable. The Democratic and Republican parties have dominated electoral competition in the United States since the 1850s; the Conservative and Labour parties have dominated British electoral politics since the 1920s. In France, by contrast, the party system has undergone almost kaleidoscopic change since the end of World War II. Broad left-wing and right-wing political tendencies remain in existence and remain recognizable; but almost every French political party since 1945 has changed its name and in other ways repositioned and reconfigured itself. To take only one example, the principal non-Communist party

---

[79] Butler and Stokes, *Political Change in Britain*, pp. 362–8; Crewe and King, "Are British Elections Becoming More 'Presidential'?" pp. 192–204. Butler and Stokes's data suggest that the differential impact of Wilson and Douglas-Home may well have tipped the outcome of the 1964 election; however, the authors themselves do not pronounce on the issue.

[80] Crewe and King, "Are British Elections Becoming More 'Presidential'?" pp. 192–204.

[81] Crewe and King, "Did Major Win? Did Blair Lose?" p. 144.

of the left was known as the SFIO (Section française de l'internationale ouvrière) from its formation in 1905 until 1969, when it became the French Socialist Party.[82]

One source of these kaleidoscopic changes in the parties has been the endemic personalism of French politics, with parties forming and reforming to meet the personal requirements of individual leaders and their followers. Charles de Gaulle, in particular, established the Rally of the French People (Rassemblement du peuple français) in 1946 only to disband it when he retired from active politics in 1953. On his return in 1958, a core of his sup- porters created a new party which they christened the Union for the New Republic (Union pour la nouvelle république). In 1976 the Union for the New Republic duly became, in its turn, the Rally for the Republic (Rassemblement pour la république). Significantly, none of these three organizations chose to call itself a "party." Equally significantly, all of them were known universally simply as "the Gaullists" after their founder and patron saint.

This degree of personalism and these changes in the French party system have one known effect and raise one possibility. The known effect is to lower the levels of party identification in France below what they would otherwise probably be; it is hard for voters to form stable long-term attachments to political parties when the parties themselves, the putative objects of these attachments, change so much and so often.[83] The possibility is that, absent a stable party system and absent high levels of party identification, French voters may be more liable than voters in other countries to be swayed by party leaders and presidential candidates—by their personalities and other personal characteristics as well as their issue positions. It is also possible that voters in France are in any case, because of the personalist tradition in French politics, more receptive than voters in other countries to electoral appeals based on individual candidates' real or imagined leadership qualities.

As early as 1958 Philip E. Converse and Georges Dupeux noted that fully 40 percent of the French public, when asked before the constitutional refer- endum of that year whether they would be voting on the basis of the consti- tution that had been drafted for the new Fifth Republic or on the basis of General de Gaulle's personality, confessed that they would be casting a per- sonality vote. "Since this was clearly not the 'proper' political response," Converse and Dupeux add, "one can be sure that many others felt the same

---

[82] On the changing face of the French party system since 1945, see Vincent Wright, *Government and Politics of France*, chaps. 9–10.

[83] Early evidence of the difficulty that many French voters have in "identifying" with a polit- ical party was provided by Philip E. Converse and Georges Dupeux in "Politicization of the Electorate in France and the United States" in Angus Campbell, Philip E. Converse, Warren E. Miller, and Donald E. Stokes, *Elections and the Political Order* (New York: John Wiley, 1966), pp. 277–83. Rather than using the term "party identification," many students of voting patterns in France prefer to use the looser term "party affection." As in most other democratic countries, such bonds as did exist between parties and voters in France have become more frayed in recent years.

way but concealed the fact."[84] Converse and Dupeux also noted that French voters, when asked at roughly the same time to say what they liked and disliked about de Gaulle, responded overwhelmingly in terms of his personal attributes, his leadership qualities, and his war record and not in terms of his policy positions.[85]

Roy Pierce in *Choosing the Chief*, published a generation later, also drew attention to the importance of "overall candidate evaluations" in influencing voters' decisions in the 1988 French presidential election, though these appear to have been more important on the second ballot than on the first. On the first ballot, probably because there were more candidates standing, representing a wider range of political parties, voters appear to have been guided to a greater extent by their initial party identifications. However, on the second ballot, when several of the parties' candidates had been forced to drop out and when only the candidates who had finished either first or second on the first ballot were still available to be voted for, the role of party identification appeared to decline and the role of candidate evaluations to increase.[86] Pierce notes that in both France and the United States, in a pair of roughly comparable presidential elections, "candidate evaluations emerge[d] as the main factor in candidate choice."[87]

Unfortunately, the question of the relative importance of leader and candidate evaluations in France in determining both individuals' vote decisions and the overall outcomes of French parliamentary and presidential elections has never really been followed up. Exhaustive survey-based studies of elections are considerably sparser in France than in many other democratic countries, and even those political scientists who are interested in the subject have not, with the partial exceptions of Converse and Dupeux, sought to "strip out," so to speak, those aspects of candidate evaluations that are based on the candidates' strictly personal qualities and those that are based on their issue positions, their appeals to specific groups in the electorate, and so forth. There is more talk in France of the importance of individual leaders than there is hard evidence of their electoral significance.

Germany

If France's executive institutions are strangely bicephalous (with two people, the president and the prime minister, sharing power in an often uneasy relationship), Germany's are more conventional. The political parties compete in

---

[84] Philip E. Converse and Georges Dupeux, "De Gaulle and Eisenhower: The Public Image of the Victorious General," in Campbell, Converse, Miller, and Stokes, *Elections and the Political Order*, p. 295.

[85] Converse and Dupeux, "De Gaulle and Eisenhower," pp. 298–9.

[86] Roy Pierce, *Choosing the Chief: Presidential Elections in France and the United States* (Ann Arbor: University of Michigan Press, 1995), pp. 136–8.

[87] Pierce, *Choosing the Chief*, p. 139.

elections. Each party's leader at each election is that party's chancellor-candidate. Whichever party wins the election forms the government, usually in combination with at least one other party, and the leader of the largest party in the government becomes chancellor. The research question is therefore straightforward (and also quite familiar by now): To what extent do the personal qualities of the major party leaders influence the decisions of individual German voters and determine the outcomes of German elections?

The question is especially interesting in the German context because German politics since the creation of the Federal Republic in 1949 has been dominated by a tiny number of remarkable and extraordinarily long-serving leaders: Konrad Adenauer (*"Der Alte"*), chancellor from 1949 until 1963, Helmut Schmidt, chancellor from 1974 until 1982, and Helmut Kohl, chancellor from 1982 until 1998. In other words, during nearly forty of the Federal Republic's first fifty years one or other of only three men occupied the chancellor's office. It therefore becomes important to gauge the extent to which German elections during the long postwar period constituted, in effect, referendums on the leadership qualities, as well as on the actual performance in office, of Adenauer, Schmidt, and Kohl. If leaders' personal characteristics are ever electorally significant, modern Germany ought to be one place where that is so.

But the bulk of the academic research that exists on the subject suggests that it is not. More precisely, it suggests that the outcomes of federal elections in Germany are only very occasionally determined—or even substantially influenced—by voters' relative leader preferences. As in the British case, reliable German survey data are available only for the period since the early 1960s. Writing as early as 1978, Hans-Dieter Klingemann and Charles Lewis Taylor reviewed the evidence from the five federal elections held between 1961 and 1976 and concluded that the relative personal standings of the two main parties' chancellor-candidates had had little or no bearing on the outcomes of three of the five: those of 1961, 1965, and 1976.[88] However, in 1972 voters' preferences for the incumbent chancellor, Willy Brandt, the candidate of the Social Democratic Party (SPD), over Rainer Barzel, his Christian Democratic Union (CDU) rival, may possibly have tipped the outcome of that election in the SPD's favor. Klingemann and Taylor suggest that the contrast between Brandt and Barzel in voters' eyes afforded the SPD an advantage of 2.6 percentage points; the gap between the two parties in second votes that year was less than 1 point.[89] But the real outlier was 1969. At that election, Klingemann

---

[88] Hans D. Klingemann and Charles Lewis Taylor, "Partisanship, Candidates and Issues," in Max Kaase and Klaus von Beyme, eds., *Elections and Parties*, German Political Studies, Vol. 3 (London: Sage, 1978).

[89] Klingemann and Taylor, "Partisanship, Candidates and Issues," p. 118. The phrase "second votes" refers to the votes that German electors cast for party lists in addition to the votes they cast for individual candidates in geographical districts. It is the tally of these second votes that mainly determines the partisan composition of the Bundestag.

and Taylor argue, Kurt-Georg Kiesinger's personal standing relative to that of Willy Brandt was worth a massive 5.0 percentage points to the CDU and, in terms of second votes, probably contributed decisively to the CDU's net advantage over the SPD of 3.4 points.[90] Unfortunately for Kiesinger, the SPD had fought the election in informal alliance with the Free Democratic Party and went on after the election to form a governing coalition with that party. It was Brandt, not Kiesinger, who served as chancellor from 1969 onward.[91]

The subsequent period, if anything, seems to have witnessed a decline in the personal influence of chancellor-candidates as compared with their parties, their parties' policies, and their parties' records in office. Angelika Vetter and Oscar W. Gabriel, in a paper published in 1998, noted that in every German election until 1983 "the candidate preferred by the majority of the electorate always became chancellor during the following parliamentary term."[92] That pattern was broken, however, in 1987. In the period between 1987 and 1994— which included three federal elections (and also the reunification of Germany)—"candidates," according to Vetter and Gabriel, "did not play a central role in influencing election outcomes . . . Relatively low ratings of [Helmut] Kohl did not prevent his party from winning elections."[93]

During this same period, in an article entitled "Is There Personalization in Politics?", Max Kaase asked more generally whether there was evidence that the personalization of politics was proceeding apace in parliamentary polit-ical systems like the German as well as in (as he believed) presidential systems like that of the United States.[94] He asked the question having in mind the widespread belief among political scientists that "television, inherently averse to sophisticated explanations of complicated matters, is bound to emphasize the outer appearance and performance of leaders."[95] He was also sensitive to the possibility that, as enduring psychological attachments to the political parties wane in Germany, as they do elsewhere, voters might be more prone to be swayed by the personal characteristics of the parties' leaders rather than by the parties as such.[96]

[90] Klingemann and Taylor, "Partisanship, Candidates and Issues," p. 118.

[91] For a brief account of the 1969 election and its aftermath, see Peter Pulzer, *German Politics, 1945–1995* (Oxford: Oxford University Press, 1995), pp. 86–8. The obvious point should made in this context that, in political systems dominated by interparty alliances and coalition governments, the outcomes of elections and the formation of governments are less likely than in majoritarian democracies like the American and British to be determined by voters' responses to leaders' per-sonal characteristics. This fact is somewhat obscured by the fact that all six countries covered in this volume, with the partial exception of Germany, are predominantly of the majoritarian type.

[92] Angelika Vetter and Oscar W. Gabriel, "Candidate Evaluations and Party Choice in Germany, 1972–94: Do Candidates Matter?" in Christopher J. Anderson and Carsten Zelle, eds., *Stability and Change in German Elections: How Electorates Merge, Converge, or Collide* (Westport, Conn.: Praeger, 1998), p. 81.

[93] Vetter and Gabriel, "Candidate Evaluations and Party Choice in Germany," p. 84.

[94] Kaase, "Is There Personalization in Politics?" p. 212.

[95] Kaase, "Is There Personalization in Politics?" p. 213.

[96] Kaase, "Is There Personalization in Politics?" p. 221.

Kaase could not, however, on the basis of survey data drawn from the eight federal elections between 1961 and 1987, find any evidence to support either the idea that German electoral politics were becoming more "presidential" over time or the idea that German voters, at whatever time, were greatly swayed by leader rather than partisan preferences. Kaase wrote:

The substantive conclusion from these data is straightforward. Not only is the short-term (issue and candidate) component of the voting intention in comparison to partisanship insubstantial (in terms of explained variance); it also does not systematically increase in importance over time, as a personalization concept would require.[97]

Kaase adds: "The German case gives little support for the speculation that individual-related preferences by the electorate are substantially gaining ground in determining electoral choices."[98]

To date the Kaase paper, published in 1994, represents the most comprehensive attempt to assess the importance of leader and candidate effects in Germany; but it is worth noting that Hans-Dieter Klingemann and Martin P. Wattenberg, in a comparison of the German and American electorates which covered an extended historical period, arrive at broadly the same conclusion.[99] They report that German voters are considerably more likely than American voters to have leader preferences that coincide with their party preferences and that they are also considerably more likely, when their leader and party preferences diverge, to vote for their preferred party rather than their preferred leader. Unsurprisingly, Klingemann and Wattenberg refer generally to "the lack of a candidate focus for German voters."[100] Referring more specifically to Helmut Kohl's tight grip on the chancellorship before 1998, they say:

In particular, Helmut Kohl has held steadfastly to power not via national popularity but rather by his ability to work the party machinery deftly. Had there been a one-on-one popularity contest with the leader of the Social Democrats, survey evidence shows that Kohl would have lost in both 1983 and 1987.[101]

In short, if evidence exists that any large number of German elections is swayed by the personal characteristics of the rival chancellor-candidates, it is very hard to locate.

[97] Kaase, "Is There Personalization in Politics?" p. 226.

[98] Kaase, "Is There Personalization in Politics?" p. 226–7.

[99] Hans-Dieter Klingemann and Martin P. Wattenberg, "Decaying Versus Developing Party Systems: A Comparison of Party Images in the United States and West Germany," *British Journal of Political Science*, 22 (1992), 131–49.

[100] Klingemann and Wattenberg, "Decaying Versus Developing Party Systems," p. 142.

[101] Klingemann and Wattenberg, "Decaying Versus Developing Party Systems," p. 144.

Canada

Compared with the countries we have looked at already, Canada is something of a hybrid. On the one hand, it is a stable democracy and one that also had a remarkably stable party system, at least until the mid 1980s; in these respects, Canada closely resembles the United States and Great Britain. On the other hand, the Canadian party system has been in turmoil ever since the mid 1980s, with both the Canadian electorate as a whole and individual Canadian voters exhibiting remarkably high levels of volatility; in these respects, though in few others, Canada resembles France and post-Soviet Russia.

The changes in the Canadian party system over the past quarter-century are worth emphasizing. Until the federal elections of the mid 1980s, Canadian electoral politics were dominated—and had been dominated for more than a century—by the Liberal Party and the Progressive Conservative Party. These were Canada's two "major parties" in the British sense of the term. Third parties rose and fell, but only one of them, the Cooperative Commonwealth Federation, later renamed the New Democratic Party (NDP), consistently won both 10 percent or more of the national vote and a number of seats—sometimes quite a large number—in parliament. The amplitude of the electoral swings between the two major parties was relatively small, more or less in line with that in Great Britain and other established parliamentary democracies.

But all that changed with the federal election of 1984, and Canadian electoral politics ever since has been among the most volatile and unpredictable in the democratic world. At the 1984 election, the Liberals' share of the vote fell below 30 percent, and they lost nearly three-quarters of their seats in the House of Commons. In 1988, the NDP's vote exceeded 20 per cent for the first time, and it won a record number of seats. In 1993, the Progressive Conservatives, who had been in power for the previous nine years, saw their share of the vote plummet from 43 percent to 16 percent (*sic*) and their parliamentary representation from 169 to two (also *sic*). In 1993, the Bloc Québécois, hitherto unrepresented in the federal parliament, became the official opposition, and the new Reform Party, also hitherto unrepresented in parliament, succeeded in more or less obliterating the NDP. Four years later, at the 1997 election, the Progressive Conservatives and the NDP both staged modest recoveries, but the Reform Party—which only a decade before had won only 2 percent of the popular vote and not a single seat in the Commons—now proceeded to supplant the Bloc Québécois as the official opposition. In 1984, the rank order of Canada's parties—in terms of their parliamentary strength—had been Progressive Conservatives, Liberals, NDP, with the rest nowhere. By 1997, the rank order was Liberals, Reform Party, Bloc Québécois, NDP, Progressive Conservatives. In other words, a long-established two-party-dominant system had effectively become, within a generation, a five-party system. Not only that, but the top party of 1984 was now, in 1997, the bottom party.[102]

In such a volatile environment, the personal qualities of party leaders might be expected to be of considerable electoral significance, and even before 1984 Canadian political scientists were suggesting that party leaders in Canada might count for more electorally than their counterparts in other democracies. They pointed out, in particular, that Canadian voters' strength of party identification was less than elsewhere, that in a country as deeply divided as Canada the political parties had every incentive to avoid addressing contentious issues and to try instead to build winning coalitions around the personalities of their leaders and that, in any case, the organizational disunity of Canada's political parties at the federal level more or less compelled them to embody themselves in their leaders' personas.[103]

Unlike in the United States, there is something of a conventional wisdom in Canada concerning the electoral importance of party leaders, but it is a wisdom tempered by dubiety. For the kinds of reasons just given, most students of Canadian politics take it for granted that Canadian party leaders count for a great deal in determining individual vote choices and overall election outcomes, but many of them at the same time seem uneasily aware that all may not be quite as it seems. For example, the authors of a survey-based study of the 1988 federal election note wryly that, while that election "put leadership on the table in a wholly new way," the most popular leader of all "seemed to be Ed Broadbent, leader of the system's weakest party [the NDP]."[104] They also note that the only leader who apparently rose in voters' esteem during the 1988 campaign was the Liberals' John Turner. But the Liberals lost—badly.[105]

The only sustained effort made so far to assess Canadian party leaders' personal contributions both to individual vote decisions and to overall election outcomes is the one made in the 1970s by Harold D. Clarke and his associates.[106] Their data indicate that at both the 1968 and 1974 federal elections considerable numbers of party identifiers who positively preferred the leader of another party, or else held their own party's leader and the leader of another party in equal esteem, chose to vote for the party whose leader they preferred rather than for their own.[107] More generally, they observed that the scale of such leadership effects tended to vary substantially over time and

---

[102] Canadian election data for the period 1957–88 can be found in Thomas T. Mackie and Richard Rose, *The International Almanac of Electoral History*, 3rd edn. (Basingstoke, Hants.: Macmillan, 1991). Data relating to the 1993 and subsequent elections can be found on the Elections Canada web page.

[103] Harold D. Clarke, Jane Jenson, Lawrence LeDuc, and Jon H. Pammett, *Political Choice in Canada* (Toronto: McGraw-Hill, Ryerson, 1979), p. 207.

[104] Richard Johnston, André Blais, Henry E. Brady, and Jean Crête, *Letting the People Decide: Dynamics of a Canadian Election* (Stanford, Calif.: Stanford University Press, 1992), p. 169.

[105] Johnston *et al.*, *Letting the People Decide*, esp. chap. 6.

[106] Clarke *et al.*, *Political Choice in Canada*, p. 91.

[107] Clarke *et al.*, *Political Choice in Canada*, pp. 327–8.

depended to a large extent on the strength of individual voters' partisan attachments. With specific reference to the 1974 election, they concluded that the pull of the major parties' leaders was considerable at the individual level and, moreover, that among the electorate as a whole the balance of opinion was heavily skewed in favor of Pierre Trudeau and the Liberals. The Liberals won, and Clarke and his associates conclude, on the basis of their data, that "the movement toward the Liberals among the more leader-oriented segment of the electorate . . . [was] large enough to be of potential significance in the outcome."[108]

This view—which emphasizes the actual or potential importance of party leaders in Canada—constitutes the conventional wisdom, but it has been challenged on at least one occasion, albeit at the provincial rather than the federal level. David K. Stewart and R. K. Carty analysed 136 changes of party leadership in Canadian provincial parties over the period 1960–92.[109] They did so in the light of the widespread presumption in Canada that party leaders are of enormous electoral significance:

Canadian political parties have always been leader-focussed electoral machines and as a consequence quick to attribute their electoral success, or failure, to their leaders . . . As a consequence it has become the conventional wisdom that changing leaders will pay an electoral dividend since a new leader provides a new face for the easily jaded electorate.[110]

Stewart and Carty's findings, however, by no means pointed in the expected direction, and their conclusion is worth quoting in full:

Leadership changes and conventions do not provide a guarantee of future electoral success nor are they a panacea for an unpopular governing party. Though Canadian parties often attempt to redefine both their policies and their image by changing their leaders, the evidence indicates that such changes will not catapult an opposition party into power nor ensure that a governing party retains its position. While parties not in power usually see their vote and seat shares increase after a leadership change, these changes are typically very small. In terms of providing electoral boosts, conventions and leadership changes are largely failures: the conventional wisdom is wrong.[111]

Russia

Leaders' personalities and other personal characteristics ought, on the face of it, to count for an enormous amount in post-Soviet Russia. For most of Russian history, individual autocrats—imperial tsars, then Communist dictators—utterly dominated the country's political life. The man or woman in

---

[108] Clarke *et al.*, *Political Choice in Canada*, p. 375.

[109] David K. Stewart and R. K. Carty, "Does Changing the Party Leader Provide an Electoral Boost? A Study of Canadian Provincial Parties: 1960–1992," *Canadian Journal of Political Science*, 26 (1993), 313–30.

[110] Stewart and Carty, "Does Changing the Leader Provide an Electoral Boost?" p. 313.

[111] Stewart and Carty, "Does Changing the Leader Provide an Electoral Boost?" p. 329.

the Kremlin, whoever he or she was, exercised personal power on a scale inconceivable in a constitutional state. In most of the rest of Europe or the Americas there were no real analogues to Catherine the Great, Nicholas I, Lenin, and Stalin. Even today, the belief is widely held that the mass of the Russian people continue to hunger for strong leadership and, therefore, for strong leaders.

Leaders' personalities might also be expected to count for a great deal in Russia because the Russian party system is still in its infancy. Many of the political parties in Russia are themselves unstable; they come and go—and change their names—with bewildering frequency. In addition, even if the political parties themselves were more stable, most Russian voters, unlike voters in the United States, Britain, Germany, and other democracies, have not yet had the time to develop stable attachments to them. Strong voter identification with political parties is typically built up over years, even generations, and the first free presidential election in post-Soviet Russia was not held until 1991. Under these circumstances, voters might be expected to take their electoral cues, not from organized political parties, which, apart from the Communists, scarcely exist, but from the personal qualities of the skillfully projected individual politicians who compete for the presidency.

Political scientists who have studied Russian elections have to a large extent, based on their empirical research, accepted the central thrust of this argument. Some have gone further and argued that, whereas in established democracies preexisting party identifications tend to color judgments of party leaders, in Russia judgments of party leaders may actually help give rise to party identifications: stable, enduring attachments to particular political parties. In the words of two Russian scholars:

Electoral uncertainty combined with the lack of commonly recognized meaningful cleavages, in the absence of party affiliation or even general political affiliation, makes personalities of politicians the key feature that distinguishes numerous political parties with similar electoral platforms from one another. Personalities thus become the essential asset of a "new" political party.[112]

Arthur H. Miller, William M. Reisinger, and Vicki L. Hesli strongly support this view. In a paper published in 1998, Miller and his colleagues note the high correlations in Russia between the nascent party identifications of ordinary voters and their favorable or unfavorable views of the various parties' leaders.[113] They also note that voters' generalized judgments of the parties' leaders tend to be based on more specific judgments about the leaders' personal traits: for instance, on whether each was or was not seen to be "trustworthy," "caring," or

---

[112] Quoted in Arthur H. Miller, William M. Reisinger, and Vicki L. Hesli, "Leader Popularity and Party Development in Post-Soviet Russia," in Matthew Wyman, Stephen White, and Sarah Oates, eds., *Elections and Voters in Post-communist Russia* (Cheltenham: Edward Elgar, 1998), p. 101.

[113] Miller, Reisinger, and Hesli, "Leader Popularity and Party Development in Post-Soviet Russia."

"a man of action." They conclude that "public assessments of performance-related traits associated with political leaders appear to be a major explanation for the partisan identification rapidly emerging among post-Soviet Russian citizens."[114] They maintain that this conclusion holds good even when other possible sources of party identification, such as socioeconomic status, ideological dispositions and views about the future organization of Russia's economy, are controlled for.

To the obvious objection that the causal arrow may point the other way and that voters' assessments of the party leaders are likely to be heavily influenced by their prior assessments of the parties, Miller and his colleagues respond that, while this may be true up to a point of the Communist Party and its leaders, given that the Communist Party is a long-established feature of the Russian political landscape, it is most unlikely to be true of the other parties, which have emerged in recent years at much the same time as their leaders—indeed in several cases *after* their leaders. Readily conceding that in the mid 1990s preferences for the Communist leader, Gennadii Zyuganov, may have been colored by preexisting preferences for the Communist Party, Miller and his colleagues add immediately: "The other parties, however, have appeared so recently that surely this cannot apply to them."[115] If Miller and his colleagues are right, Russian electoral politics is likely to bear the impress for generations to come of those politicians, most notably Boris Yeltsin and Gennadii Zyuganov, who happened to be politically prominent at the time that Russia became a democracy. The thought is not wholly far-fetched. After all, the Republican Party in the United States became identified in its earliest years with the person of Abraham Lincoln, and it remained "the party of Lincoln" for decades thereafter.

Hypotheses

As we have just seen, some political scientists believe that leaders' and candidates' personal characteristics matter a lot; others believe that they matter scarcely at all. Concerning the United States, opinion is divided. Concerning Great Britain, opinion is also divided. Concerning France, not a great deal has so far been written but the general view is that leaders and candidates are important. Concerning Germany, it seems generally agreed that party loyalties count for more than leader evaluations. Concerning Russia, it seems generally agreed that leaders count for a great deal. Concerning Canada, the same broad consensus seems to exist (except at the provincial level).

---

[114] Miller, Reisinger, and Hesli, "Leader Popularity and Party Development in Post-Soviet Russia," p. 126.
[115] Miller, Reisinger, and Hesli, "Leader Popularity and Party Development in Post-Soviet Russia," p. 131.

Confronted with such substantial and widespread disagreements, one is tempted to say that both views—the view that attributes maximal electoral importance to leaders' and candidates' characteristics and the view that, on the contrary, accords them minimal importance—cannot be right. But, of course, they can. Implicit in all of the above discussion has been the possibility that the characteristics and qualities of leaders and candidates are important under some circumstances and unimportant, or considerably less important, under others. The task then becomes, not to choose between two competing schools of thought, but to specify the conditions under which leaders' characteristics are, and are not, likely to be electorally significant, always bearing in mind that large numbers of individual voters' decisions at an election may be affected by leaders' characteristics without the overall outcome of that election being seriously affected. The distinction between "gross" and "net" in this context is crucial, and we shall return to it repeatedly in the pages that follow.

At each of these two levels, one can advance a number of hypotheses. Set out in simple language, they may seem obvious, even trite, but their implications are enormous.

At the gross level—the level of individuals' vote decisions—it seems reasonable to suggest that *the impact of leaders' personalities and other personal characteristics will be greatest when large numbers of voters perceive large differences between the competing leaders' or candidates' leadership-related capabilities*, however these things are measured. In other words, if large numbers of voters think one leading contender for the prime ministership, the presidency, or whatever is a great statesman while the other is a complete idiot, many of them are likely to act on the basis of that judgment. Note that this is already a somewhat stringent test, since, as was pointed out earlier, political parties are unlikely in practice to elect as their leaders or nominate as their candidates individuals who are ill equipped by temperament or intellect to hold high office. The example of Michael Foot in Great Britain in 1983 (Foot having been ill regarded not only by most ordinary electors but by his closest parliamentary colleagues) is unusual.

It also seems reasonable to suggest that *the impact of leaders' personalities and other personal characteristics will be greatest when voters' emotional ties to parties are at their weakest*. Strong party attachments typically mean either that most voters disregard the personal qualities of the competing leaders or else view them largely through the prism of their already established party preferences. If, however, party attachments among the electorate are weak— because the party system itself is new or in flux, or because previously strong party attachments have been eroded for some reason—then many voters may be expected to use the personal qualities of the competing leaders as the basis, or at least as *a* basis, for making their vote decisions.

Similarly, it might be hypothesized that *the impact of leaders' and candidates' personal qualities will be greatest when voters can discern few other grounds—whether grounds of performance or of policy—for choosing among either the parties or the leaders.* If, on the one hand, parties and candidates are sharply differentiated on policy grounds, or if voters have reason to believe that one party is almost certain to outperform the other(s) in connection with, say, managing the economy or fighting crime, then the competing leaders' personal characteristics are unlikely to count for much. If, on the other hand, the parties and candidates have taken up almost identical policy positions and/or appear likely, if elected, to govern in a highly similar manner, then voters might choose to use the leaders' or candidates' personal characteristics as, so to speak, a "tie-breaker."

At the more important, net level—the level of overall election outcomes—it goes without saying that *the impact of leaders' characteristics will be greatest when large numbers of individual voters are influenced by such characteristics and,* at the same time, *their preferences are heavily skewed in favor of one leader or candidate rather than another (or others).* Clearly, both of these conditions have to be met. Large numbers of voters have to be susceptible to the leaders' or candidates' personal appeals, *and* those susceptible voters have to be disproportionately susceptible to one leader or candidate's appeal rather than others'. Again, it is worth noting that these conditions, taken together, constitute a single, stringent condition, one that, on the face of it, seems unlikely to be fulfilled more than occasionally.

It also goes without saying—or should go without saying—that *the impact of leaders' characteristics will be at its greatest, and is most likely to be decisive, when the outcome of the election under consideration would in any case have been extremely close.* Under these circumstances, almost any factor can be decisive, and there is no reason why the comparative appeal of competing leaders should not on occasion be the factor that decides the outcome. We have already seen that most British observers are agreed that, in the extremely close-fought general elections of 1964 and February 1974, the differential appeals of Harold Wilson and Sir Alec Douglas-Home in the first instance, and of Harold Wilson and Edward Heath in the second, may have made all the difference.

One final point is worth making. It happens from time to time that the party with the most highly regarded leader loses a national election to a party that has a less highly regarded leader. Two such cases, according to Klingemann and Wattenberg, were the 1983 and 1987 elections in Germany, when the Christian Democrats under Helmut Kohl won despite the fact that Kohl was less popular than his Social Democrat opponent.[116] Another such case, almost certainly, was that of Great Britain in 1945, when the Labour Party under Clement Attlee defeated the Conservatives under Winston Churchill despite the fact that Churchill, as the man who had just led Britain to victory in World War II, was undoubtedly, as an individual, held in far

---

[116] See above p. 35.

higher esteem than his insignificant-seeming opponent. The inference to be drawn from such instances is obvious and has already been referred to in passing. If the party with the less well-esteemed leader wins, then the outcome of that election *cannot* have turned on voters' judgments of the respective qualities of the various parties' leaders or candidates. Leadership effects *cannot* have been decisive; they can, at most, only have reduced the victor's margin of victory. Full stop, end of story. The point is indeed obvious but is sometimes overlooked by political scientists who concentrate on the dynamics of individuals' vote decisions rather than on the determinants of overall election outcomes—which latter, of course, are of enormously greater political significance.

It is against this background that we proceed to consider the role that voters' assessments of individual political leaders play in the electoral politics of each of our six countries, starting with the United States.

2

The Impact of Candidate Traits in American Presidential Elections

LARRY M. BARTELS

One of the most familiar themes in modern electoral analysis emphasizes the potency of televised images of political candidates to sway the voting behavior of mass electorates. Beginning with the rise of television as a political force in the 1950s, political journalists and campaign consultants have suggested that the "old politics" of socially and ideologically based party coalitions has given way to a "new politics" centering on the personal qualities of individual candidates, as conveyed, or even *created*, through the medium of television. Thus, by the early 1960s, one leading political scientist felt it necessary to deny that American voters were "moved by subconscious urges triggered by devilishly skillful propagandists."[1] A decade later, another prominent academic study decried what its authors referred to as "The Myth of Television Power in National Elections."[2]

Joe McGinniss's *The Selling of the President 1968* marked something of a watershed in popular perceptions of the modern electoral process. Its behind-the-scenes look at how even so apparently unattractive a candidate as Richard Nixon could be repackaged and sold to a gullible American electorate generated both fascination and consternation. Books with titles like *The Image Candidates*, *The Political Persuaders*, and *Polls, Television, and the New Politics* were more scholarly in tone, but reinforced the impression that the electoral process had been fundamentally altered by the rise of television.[3]

---

[1] V. O. Key, Jr., *The Responsible Electorate: Rationality in Presidential Voting 1936–1960* (New York: Vintage Books, 1966), p. 7.

[2] Thomas E. Patterson and Robert D. McClure, *The Unseeing Eye: The Myth of Television Power in National Elections* (New York: G. P. Putnam's Sons, 1976).

[3] Joe McGinniss, *The Selling of the President 1968* (New York: Trident Press, 1969); Gene Wyckoff, *The Image Candidates* (New York: Macmillan, 1968); Dan Nimmo, *The Political Persuaders: The Techniques of Modern Election Campaigns* (Englewood Cliffs, N.J.: Prentice-Hall, 1970); Harold Mendelsohn and Irving Crespi, *Polls, Television, and the New Politics* (Scranton, Penn.: Chandler, 1970).

The emphasis in the late 1960s and 1970s on candidates' "images" and the politics of personality was often interpreted as contradicting an older academic perspective emphasizing the importance of stable partisan loyalties—a perspective represented most prominently by *The American Voter*.[4] Of course, the authors of *The American Voter* were hardly unaware of the fact that the personal popularity of Dwight Eisenhower outweighed the Democratic Party's longstanding advantage in party identification in each of the two successive presidential elections they analyzed. Their own subsequent work elaborated the role of "dynamic" short-term forces, including the personal images of the competing candidates, in producing such "deviating elections."[5] However, the appropriate place of candidates' personalities within a broader understanding of voting behavior and electoral politics remained unclear.

Notwithstanding the somewhat uneasy coexistence of traditional voting research, political psychology, and popular political commentary, by the 1990s *The Rise of Candidate-Centered Politics* (to quote the title of an influential study by Wattenberg)[6] was an accepted fact among most political scientists. Television was widely viewed as the moving force behind that development. For example, Butler and Ranney concluded that "Television . . . has done more than anything else to transform electioneering." In particular, they argued, television is "more inclined to focus on visual images and personalities. It has intensified the concentration on leaders as the sole spokesmen of their parties."[7]

The impact of personality in contemporary American politics has also been accepted as a matter of faith among political observers beyond academia. As one prominent commentator, Anna Quindlen, put it in the midst of the most recent presidential campaign,

personality is key in Election 2000. . . . just as they use it to choose their friends, their spouses, the neighbors they invite over for a barbecue, the co-workers they join for lunch, so voters use their impressions of a candidate's personality to choose a president. In the next 90 days millions of people will decide, finally, whether they think Al Gore is rigid and humorless or instead serious and diligent, whether George W. Bush is straight-talking and sure of himself or simply arrogant and tactless. And that will matter. A lot.[8]

[4] Angus Campbell, Philip E. Converse, Warren E. Miller, and Donald E. Stokes, *The American Voter* (New York: John Wiley & Sons, 1960).

[5] For example, Donald E. Stokes, "Party Loyalty and the Likelihood of Deviating Elections," *Journal of Politics*, 24 (1962), 689–702; Donald E. Stokes, "Some Dynamic Elements of Contests for the Presidency," *American Political Science Review*, 60 (1966), 19–28.

[6] Martin P. Wattenberg, *The Rise of Candidate-Centered Politics: Presidential Elections of the 1980s* (Cambridge, Mass.: Harvard University Press, 1991).

[7] David Butler and Austin Ranney, eds., *Electioneering: A Comparative Study of Continuity and Change* (Oxford: Clarendon Press, 1992), p. 281.

[8] Anna Quindlen, "It's the cult of personality," *Newsweek*, August 14, 2000, p. 68.

A similar understanding of the electoral impact of personality was conveyed in a typical description in the *New York Times* of candidate Bush's efforts to portray himself as a common man rather than a scion of wealth: "in an election that many Republican and Democratic strategists believe will turn as much on personality as on policy, the way voters react to each candidate's efforts along these lines could be decisive."[9]

My aim in this chapter is to provide a systematic test of the conventional wisdom that, as Quindlen put it, "personality is key" in contemporary American electoral politics. Using survey data from the six most recent presidential elections, I shall examine the contours of the candidates' images, the bases of those images in voters' more fundamental political predispositions, and the impact of voters' assessments of the candidates' personal qualities on individual voting behavior and on aggregate election outcomes. In stark contrast with the popular conception of contemporary electoral politics as candidate-centered and image-driven, I shall argue that candidates' images are largely epiphenomenal and that they have only a modest impact on election outcomes. This conclusion is underlined by my analysis of the 2000 presidential election, in which the estimated impact of voters' assessments of the candidates' personalities was even smaller than in the previous five elections considered here—though quite probably large enough to be decisive in an election decided by a few hundred votes in a single state.

Candidate Traits

The best available data on prospective voters' personal impressions of American presidential candidates come from a battery of "candidate trait" items included in recent American National Election Study (NES) surveys.[10] In each presidential election year since 1980, NES has invited survey respondents to rate the competing presidential candidates on a series of character traits. The specific personal qualities tapped in these "trait ratings" have varied somewhat from year to year, but three traits have been included in all of the past six presidential election years and two more have been included in five of those six years. These five hardy-perennial traits are:

• moral
• knowledgeable
• inspiring
• provides strong leadership
• really cares about people like you.

---

[9] Frank Bruni, "Bush insists to voters his blood is red, not blue," *New York Times*, April 24, 2000, p. A19.

[10] The data utilized here, along with details of the study design, codebooks, and other relevant information, are publicly available through the NES website, www.umich.edu/~nes.

Considerable scholarly work has gone into conceptualizing and validating these and other specific trait questions and exploring their interrelationships.[11] However, for my purposes here it is only necessary to accept the five traits included regularly in the NES surveys as a fair sampling from the broader range of personal qualities that might conceivably be relevant to prospective voters.[12] Indeed, even readers unhappy with this selection of relevant traits may be reassured to learn that my conclusions turn out to be rather surprisingly insensitive to exactly which traits, or how many traits, are included in the analysis.[13]

The standard format of the NES trait questions requires respondents to assess how well each of a series of words or phrases describes a particular candidate. For example:

Think about Bill Clinton. In your opinion, does the phrase "he really cares about people like you" describe Bill Clinton *extremely well, quite well, not too well, or not well at all*?

In my recoding of the survey responses, *extremely well* corresponds to a score of 100, *quite well* to a score of 66.7, *not too well* to a score of 33.3, and *not well at all* to a score of zero.[14]

---

[11] Donald R. Kinder, Mark D. Peters, Robert P. Abelson, and Susan T. Fiske, "Presidential Prototypes," *Political Behavior*, 2 (1980), 315–37; Robert P. Abelson, Donald R. Kinder, Mark D. Peters, and Susan T. Fiske, "Affective and Semantic Components in Political Person Perception," *Journal of Personality and Social Psychology*, 42 (1982), 619–30; Donald R. Kinder, "Presidential Character Revisited," in Richard R. Lau and David O. Sears, eds., *Political Cognition* (Hillsdale, N.J.: Lawrence Erlbaum Associates, 1986); Donald R. Kinder and Susan T. Fiske, "Presidents in the Public Mind," in Margaret G. Hermann, ed., *Political Psychology: Contemporary Problems and Issues* (San Francisco: Jossey-Bass, 1986); Arthur H. Miller, Martin P. Wattenberg, and Oksana Malanchuk, "Schematic Assessment of Presidential Candidates," *American Political Science Review*, 80 (1986), 521–40.

[12] Miller and Shanks worried that "one of these questions (concerning 'strong leadership') presents a somewhat different criterion for evaluation than a 'personal' or non-governmental quality, for it involves an implicit standard that is hard to distinguish from 'would be a good President.'" See Warren E. Miller and J. Merrill Shanks, *The New American Voter* (Cambridge, Mass.: Harvard University Press, 1996). While recognizing the logical force of that concern, I treat the "strong leader" trait in the same way as the others in the following analysis, for two reasons. First, assessments of the candidates' leadership qualities do not turn out to be markedly more strongly related to broader political views, or to vote choices, than are some of the other trait assessments considered here. Second, including assessments of the candidates' leadership qualities in my battery of trait ratings will, if anything, exaggerate the impact of trait ratings on voting behavior, which will tend to work against the thrust of my argument that candidates' personal qualities generally have quite modest electoral effects.

[13] I repeated all of the analyses reported in this chapter using random subsets of the five-trait battery. The estimated effects of trait assessments on specific election outcomes were generally similar to those reported here, with only a very slight tendency for more extensive trait batteries to produce larger estimated effects. In the case of the 2000 election I also examined the impact of including additional traits beyond the five included regularly in previous NES surveys; the results of that exercise (detailed in due course) likewise suggest that the precise set of traits included in the analysis is relatively inconsequential.

[14] Alternative recoding schemes reflecting different assumptions about the appropriate relative distances between response categories produce results essentially similar to those reported here.

Table 2.1 provides a summary of the average ratings on the resulting 0–100 scale for each major-party presidential candidate on each of the five traits included regularly in the NES surveys. (Respondents in 1980 were not asked the "really cares" questions; respondents in 2000 were not asked the "inspiring" questions.) The trait ratings come from preelection surveys conducted in the two months preceding each November election. Given my interest in the electoral impact of trait assessments, all of the data in Table 2.1 and throughout this chapter come from NES survey respondents who reported, in a postelection reinterview, voting for one or the other of the major-party presidential candidates; those who reported not voting or voting for a minor-party candidate for president are excluded from my analysis.[15]

Table 2.1. Average trait ratings of U.S. presidential candidates, 1980–2000

	1980 Reagan/ Carter	1984 Reagan/ Mondale	1988 Bush/ Dukakis	1992 Bush/ Clinton	1996 Dole/ Clinton	2000 Bush/ Gore
Really cares						
Republican candidate	–	48.7 (0.9)	49.5 (0.8)	40.0 (0.8)	47.2 (0.8)	46.5 (0.9)
Democratic candidate	–	56.7 (0.7)	57.8 (0.7)	58.3 (0.7)	53.7 (1.0)	54.2 (0.9)
Moral						
Republican candidate	64.2 (0.9)	72.3 (0.7)	66.3 (0.7)	68.4 (0.7)	70.1 (0.7)	64.1 (0.8)
Democratic candidate	72.6 (0.9)	66.4 (0.6)	62.8 (0.6)	46.2 (0.7)	38.3 (0.9)	64.3 (0.8)
Knowledgeable						
Republican candidate	62.4 (1.0)	64.6 (0.8)	68.1 (0.6)	67.6 (0.6)	70.2 (0.6)	58.7 (0.8)
Democratic candidate	63.8 (0.9)	65.0 (0.6)	64.4 (0.6)	66.8 (0.6)	72.4 (0.8)	69.7 (0.7)
Inspiring						
Republican candidate	51.0 (1.0)	58.2 (0.8)	43.6 (0.7)	44.0 (0.8)	44.3 (0.8)	–
Democratic candidate	41.5 (1.0)	44.4 (0.7)	48.1 (0.7)	55.0 (0.7)	51.0 (0.9)	–
Strong leader						
Republican candidate	57.3 (1.0)	65.7 (0.8)	50.8 (0.8)	53.2 (0.8)	58.2 (0.8)	57.5 (0.8)
Democratic candidate	39.2 (1.0)	46.7 (0.7)	51.9 (0.7)	56.0 (0.7)	54.0 (0.9)	52.7 (0.8)

Note: Average ratings on 0–100 scale by major-party presidential voters only (with standard errors in parentheses).

[15] My analysis also excludes approximately 10 percent of the preelection respondents in each year who, for one reason or another, could not be reinterviewed after the election.

Given the large sample sizes of the NES surveys, the mean trait ratings are estimated fairly precisely—the standard errors of the estimated means are never more than 1 point on the 100-point scale. Thus, we can be fairly sure that the differences in mean ratings from candidate to candidate and from trait to trait that appear in Table 2.1 are real. However, it is worth noting that most of the differences among candidates for any given trait are relatively modest, especially for candidates of the same party. For example, the range of the six "really cares" ratings for Republicans is only from 40.0 to 49.5 (both, as it happens, for the elder George Bush), while the corresponding range for Democrats is only from 53.7 to 58.3 (both, as it happens, for Bill Clinton). The average difference in ratings for competing candidates, averaging over both traits and election years, is only a little more than 8 points on the 100-point scale, and the only cases in which any pair of competing candidates' ratings on any trait differ by as much as 20 points are the two comparisons involving Bill Clinton's ratings on the "morality" trait, which were markedly lower than those of any other candidate in the six elections covered by my analysis.

Obviously, the fact that stark differences in aggregate public perceptions of the competing candidates' personal qualities are rare tends to limit the potential impact of personalities on election outcomes. Even if voters weigh candidate traits heavily in deciding whom to vote for, the net effect of "image" considerations will be modest if prospective voters do not clearly prefer one of the competing candidates to the other. One reason why they might not is that parties presumably try to avoid nominating candidates with salient character flaws. In addition, as I shall attempt to demonstrate here, the *average* impressions of the competing candidates reported in Table 2.1 are moderated by a strong tendency for each party's partisans to think highly of their own candidate and less highly of his opponent. The result is that most of the average ratings fall in a rather narrow, mildly positive range, from about 50 to 65 on the 100-point scale.

Most of the differences that do appear in the various candidates' average trait ratings seem to be consistent with the assessments of contemporary observers regarding the candidates' personal strengths and weaknesses. For example, Ronald Reagan in 1984 received higher marks than any other recent presidential candidate for being "inspiring" and a "strong leader," while Jimmy Carter in 1980 received the lowest marks on those dimensions. Democratic candidates in every election year were more likely than their Republican opponents to be perceived as "really caring" about ordinary people. And Carter in 1980 was (by a slight margin) the most highly rated candidate with respect to "morality," while, as I have already indicated, Clinton's "morality" ratings in both 1992 and 1996 were much lower than those of any other recent presidential candidate.

In the Eyes of the Beholders:
Political Biases in Trait Ratings

The average trait ratings presented in Table 2.1 provide some evidence of real—and not unreasonable—differences in aggregate public perceptions of different candidates' personal qualities. However, those generally modest aggregate differences disguise a good deal of disagreement *among* survey respondents in any given year regarding the presidential candidates' personal qualities. Much of this disagreement presumably reflects idiosyncratic differences in individual responses to specific candidates, or even simple measurement error in the survey responses. At the same time, however, there are clear patterns in the individual responses suggesting that specific impressions of the candidates' traits are strongly affected by respondents' more general political attitudes.

The extent to which perceptions of political stimuli may be colored by political predispositions is vividly illustrated by the reactions of Patterson and McClure's survey respondents to television advertisements and news stories during the 1972 presidential campaign. Consider, for example, the following pairs of reactions to news stories and advertisements featuring George McGovern, each of which includes one reaction from a McGovern supporter followed by one from a Nixon supporter:[16]

He's a good, honest man. You can see that.
Can't believe what you see. It would be worse with him.

He looks so able. I think he's very able.
He's a weak sister. You can see that immediately.

He really cares what's happened to disabled vets. They told him how badly they've been treated and he listened. He will help them.
McGovern was talking with these disabled vets. He doesn't really care about them. He's just using them to get sympathy.

It was honest, down-to-earth. People were talking and he was listening.
Those commercials are so phoney. He doesn't care.

McGovern had his coat off and his tie was hanging down. It was so relaxed, and he seemed to really be concerned with those workers.
He is trying hard to look like one of the boys. You know, roll up the shirt sleeves and loosen the tie. It's just too much for me to take.

As Patterson and McClure aptly observed, "Different people were watching the same George McGovern on the screen, but clearly, they were not seeing

[16] Patterson and McClure, *The Unseeing Eye*, pp. 66, 114.

the same man . . . Their response was not to the image, but to the politics George McGovern personified."[17]

The perceptual biases that Patterson and McClure observed in their respondents' reactions to news coverage and advertisements also appear in a wide variety of other data on perceptions of political figures, including the trait ratings of presidential candidates collected by NES. The magnitude of these perceptual biases is illustrated in Figure 2.1, which shows how ratings of Bill Clinton as a "strong leader," "moral," and "knowledgeable" varied with the partisan loyalties of the people doing the rating in the 1992 NES survey. In each panel of the figure, the array of bars represents the percentages in each partisan group (from strong Democrats on the left to strong Republicans on the right) who said the trait in question described Clinton "extremely well" or "quite well."

The pattern of partisan bias evident in Figure 2.1 is especially striking because the measure of party identification used to differentiate voters' assessments of Clinton's personal qualities in 1992 comes from a separate NES survey conducted with the same respondents two years earlier, before Clinton had even emerged as a salient political figure. Thus, there is no question here of voters adjusting their partisanship to comport with their assessments of

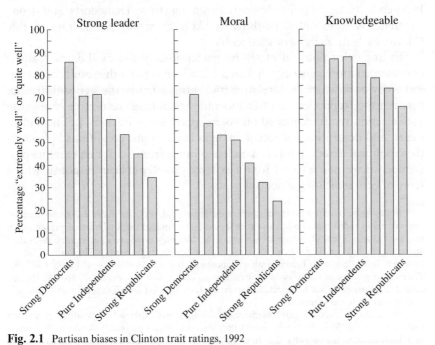

Fig. 2.1 Partisan biases in Clinton trait ratings, 1992

[17] Patterson and McClure, *The Unseeing Eye*, p. 66.

Clinton. Impressions of the candidate were strongly conditioned by political loyalties that clearly predated his arrival on the national political scene.

The largest partisan biases evident in Figure 2.1 are for assessments of Clinton as a "strong leader" and "moral," in the first and second panels respectively. For each of these traits the proportion of strong Democrats who thought the label fitted Clinton "extremely well" or "quite well" exceeded the corresponding proportion of strong Republicans by approximately 50 per- centage points, and even weak party identifiers differed in their assessments by about 25 percentage points. Short of arguing that Democrats and Republicans differed markedly in their *definitions* of what it means to be a "strong leader" or "moral"—and that Clinton just happened to exemplify the Democratic definition much better than the Republican definition in each case—it seems impossible to resist the conclusion that the trait assessments shown in Figure 2.1 reflect the biases of the voters doing the rating as much or more than they do the intrinsic qualities of the candidate being rated.

Even seemingly straightforward assessments of the candidates are subject to significant partisan biases. For example, the right-most panel of Figure 2.1 shows the percentage of each partisan group that rated Clinton as "know- ledgeable." Even among strong Republicans, 65 percent viewed Clinton as knowledgeable—but that figure was almost 20 points lower than among Independents and 27 points lower than among strong Democrats; and strong Republicans were only one-third as likely as strong Democrats to rate Clinton as "extremely" knowledgeable.

The impact of political biases on perceptions of the candidates' traits is documented more generally in Table 2.2, which reports the results of statist- ical analyses in which each relative trait rating (that is, the signed difference between the Republican and Democratic candidates' respective ratings) in each election year is regressed on voters' party identifications, political ideo- logies, and perceptions of recent changes in economic conditions.[18] Each of these political determinants is recoded to range from −1 for an extreme pro- Democratic response to +1 for an extreme pro-Republican response, with a score of zero indicating a neutral position.[19]

---

[18] Focusing on *relative* trait ratings for competing candidates (as in Table 2.2) rather than on assessments of individual candidates (as in Table 2.1) simplifies the analysis and presentation, and has the additional advantage of rendering the data impervious to idiosyncratic individual differences in the overall "generosity" of trait ratings. See Henry E. Brady, "The Perils of Survey Research: Inter-Personally Incomparable Responses," *Political Methodology*, 11 (1985), 269–91. The corresponding cost is that systematic differences in the sources or electoral impact of the two candidates' images cannot be detected from an analysis focusing on *differences* in trait ratings— a point I return to subsequently.

[19] In the case of economic perceptions, responses are scored differently depending upon which party controls the White House in order to produce the correct partisan valences in the regres- sion analyses reported in Table 2.2. In election years in which a Republican president was in office (1984, 1988, 1992) respondents who said the economy was "much better" get a score of +1, those who said the economy was "about the same" get a score of zero, and those who said the economy was "much worse" get a score of −1. In election years in which a Democratic president

Table 2.2. Political determinants of relative trait ratings, United States, 1980–2000

	1980	1984	1988	1992	1996	2000
Really cares						
Intercept	–	−10.0	−8.7	−4.0	−2.7	−5.5
		(1.0)	(1.0)	(1.5)	(1.2)	(1.2)
Republican party identification	–	31.8	27.9	35.1	34.9	39.4
		(1.5)	(1.5)	(1.5)	(1.7)	(1.8)
Conservative ideology	–	13.6	13.7	16.7	19.0	10.3
		(2.5)	(2.6)	(2.4)	(2.9)	(2.4)
Economic assessment	–	18.8	11.4	20.7	17.8	7.9
		(2.0)	(2.2)	(2.2)	(2.4)	(2.0)
Standard error of regression	–	33.9	32.9	34.0	33.1	35.6
Adjusted R^2	–	0.46	0.38	0.50	0.53	0.47
N	–	1,361	1,193	1,356	1,034	1,120
Moral						
Intercept	−10.5	4.3	3.0	27.8	34.0	1.0
	(2.2)	(0.8)	(0.9)	(1.5)	(1.3)	(1.1)
Republican party identification	19.6	16.3	14.2	22.0	32.7	23.6
	(1.8)	(1.3)	(1.3)	(1.5)	(1.8)	(1.7)
Conservative ideology	8.4	14.9	10.6	16.2	8.4	10.4
	(3.2)	(2.1)	(2.2)	(2.4)	(3.1)	(2.3)
Economic assessment	5.7	9.3	8.4	7.2	3.9	7.8
	(2.9)	(1.7)	(1.9)	(2.2)	(2.6)	(1.9)
Standard error of regression	33.6	28.3	27.8	34.3	35.0	34.0
Adjusted R^2	0.19	0.29	0.22	0.29	0.39	0.31
N	837	1,365	1,193	1,355	1,031	1,120
Knowledgeable						
Intercept	−6.0	−1.9	3.9	7.7	0.0	−10.3
	(2.2)	(0.9)	(0.8)	(1.2)	(1.0)	(1.1)
Republican party identification	21.6	19.0	15.6	16.6	17.1	20.1
	(1.8)	(1.4)	(1.3)	(1.3)	(1.5)	(1.7)
Conservative ideology	15.5	15.3	5.0	11.1	6.4	9.7
	(3.3)	(2.3)	(2.2)	(2.0)	(2.5)	(2.3)
Economic assessment	8.8	8.8	8.5	10.3	8.4	5.4
	(2.9)	(1.9)	(1.9)	(1.8)	(2.1)	(1.9)
Standard error of regression	34.1	32.1	27.5	28.9	28.3	33.8
Adjusted R^2	0.25	0.27	0.21	0.26	0.25	0.24
N	836	1,366	1,194	1,355	1,033	1,120
Inspiring						
Intercept	2.7	11.1	−4.2	−1.8	−3.2	–
	(2.4)	(1.0)	(1.0)	(1.4)	(1.3)	
Republican party identification	28.5	25.3	21.1	26.7	28.4	–
	(2.0)	(1.6)	(1.5)	(1.5)	(1.9)	
Conservative ideology	14.6	14.4	7.2	14.6	13.8	–
	(3.6)	(2.5)	(2.6)	(2.4)	(3.2)	

Table 2.2 (*cont.*): Political determinants of relative trait ratings, United States, 1980–2000

	1980	1984	1988	1992	1996	2000
Inspiring (*cont*):						
Economic	19.9	20.7	11.4	12.8	16.2	–
assessment	(3.2)	(2.0)	(2.2)	(2.2)	(2.7)	
Standard error						
of regression	37.3	34.6	32.2	33.6	37.0	–
Adjusted R^2	0.31	0.39	0.27	0.37	0.37	–
N	836	1,365	1,190	1,356	1,032	–
Strong leader						
Intercept	8.8	16.0	−1.0	8.4	7.8	6.8
	(2.5)	(1.0)	(1.0)	(1.4)	(1.3)	(1.2)
Republican party	34.4	27.4	25.6	26.9	29.8	35.4
identification	(2.1)	(1.6)	(1.5)	(1.5)	(1.8)	(1.8)
Conservative	14.1	9.8	10.7	11.8	9.8	10.0
ideology	(3.7)	(2.5)	(2.7)	(2.4)	(3.1)	(2.4)
Economic	19.1	26.2	13.3	16.0	13.2	8.1
assessment	(3.3)	(2.0)	(2.3)	(2.1)	(2.6)	(2.0)
Standard error						
of regression	38.3	34.7	33.2	33.5	35.2	35.8
Adjusted R^2	0.37	0.43	0.34	0.38	0.38	0.43
N	837	1,363	1,189	1,355	1,033	1,120

Note: Regression coefficients based upon major-party presidential voters only (with standard errors in parentheses).

Given this coding of the variables measuring political predispositions, the intercepts in Table 2.2 represent the relative trait ratings of the competing candidates in each election by "neutral observers"—survey respondents without partisan attachments who are ideologically moderate and who view the state of the national economy as essentially unchanged from the preceding year. If trait assessments were simple reflections of the intrinsic qualities of the candidates, we would expect these intercepts to vary markedly from trait to trait and from year to year with the personal qualities of the two candidates in each election. But we would not expect the coefficients for partisanship, ideology, and economic perceptions to reflect any strong relationship between voters' general political views and their specific assessments of the candidates' traits. In fact, however, there is much more systematic variation evident *among* voters in each election than there is *across* election years. This

was in office (1980, 1996, 2000) respondents who said the economy was "much better" get a score of −1, those who said the economy was "about the same" get a score of zero, and those who said the economy was "much worse" get a score of +1. Given this coding scheme, the expected impact of economic perceptions on relative (Republican minus Democratic) trait ratings under the hypothesis of partisan bias is positive in every election year.

pattern is most striking in the case of empathy ratings, where variations in "neutral observer" ratings from year to year amounted to only a few points, but strong partisans on each side gave their respective candidates an edge amounting to about 30 points on the -100 to $+100$ scale (by comparison with pure independents). For readers enamored of "statistically significant" parameter estimates, the *average* *t*-statistic for the twenty-eight separate Republican Party Identification coefficients in Table 2.2 is 15.8. The corresponding *average* *t*-statistics for the Conservative Ideology and Economic Assessment coefficients are 4.6 and 5.6, respectively.

The "neutral observer" trait ratings represented by the intercepts in Table 2.2 are presented in graphical form in Figure 2.2.[20] The figure differs from the table in presenting separate ratings for each presidential candidate, rather than comparative ratings of the two competing candidates in each election year. However, the basic aim is similar in both cases—to summarize public perceptions of the candidates' personal qualities purged of the biases attributable to partisanship, ideology, and retrospective economic evaluations.

The "neutral observer" ratings in Figure 2.2 differ in some significant respects from the *average* trait ratings presented in Table 2.1. For example, Jimmy Carter's unusually low ratings with respect to "strong leadership" in Table 2.1 appear to be largely attributable to the circumstances in which he ran for reelection; indeed, the "neutral observer" ratings of five different Democratic candidates in six different election years display very little variation in leadership assessments, suggesting that most of the variation in average leadership ratings in Table 2.1 reflects differences in political context rather than differences in the various candidates' intrinsic personal qualities.

It is striking that the major-party presidential candidate with the least impressive public image in the twenty years of systematic readings by NES is the one who has so frequently been referred to by journalists as a master campaigner and "once-in-a-lifetime political performer," Bill Clinton.[21] As a challenger in 1992, Clinton was rated only slightly higher than Walter Mondale in 1984 or Michael Dukakis in 1988 as "caring," and "knowledgeable," and much lower as "moral." His higher ratings than his predecessors as "inspiring" and a "strong leader" were largely due to the fact that he ran in a period of widespread economic discontent. What is even more surprising is that, allowing for the differences in circumstances between the two years, Clinton was viewed less favorably in 1996 than in 1992 on four of the five traits: less moral, less caring, less inspiring, and a less strong leader. The only respect in which his image improved during his first term in office is that he

[20] The "neutral observer" ratings for assessments of each candidate as "inspiring" are omitted from Figure 2.2 in order to conserve space. They generally parallel the "strong leader" ratings, except that George Bush in 1992 and Bob Dole in 1996 were each viewed as being slightly *less* inspiring than Bill Clinton.

[21] Caryn James, "Presenting a masterpiece in political theater, with a scene from 'Camelot'," *New York Times*, August 16, 2000, p. A26.

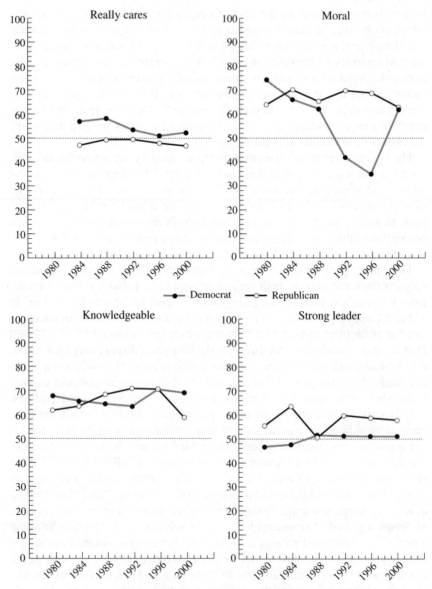

Fig. 2.2 "Neutral observer" trait ratings for presidential candidates, United States, 1980–2000

was more likely to be considered "knowledgeable"—as were Ronald Reagan in 1984 and George Bush in 1992 after four years in the White House.

In 2000, both of the competing candidates were viewed as fairly typical nominees of their respective parties, with the notable exception of George W. Bush's unusually low rating as "knowledgeable." Al Gore was perceived as more knowledgeable (by 69 to 59 on the 100-point scale) and caring (by 52 to

47), while Bush was viewed as a stronger leader (by 58 to 51) and slightly more moral (by 64 to 63). Thus, as in each of the other elections considered here, the net impact of candidate traits on the election outcome was dependent on the relative weight attached to different specific traits, and mitigated by the fact that neither candidate enjoyed a more favorable public image than his opponent across the whole range of traits likely to be considered relevant by prospective voters.

The Causal Status of Trait Ratings

My claim that specific impressions of the competing candidates are power-fully shaped by more basic political predispositions is reminiscent of the "fun-nel of causality" framework proposed by the authors of *The American Voter* and subsequently elaborated in a series of articles by Miller and Shanks cul-minating in their book-length study of *The New American Voter*.[22] Like Miller and Shanks, I argue that any reasonable assessment of the causal impact of candidate traits must take systematic account of the extent to which prospective voters' trait assessments are epiphenomenal.

More specifically, I shall follow Miller and Shanks in constructing a multi-stage causal model of voting behavior in which basic political predispositions may have powerful indirect effects by virtue of their importance in shaping more specific political opinions and impressions. In Miller and Shanks's for-mulation, eight distinct categories of explanatory variables are arrayed in a causal sequence with six distinct stages leading up to the ultimate decision to vote for one candidate or another. For my purposes here, that much com-plexity seems both unnecessary and potentially counterproductive.[23] Thus, my own analysis simply distinguishes between two categories of potential influences on voting behavior—assessments of the candidates' personal traits,

---

[22] Miller and Shanks, *The New American Voter*. See also Warren E. Miller and J. Merrill Shanks, "Policy Directions and Presidential Leadership: Alternative Interpretations of the 1980 Presidential Election," *British Journal of Political Science*, 12 (1982), 299–356; J. Merrill Shanks and Warren E. Miller, "Policy Direction and Performance Evaluation: Complementary Explanations of the Reagan Election," *British Journal of Political Science*, 20 (1990), 143–235; J. Merrill Shanks and Warren E. Miller, "Partisanship, Policy and Performance: The Reagan Legacy in the 1988 Election," *British Journal of Political Science*, 21 (1991), 129–97.

[23] Miller and Shanks, *The New American Voter*, chap. 8. Miller and Shanks included a much richer set of explanatory variables in their analyses than I employ here, but at the cost of making a variety of potentially problematic assumptions about causal ordering. For example, on the one hand, their analytic framework treated voters' retrospective evaluations of presidential perform-ance as potential causes, but not potential consequences, of their impressions of the candidates' personal qualities; on the other hand, voters' prospective evaluations of how the competing can-didates would perform in office were treated as potential consequences, but not potential causes, of their assessments of the candidates' personal traits. In the absence of good evidence regarding the nature of the causal relationships among these various explanatory factors, it seems desirable to simplify the analysis as much as possible by limiting the number of explanatory variables and assumptions of causal priority.

and the more basic political attitudes (party identification, ideology, and economic assessments) employed as explanatory variables in the regression analyses reported in Table 2.2.

I assume here that the strong relationships reported in Table 2.2 between trait assessments on the one hand and partisanship, ideology, and economic assessments on the other reflect the impact of political predispositions on specific impressions of the candidates. In that case, it seems reasonable to discount the apparent impact of trait assessments on voting behavior to allow for the fact that trait assessments are, in significant part, simply reflections of more basic partisan, ideological, and economic views rather than independent reactions to the candidates' intrinsic personal qualities. However, an alternative explanation for the observed relationship between political attitudes and trait ratings is that personal impressions of the candidates influence prospective voters' partisanship and (perhaps less directly) their ideological views and perceptions of economic conditions. If that interpretation is correct, then my analysis will understate the electoral impact of trait perceptions by misattributing to partisan, ideological, and economic bias some of the direct effect of trait assessments on votes. Thus, it seems prudent to determine which of these contrasting causal interpretations seems most tenable.

Making convincing inferences about causal connections between political attitudes and opinions using survey data collected at a single point in time is notoriously difficult. Fortunately, in this case it is possible to bring some additional leverage to bear by analyzing data from repeated surveys with the same respondents over a period of several months. The 1980 National Election Study included an election-year panel survey in which the same respondents were interviewed in January or February, again in June, and again during the fall campaign. By relating their political attitudes and trait assessments in the fall interview to the answers they gave to the same questions before the first primary votes were cast in early spring, we can gauge the extent to which changes in trait assessments over the course of the election year flow from pre-existing partisan, ideological, and economic attitudes— and, conversely, the extent to which changes in partisanship, ideology, and economic assessments flow from preexisting attitudes regarding the candidates' personal qualities.

Tables 2.3 and 2.4 present the results of parallel regression analyses in which each of the attitudes employed as explanatory variables in my analysis of vote choice in the 1980 election appear as dependent variables, with the entire set of corresponding attitudes as measured before the first primaries in early spring appearing as explanatory variables. Table 2.3 includes the results for the four fall trait ratings; Table 2.4 provides the parallel results for the fall measures of partisanship, ideology, and economic perceptions. If partisanship, ideology, and economic perceptions are causally prior to candidate trait assessments, as I have asserted, then we should see some tendency in Table 2.3 for trait assessments in the fall to be influenced by political attitudes at the beginning of the election year, even with pre-primary trait assessments included in the regression analyses. Conversely, if partisanship, ideology, and economic perceptions are significantly influenced by perceptions of the candidates' personalities, then we should see significant coefficients for trait ratings in Table 2.4, even with prior levels of partisanship, ideology, and economic perceptions included in the regression analyses.

The results in Table 2.3 provide very strong evidence that candidate trait ratings are affected by partisan bias and fairly consistent evidence for ideological bias as well. On average, and other things being equal, strong Republicans and strong Democrats diverged by about 28 points between January and September in their assessments of Reagan and Carter on each of the four 200-point relative trait scales. Even with fewer than 500 respondents in the panel analysis, the average *t*-statistic for the four separate partisan bias estimates is 5.9. The magnitudes of the corresponding ideological bias estimates are a good deal smaller, and the average *t*-statistic for these four effects is only 1.0; nevertheless, the consistency of the estimated effects across three of the four traits makes it very unlikely that they are merely due to chance. By comparison, the estimated effects of economic assessments on subsequent changes in trait ratings are both small and inconsistent, suggesting that trait

Table 2.3. Impact of pre-primary party identification, ideology, economic assessment, and trait ratings on fall trait ratings, United States, 1980

	Moral	Knowledgeable	Inspiring	Strong leader
Intercept	−4.9	−0.1	6.3	14.4
	(2.6)	(2.8)	(3.1)	(3.2)
Republican identification	10.1	9.1	16.6	19.5
	(2.0)	(2.2)	(2.5)	(2.5)
Conservative ideology	4.1	5.9	5.0	0.7
	(3.6)	(3.8)	(4.3)	(4.4)
Economic assessment	−0.9	−1.8	−2.9	4.2
	(3.4)	(3.7)	(4.1)	(4.2)
Moral	0.350	0.076	0.173	0.112
	(0.050)	(0.054)	(0.060)	(0.062)
Knowledgeable	−0.027	0.263	0.151	0.171
	(0.048)	(0.051)	(0.057)	(0.059)
Inspiring	0.036	0.115	0.173	0.167
	(0.044)	(0.047)	(0.053)	(0.055)
Strong leader	0.163	0.053	0.194	0.324
	(0.045)	(0.049)	(0.055)	(0.057)
Standard error of regression	27.8	30.0	33.6	34.7
Adjusted R^2	0.30	0.27	0.39	0.45
N	478	475	476	477

Note: Regression coefficients based upon major-party presidential voters only (with standard errors in parentheses).

Table 2.4. Impact of pre-primary attitudes and trait ratings on fall party identification, ideology, and economic assessment, United States, 1980

	Republican identification	Conservative ideology	Economic assessment
Intercept	0.052	0.059	0.420
	(0.032)	(0.027)	(0.037)
Republican identification	0.888	0.110	0.062
	(0.025)	(0.022)	(0.029)
Conservative ideology	0.030	0.551	0.037
	(0.044)	(0.038)	(0.052)
Economic assessment	0.061	−0.037	0.261
	(0.041)	(0.036)	(0.049)
Moral	0.0013	0.00054	−0.00059
	(0.00061)	(0.00053)	(0.00072)
Knowledgeable	0.00004	0.00004	0.00107
	(0.00058)	(0.00050)	(0.00068)
Inspiring	−0.00031	0.00097	−0.00075
	(0.00054)	(0.00046)	(0.00063)
Strong leader	0.00056	0.00005	0.00176
	(0.00056)	(0.00048)	(0.00066)
Standard error of regression	0.343	0.297	0.406
Adjusted R^2	0.78	0.42	0.11
N	488	488	489

Note: Regression coefficients based upon major-party presidential voters only (with standard errors in parentheses).

assessments (with the possible exception of leadership ratings) are insensitive to perceptions of economic conditions over the course of an election year.

The corresponding results in Table 2.4 suggest that the political attitudes treated as causally prior in my analysis are largely but not entirely unaffected by perceptions of the candidates' personal qualities. Six of the twelve relevant parameter estimates (in the bottom half of Table 2.4) have t-statistics greater than or equal to 1.0, but these potentially significant effects are scattered among the columns and rows of the table in a way that suggests no clear pattern. Even for the most general of the traits, "strong leadership," the effects on broader political attitudes are small and statistically uncertain (with an average t-statistic of 1.3).

Taken together, the results presented in Tables 2.3 and 2.4 provide considerable support for treating trait assessments as partly "caused" by party identification and other more basic political attitudes that are themselves largely unaffected by personal reactions to the candidates. Since my primary interest here is in the independent electoral impact of candidates' traits, I will attempt to specify the extent to which the apparent effects of trait assessments reflect the personal qualities of the competing candidates rather than the political biases of the voters doing the assessing. While political biases are by no means inconsequential, they seem to me (as to Miller and Shanks) to be more properly counted as effects of partisanship, ideology, or economic considerations than as evidence of the political significance of personal images.

The Impact of Trait Ratings on Voting Behavior

The "neutral observer" trait ratings in Figure 2.2 are intended to provide a summary of each recent presidential candidate's distinctive public image, shorn of positive or negative biases attributable to partisanship, ideology, and economic assessments. My aim in the remainder of this chapter is to gauge the impact of those public images on voting behavior and on the outcomes of recent presidential elections. To that end, Table 2.5 presents the results of separate probit analyses of vote choice in each of the six presidential elections from 1980 through 2000. The analyses are, once again, limited to NES survey respondents who reported voting for a major-party presidential candidate. The explanatory variables include party identification, ideology, and economic assessments, as well as relative ratings of the competing presidential candidates on the five character traits included most regularly in recent NES surveys.

The parameter estimates for party identification, ideology, and economic assessments in Table 2.5 offer few surprises. All have the expected (positive) sign, and the magnitudes of the estimated effects are reasonably stable from year to year. (The 2000 election is something of an outlier in this respect, with party identification having a stronger impact and ideology and economic assessments having weaker effects than in other recent election years.)

The parameter estimates for the various candidate traits included in Table 2.5 are also uniformly positive, though a few are smaller (and a few more are only slightly larger) than their respective standard errors. These estimates are graphically summarized in Figure 2.3, which shows the estimated impact of each trait in each election year. The magnitudes of the effects vary from year to year, reflecting some combination of election-specific salience effects and pure sampling error.[24] However, the general tendency is for "really cares" to have the largest electoral impact, followed in descending order by "strong leader," "moral," "inspiring," and "knowledgeable."

The estimated effects of trait ratings on vote choice presented in Table 2.5 are derived from a very simple model in which the weights attached to trait assessments are allowed to vary across traits and across elections, but are assumed to be equal for both candidates and for all voters in any given election. I have also examined somewhat more complicated models in which the competing candidates in each election may be evaluated on the basis of different traits, or in which different voters may attach different weights

---

[24] Since the standard errors of the probit coefficients range from about 0.002 to 0.003, many of the year-to-year variations in the impact of each trait evident in Figure 2.3 are too large to be plausibly attributable solely to sampling error.

Table 2.5. Impact of relative trait ratings on vote choice, United States, 1980–2000

	1980	1984	1988	1992	1996	2000
Intercept	−0.018	0.313	0.237	−0.206	−0.457	−0.027
	(0.122)	(0.074)	(0.066)	(0.109)	(0.113)	(0.077)
Republican identification	0.927	0.832	0.963	1.066	0.990	1.317
	(0.116)	(0.099)	(0.096)	(0.100)	(0.126)	(0.124)
Conservative ideology	0.554	0.547	0.559	0.974	0.701	0.365
	(0.196)	(0.169)	(0.171)	(0.178)	(0.221)	(0.156)
Economic assessment	0.384	0.365	0.203	0.147	0.472	0.093
	(0.155)	(0.127)	(0.138)	(0.136)	(0.185)	(0.123)
Really cares	—	0.01792	0.01198	0.01242	0.01738	0.00930
		(0.00222)	(0.00232)	(0.00216)	(0.00230)	(0.00236)
Moral	0.00829	0.00690	0.01057	0.00845	0.00889	0.00890
	(0.00236)	(0.00252)	(0.00266)	(0.00197)	(0.00236)	(0.00238)
Knowledgeable	0.00242	0.00585	0.00259	0.00254	0.00772	0.00285
	(0.00227)	(0.00214)	(0.00266)	(0.00260)	(0.00345)	(0.00229)
Inspiring	0.00552	0.00177	0.00738	0.00309	0.00519	—
	(0.00223)	(0.00214)	(0.00234)	(0.00228)	(0.00267)	
Strong leader	0.01700	0.01100	0.01128	0.01119	0.00256	0.01476
	(0.00229)	(0.00221)	(0.00232)	(0.00231)	(0.00279)	(0.00237)
Log likelihood	−236.2	−326.6	−306.0	−285.0	−187.6	−234.6
Pseudo-R^2	0.59	0.65	0.63	0.69	0.73	0.70
N	835	1,355	1,183	1,349	1,031	1,120

Note: Probit coefficients for (Republican) presidential vote choice (with standard errors in parentheses).

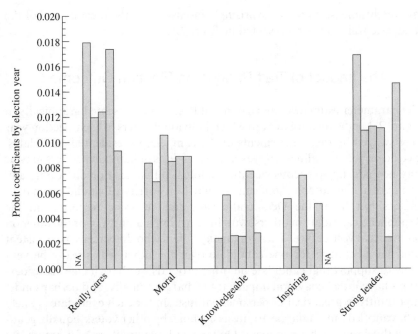

Fig. 2.3 The impact of candidate traits on presidential votes, United States, 1980–2000
Note: The election years were 1980, 1984, 1988, 1992, 1996, and 2000.

to the same trait.[25] However, these more elaborate models produce only modest improvements in fit over the simpler model presented in Table 2.5,[26] and their implications with respect to the aggregate impact of candidate traits on election outcomes are quite similar to those reported here.[27] Thus,

[25] Each of these more elaborate model specifications included twice as many trait effects as the basic model presented in Table 2.5. The first alternative model included separate trait effects for Republican and Democratic candidates in each election. The second alternative model included interactions between each relative trait rating and voters' party identification, allowing Republican and Democratic voters to attach different weights to each trait in each election. The third alternative model included interactions between each relative rating and the strength of voters' partisanship, allowing strong partisans and independents to attach different weights to each trait in each election. I am grateful to Tali Mendelberg, Karen Stenner, and Mark Fischle for suggesting these alternative model specifications.

[26] Only three of the eighteen likelihood ratio tests (for the three alternative models applied to each of six elections) reflect "statistically significant" improvements in fit (at the conventional 0.05 level), and the average p-values (over the six elections) range from 0.15 for the second (party-specific) alternative specification to 0.53 for the third (strength-of-partisanship) model.

[27] For the second (party-specific) and third (strength-of-partisanship) alternative models the estimated net effects of candidate traits are practically identical to those for the basic model, never differing by more than 0.2 percentage points. The first (candidate-specific) alternative model produces somewhat different estimates, but even these differ from the corresponding estimates in Table 2.6 by an average of less than 1 percentage point, and the average magnitude of the estimated net effects is only 1.5 percentage points (as against 1.6 percentage points for the simpler model in Table 2.6).

my conclusions seem to be surprisingly insensitive to the precise form of the candidate trait effects represented in Table 2.5.

The Impact of Trait Ratings on Election Outcomes

The parameter estimates reported in Table 2.5, and presented graphically in Figure 2.3, indicate the extent to which individual voters in each election year were swayed by their assessments of the competing presidential candidates' specific personal qualities. However, the reactions of individual voters may or may not add up to a consequential political outcome. For one thing, any given voter may attach significant weight to a variety of candidate characteristics but favor the Democratic candidate in some respects and the Republican candidate in others, with little net impact one way or the other on her eventual vote choice. Then too, many voters who do perceive a consistent personal advantage for one candidate over the other will already be very likely to support that candidate on other grounds, so that "image" considerations have little behavioral impact at the margin. Finally, and perhaps most importantly, a great deal of personal enthusiasm for each candidate is likely to be canceled out, in the electorate as a whole, by other voters' equally genuine enthusiasm for his opponent. Only when large numbers of more or less uncommitted voters are in substantial agreement regarding the personal superiority of one candidate to the other are their assessments likely to have a significant impact on the election result.

Gauging the impact of candidates' personal traits in a given election requires an assessment of how that election *would have* turned out if the candidates had had different personal qualities from those they actually had. The most relevant counterfactual would seem to be a (hypothetical) election in which the competing candidates were viewed equally favorably (or unfavorably) on each potentially relevant trait dimension by a "neutral observer" unaffected by partisan, ideological, or economic biases. To the extent that the actual election outcome departs from the hypothetical outcome, it seems reasonable to conclude that the candidates' personalities had a politically consequential impact. Thus, my approach here is to compare the estimated probability of casting a Republican vote for each voter in each NES survey, as estimated from the probit analyses reported in Table 2.5, with a counterfactual probability calculated by adjusting the voter's relative trait assessments to remove the effect of differences in the competing candidates' personal qualities as judged by "neutral observers"—differences of the sort illustrated in Figure 2.2. I take the difference between these two probabilities to represent the impact of the candidates' "objective" personal strengths and weaknesses on each voter's choice, and the average difference for all the voters in a given election year to represent the net electoral impact of candidate traits on the outcome of that election.

My estimates of the net impact of candidate traits on the outcomes of the six presidential elections considered here are presented in Table 2.6. The estimate in each case is of the net impact of trait assessments on the Republican share of the major-party presidential vote; thus, a positive entry implies that the election outcome was more favorable to the Republican candidate than it would have been if "neutral observers" had perceived the two candidates as equally attractive on each trait dimension, while a negative entry implies a net personal advantage for the Democratic candidate.

The most striking feature of the estimates in Table 2.6 is that the net effects of candidate trait assessments are generally quite modest in magnitude. The average effect for the six elections is 1.6 percentage points, and the *largest* effect (in 1992) is only 3.5 percentage points. By comparison, the average margin of victory in these six elections (that is, the winning candidate's plurality of the two-party popular vote, including George W. Bush's small negative plurality in 2000) was 8.7 percentage points, and the average inter-election vote swing was about 5 percentage points. In three of the six elections—including the two with the largest net trait effects—the winning candidate would quite probably have won by a *larger* margin had personal qualities played no role in determining the election outcome. The only case in which it seems at all likely that perceptions of the candidates' personal qualities had a decisive impact on the election outcome is the 2000 election, where Bush's half-point advantage with respect to candidate traits was probably one of many "decisive" factors contributing to his razor-thin victory.

A second important point to note about the estimates of net electoral impact in Table 2.6 is that they comport rather poorly with conventional wisdom regarding the political and personal qualities of the various candidates

Table 2.6. Net electoral impact of candidate traits, United States, 1980–2000

	Estimated Republican vote gain or loss (%)	Candidate advantaged	Winning candidate	Decisive impact?
1980	+1.0 (1.0)	Reagan	Reagan (55.3%)	No
1984	+0.5 (0.8)	Reagan	Reagan (59.2%)	No
1988	−1.5 (0.5)	Dukakis	Bush (53.9%)	No
1992	+3.5 (0.7)	Bush	Clinton (53.5%)	No
1996	+2.6 (0.9)	Dole	Clinton (54.6%)	No
2000	+0.4 (0.5)	Bush	Bush (49.7%)	Probably

Note: Estimated net impact of candidate traits on Republican share of two-party presidential vote (jackknife estimates with standard errors in parentheses).

in these six presidential elections. Ronald Reagan, the "great communicator" and consummate actor, had a net advantage of only 1 percentage point over Jimmy Carter in 1980 and a net advantage of less than 1 percentage point over Walter Mondale in 1984. Michael Dukakis, widely regarded as cold and politically inept, appears here to have been the only Democratic presidential candidate in the past two decades to enjoy a more favorable personal image than his Republican opponent. And Bill Clinton, "a once-in-a-lifetime political performer,"[28] appears to have had the *worst* personal image of any presidential candidate in recent American history, at least as measured by the impact of trait assessments on election outcomes. The estimates in Table 2.6 suggest that Clinton lost about 3.5 percentage points to George Bush in 1992 and about 2.5 percentage points to Bob Dole in 1996.

The assessments of electoral impact offered in Table 2.6 differ in some important details from those produced by Miller and Shanks for some of the same elections using much the same data and similar methods of analysis, and summarized in Table 1.2 of the present volume. For example, Miller and Shanks estimated that Jimmy Carter had a slight net advantage over Ronald Reagan due to trait assessments in 1980 and that the independent contribution of personal qualities was "close to invisible" in 1992.[29] My estimates in Table 2.6 imply that Reagan probably had a slight net advantage over Carter in 1980 (increasing Reagan's vote share by about 1 percentage point) and that George Bush had an unusually large net advantage over Bill Clinton in 1992 (increasing Bush's vote share by about 3.5 percentage points).[30]

In some cases, these differences reflect differences in the specific set of candidate traits included in each analysis; whereas I focus here on the subset of traits included most consistently in the NES surveys since 1980, Miller and Shanks considered all of the traits included in each election year, eventually dropping those with statistically "insignificant" effects. The differences in results also reflect different assumptions about the impact of other political factors Miller and Shanks's analysis included a wider variety of explanatory factors and a more heroic set of assumptions regarding the causal ordering of those explanatory factors than I employ here.

Despite these differences in detail, my analysis generally tends to confirm and reinforce Miller and Shanks's central claims that "[m]ost of the statistical

---

[28] See James, "Presenting a Masterpiece in Political Theater."

[29] Miller and Shanks, "Policy Directions and Presidential Leadership;" Miller and Shanks, *The New American Voter*, p. 480.

[30] Additional differences appear with respect to individual trait assessments in specific election years. For example, Miller and Shanks reported in *The New American Voter* (p. 425) that "honest," "inspiring," and "really cares" were "the *only* traits for which the comparative evaluations of the two candidates . . . exhibited a significant relationship to the vote" in 1992, net of other factors; the corresponding results in Table 2.5 show fairly strong and statistically significant effects for "really cares," "strong leader," and "moral" and considerably weaker effects for "inspiring" and "knowledgeable." (Assessments of honesty are not included in my analysis because that trait did not appear consistently in the NES surveys employed here.)

relationships between vote choice and comparative evaluations of the candidates' personal qualities should be seen as misleading or spurious" and that "media emphasis on candidates' personal attributes and voters' volunteered appraisals of candidates' personalities should not be taken at face value" by electoral analysts.[31] Voters' impressions of the candidates' personalities are strongly shaped by more basic political predispositions. A candidate's net advantage with respect to one personal trait is not infrequently offset by a net disadvantage with respect to some other equally important trait. And pundits' assessments of the candidates' personal qualities, and of the electoral relevance of those qualities, are likely to be significantly distorted by *post hoc* reasoning from observed effects to putative causes. For all of these reasons, the electoral impact of candidates' traits is likely to be less than meets the eye.

Bush vs. Gore

If the estimated candidate trait effects in Table 2.6 are even approximately right, how could conventional wisdom about the personal qualities of recent presidential candidates—and about the impact of those qualities on election outcomes—be so wrong? The crucial point, I suspect, is that in every election conventional wisdom seems to have overestimated the relative personal qualities of the winning candidate. Ronald Reagan *must* have been a strong, charismatic candidate because he defeated a sitting president and then won reelection in a landslide. Michael Dukakis *must* have been cold and inept because he blew a double-digit lead in the polls. Bill Clinton *must* have been an inspiring, empathetic political performer because he returned the Democrats to the White House after the long hiatus of the Reagan era. In each case, the *post hoc* assessment of the candidates' personal strengths and weaknesses simultaneously validated and was validated by the notion that, as Quindlen put it, "voters use their impressions of a candidate's personality to choose a president."

Quindlen's own application of the "cult of personality" thesis to the 2000 presidential campaign hints at how the thesis can easily become self-fulfilling. "In the next 90 days," she wrote in August 2000, "millions of people will decide, finally, whether they think Al Gore is rigid and humorless or instead serious and diligent, whether George W. Bush is straight-talking and sure of himself or simply arrogant and tactless." How are we to know what they decided? Presumably, since "personality is key in Election 2000," by seeing how they voted.

The potential fluidity of assessments of candidates' personal strengths and weaknesses was clearly illustrated by changing impressions of the competing candidates over the course of the 2000 campaign. Al Gore was widely

---

[31] Miller and Shanks, *The New American Voter*, pp. 501–2.

portrayed as rigid and humorless when Bill Bradley seemed likely to derail his nomination, but became serious and diligent when he surged in the polls following the Democratic convention. Conversely, George W. Bush was affable and charismatic through most of the spring and summer before becoming lazy and confused in late August and September—that is, at just the point when he began to trail Gore in the polls. As one prominent reporter admitted,

There is something of a circular phenomenon here. Mr. Bush's gaffes on the stump are nothing new, but they are being picked up more by the media because the context of the campaign has changed and the governor is no longer viewed as the towering favorite.[32]

In the end, of course, Bush did manage to win the election—not in the national popular vote, but in the Electoral College (probably), and, more importantly, in the U.S. Supreme Court. Thus, analysts and commentators after the election focused on "explaining" his victory and, even more, Gore's defeat. How could the nominee of the incumbent party not have triumphed easily in a period of peace and apparent economic prosperity? One common explanation focused on Gore's putative personal weaknesses—including many of the same weaknesses that had loomed large the previous spring but receded with Gore's rise in the polls in late summer and early fall. Gore was too wooden; prone to fibbing; not a strong leader. As Berke himself put it, Gore was "a flawed candidate who squandered a prime opportunity to capture the White House."[33]

On the one hand, the estimate presented in Table 2.6 suggests that Gore *was* a less attractive candidate than Bush, all in all, but only by less than 0.5 percentage points. Of course, given the extraordinary closeness of the election, it is quite probable that that sliver of personal advantage was essential to Bush's victory. In an election "decided" by a few hundred votes in Florida, any advantage, however slight, can reasonably be considered decisive. On the other hand, given the precision of the estimate in Table 2.6, it is also quite possible that Gore rather than Bush was the "real" winner of the 2000 popularity contest. (The relevant probability is a little over 20 percent.) What is clear is that neither candidate enjoyed a major electoral advantage on the basis of personality. Even more than in the other presidential elections covered by my analysis, the importance of candidate images among the various factors shaping the outcome of the 2000 election outcome was remarkably modest.

Partisans of candidate-centered politics may resist this conclusion on the grounds that the specific candidate traits included in Table 2.5 did not really tap the dimensions of personal evaluation that were most salient in the 2000 election. In order to test that possibility, I repeated my analysis of the 2000 outcome using a somewhat richer collection of trait assessments than in the analysis reported in Table 2.5. Respondents in the 2000 NES survey were

[32] Richard L. Berke, "Tested and occasionally tripped, Bush may yet rue a mirror crack'd," *New York Times*, September 18, 2000, p. A16.

[33] Richard L. Berke, "Many seem skeptical of Gore's future," *New York Times*, December 17, 2000, p. A1.

invited to rate the presidential candidates as "dishonest," "intelligent," and "out of touch" in addition to the four traits included in Table 2.5.

Perhaps unsurprisingly, given the events of the campaign, Bush had a modest (5-point) advantage (among major-party voters) with respect to perceived honesty, while Gore had a modest (7-point) advantage with respect to perceived intelligence. Gore was also perceived as slightly more "in touch." Adding voters' comparative assessments of the candidates on those traits to the set of explanatory variables included in Table 2.5 produced a significant estimated effect for being "in touch" (roughly similar in magnitude to the effects for "moral" and "really cares"), a smaller estimated effect (about half as large) for honesty, and an even smaller (indeed, negative, albeit imprecise) estimated effect for intelligence.

What is most important for my purposes here is that the net impact of these additional trait ratings on the outcome of the 2000 presidential election seems to have been very modest. Whereas the calculation reported in Table 2.6, based upon four comparative trait assessments, suggested that Bush gained about 0.4 percentage points due to voters' reactions to the candidates' personal qualities, the corresponding estimate based upon all seven comparative trait assessments is only slightly larger—about 0.6 percentage points.[34] Needless to say, this estimate is statistically indistinguishable from the estimate presented in Table 2.6, and, for that matter, only roughly distinguishable from zero; nevertheless, it is precise enough to make it quite clear that the electorate was not swayed far in either direction by the candidates' personalities.

In short, my analysis suggests that the 2000 election was a virtual dead heat with respect to the candidates' personal qualities, as in almost every other respect. What is surprising is not that the electoral impact of candidate traits in 2000 was modest, since that has generally been the case in recent presidential elections. What is surprising is that in 2000 the modest effect of candidate traits was, quite probably, large enough to be decisive.

Acknowledgment

The research reported in this chapter was supported by Princeton University's Woodrow Wilson School of Public and International Affairs. Mark Fischle, Tali Mendelberg, Karen Stenner, and participants in seminars at Princeton and at the University of Washington provided helpful reactions to earlier versions of the analysis.

[34] The precise estimate is 0.59 percentage points (pro-Bush), which is in reasonably close agreement with the out-of-sample estimation error of 0.56 percentage points (pro-Bush) from Bartels and Zaller's analysis of the 2000 presidential election in historical perspective. See Larry M. Bartels and John Zaller, "Presidential Vote Models: A Recount," *PS: Political Science & Politics*, 34 (2001), 9–20. The agreement is, of course, coincidental; but the results presented here lend some support to Bartels and Zaller's assertion (p. 19) that there is "no need, and little warrant, to posit either unusual incompetence on Gore's part or unusual skill on Bush's part" in order to account for the outcome of the 2000 election.

3

The Impact of Party Leaders in Britain: Strong Assumptions, Weak Evidence

JOHN BARTLE AND IVOR CREWE

It is easy to understand the widespread assumption that leaders' personalities must influence election results in presidential systems such as those of the United States, France, and Russia. In those countries, voters select individuals to exercise wide-ranging executive powers, whether it be to wage war, appoint the senior judiciary or dissolve the legislature. These sorts of decisions are very likely to be heavily influenced by the personal qualities and quirks of the decision maker. It might therefore be supposed that it is only natural for voters to take into account the personal traits of presidential candidates—their intelligence, honesty, political acumen, and sheer likeability—when deciding for whom to vote.

The assumption that leaders' personalities matter in parliamentary systems such as Britain's, however, is less obviously correct. British prime ministers are not directly elected by the electorate as a whole. Like every other member of Parliament, they owe their membership of the House of Commons to the seventy thousand or so electors in their own constituency. They owe their position as prime minister to election by their party as its leader and, once in office, to the continuing support of their senior cabinet colleagues and parliamentary party.[1] Formally, at least, British government is party government: a collective enterprise in which the prime minister is merely *primus inter pares*. Margaret Thatcher's ignominious departure from office in 1990 well illustrates a prime minister's fundamental dependence on cabinet and party.

In recent years, however, most informed observers of British politics, with the important exception of academic political scientists, have taken it as axiomatic that the personalities of party leaders strongly influence the way people vote and therefore the result of elections. Some make the point that a

---

[1] Both parties now give the wider party a role to play in the election of the party leader. See Keith Alderman and Neil Carter, "The Labour Party Leadership and Deputy Leadership Elections of 1994," *Parliamentary Affairs* (1995), 438–55; The Conservative Party, *The Fresh Future* (London: Conservative Party, 1997).

prime minister's control of the cabinet agenda, coupled with his extensive powers of appointment, has replaced cabinet government by prime ministerial government.[2] Others go further and refer to the "presidentialization" of British politics and, in particular, British elections: the parties and media, they argue, have come to organize and depict election campaigns as a contest between the Labour and Conservative leaders.[3] The personalities of party leaders have come to be thought of as looming every bit as large in the consciousness of British voters as they do among the voters of the United States, France, and Russia. This view of British politics is not confined to foreign commentators, tempted to construe British parliamentary elections in more familiar presidential terms. Nor is it confined to saloon bar discussions or the ruminations of tabloid journalists.[4] Writing in 2000, one highly respected commentator, Hugo Young of the *Guardian*, expressed the firm belief that there is an identifiable personality component in the vote:

In modern [British] politics, nothing matters more than the leader. We have a parliamentary system but a presidential impulse. This takes a certain view about power, but a determining one about style. Think of the Tories and you get William Hague: bald, struggling, robotic, Yorkshire. Think of Labour, and there's only one face in front of it and one mind behind. Almost the entire apparatus of party presentation is devoted to the daily manicuring, weekly shaping and permanent controlling, down to the finest detail, of the impression these leaders make on the voting public.[5]

Communications advisors take it as axiomatic that leaders' physical appearance, the clothes they wear, their accent and their tone of voice all help to create positive or negative impressions. Many politicians apparently agree and are therefore willing to undergo "makeovers" in order to improve their appeal.[6] Moreover, a failure on the part of a leader to project the right image, it is supposed, can have disastrous consequences. Neil Kinnock attributed Labour's defeat in 1992, at least in part, to voters' assessments of him as a leader: "One of the reasons [voters] eventually put their crosses by the Conservative candidate was this innate feeling among a relatively small number of people that they couldn't see me as prime minister. It's just there in the biochemistry, as it were. It's a pity but it's a fact of life I recognise."[7] In a similar vein William Hague attributed the Conservative Party's defeat in June 2001 to his personal failure "to persuade sufficient numbers that [he was] their

---

[2] R. H. S. Crossman, "Introduction," in Walter Bagehot, *The English Constitution* (London: Collins, 1963), pp. 1–57.

[3] Anthony Mughan, "Party Leaders and Presidentialism in the 1992 Election: A Post-War Perspective," in David Denver, Pippa Norris, Colin Rallings, and David Broughton, eds., *British Elections and Parties Yearbook, 1993* (Hemel Hempstead, Herts.: Harvester Wheatsheaf, 1993), pp. 193–204.

[4] See Sion Simon, "Hague's a loser just like Kinnock," *News of the World*, July 16, 2000.

[5] Hugo Young, "Romsey is more important than the London result," *Guardian*, May 9, 2000.

[6] George Trefgarne, "New leader, new image," *Daily Telegraph*, July 5, 1997.

[7] Nicholas Watt, "Putting it baldly: Kinnock looks back on lost election—and advises Hague to ditch baseball cap," *Guardian*, June 17, 1999.

alternative prime minister." Indeed, his subsequent resignation was based, at least in part, on the belief that the Conservatives needed a leader who could "command a larger *personal following* in the country."[8]

Many ordinary voters share this belief. One member of a *Guardian* focus group in late 1998 expressed the view that "Labour consists of one person— Blair. He's able to sway people with his oratory. But the people around him haven't a clue what to do."[9] The belief that there is an identifiable personality component of the vote is, as Anthony King suggested in Chapter 1, part of the culture, seldom questioned, and completely taken for granted.[10]

The remarkable tenacity of people's belief in leadership effects can, at least in part, be attributed to a failure to distinguish between direct and indirect effects. However, certain features of the British political system also serve to sustain the belief that leaders' personalities matter. The bear pit that is Prime Minister's Question Time, broadcast live on television from the House of Commons since 1989, provides voters with a ready opportunity to compare the cleverness, quick-wittedness and knowledge of the party leaders.[11] Moreover, it could be argued that, since there is often no other benchmark by which to judge leaders, voters not unnaturally compare leaders with each other.[12]

The media further encourage the personalization of politics by focusing on the leaders, especially during election campaigns. Newspapers and television alike report elections as if they were gladiatorial combats between two generals rather than battles between two armies.[13] This focus partly reflects journalists' fascination with politicians as individuals; but it may also reflect a belief that their readers or audience have a deep-seated need for human interest stories to stimulate their interest in politics. Moreover, the point–counterpoint style of reporting, whereby the speeches, comments, or

[8] Hague's resignation speech from the *Guardian* website. Emphasis added. http://politics.guardian.co.uk/election2001/story/0,9029,503732,00.html

[9] Peter Hetherington, "Strong Blair escapes voters' blame," *Guardian*, September 28, 1998.

[10] However, see the following for more skeptical notes: John Bartle, "The MPs who owe their seats to Tony Blair," *Times Higher Educational Supplement*, October 3, 1997; John Gray, "A trap from which no leader can deliver them," *Guardian*, September 1, 1999; Anthony King, "Hague the scapegoat for unpopular Tories," *Daily Telegraph*, September 3, 1999; Philip Oppenheim, "If the Tories are feeling sick Matron Widdecombe will make them feel sicker," *Sunday Times*, August 29, 1999; Alice Thomson, "Looking for votes," *Spectator*, October 25, 1997.

[11] Prime Minister's Question Time now takes the form of a half-hour question and answer session on Wednesdays at 3 p.m. Proceedings are dominated by exchanges between the prime minister and the leader of the official opposition. However, the leader of the Liberal Democrats is also able to ask up to two questions of the prime minister.

[12] Richard Nadeau, Richard G. Niemi, and Timothy Amato, "Prospective and Comparative or Retrospective and Individual? Party Leaders and Party Support in Great Britain," *British Journal of Political Science*, 26 (1996), 245–58; cf. Donald R. Kinder, Mark D. Peters, Robert Abelson, and Susan T. Fiske, "Presidential Prototypes," *Political Behaviour*, 2 (1980), 315–37.

[13] See Peter Riddell, "Hague fails to gain as Blair image fades," *The Times*, April 26, 2000; Anthony King, "Blair losing sparkle, but Hague is no boy wonder," *Daily Telegraph*, April 14, 2000.

sound bites of one party leader are immediately followed by those of another emphasizes the tendency to look upon an election as effectively a choice between alternative prime ministers.[14]

The parties themselves encourage this same tendency by fighting leader-centered campaigns. In the postmodern campaign, leaders are not simply the mouthpieces for the party's values and policies but have become part of the message. Their personality is managed and manufactured by the party organization to project an image of the party they lead. Attempts to create the impression that William Hague, the former Conservative leader, was a down-to-earth, no-nonsense man of action, fit to be prime minister—as distinct from being a precocious "anorak" and "something of a prat"—included the wearing of a baseball cap during a visit to a theme park, a much photographed ascent of Ben Nevis with his wife, and his claim to have occasionally drunk as many as fourteen pints of beer a day as a teenager.[15] Parties and the media are locked into an interdependent relationship. Television craves pictures. The parties, craving exposure for their leaders, provide them.

The common belief that leaders' personalities influence the outcome of British elections appears to be corroborated by survey evidence. A MORI poll conducted in August 1999 revealed that an impressive 98 percent of respondents recognized a picture of Tony Blair and 97 per cent knew that he was prime minister. Fully 84 percent recognized William Hague and 84 per cent, again, knew that he was leader of the Conservative opposition. Recognition of secondary leaders such as Gordon Brown (45 percent) and Michael Portillo (42 per cent) was far fainter. In contrast, the British Election Study, the major academic survey of opinion at each general election, revealed that the proportion of the electorate who associated even the most distinctive policies with the correct party was often far lower. Only 36 percent correctly identified the Liberal Democrats as the party "most in favour of proportional representation," and only 32 percent identified the SNP as the party "most in favour of independence for Scotland."[16] While some voters evidently find it difficult to assess politicians' policies, they undoubtedly find it much easier to assess their personalities.

Additional evidence for the electoral importance of voters' evaluations of leaders is seemingly provided by questions that ask respondents how they would react if a named politician were to lead a party or if the existing party leader were replaced by some unspecified individual. The answers to these questions seem to show that such changes could make a significant difference to the party's electoral prospects. Certainly, quasi-experimental "trial heat"

---

[14] Nadeau *et al.*, "Prospective and Comparative or Retrospective and Individual," p. 258.

[15] Gillian Harris and Tom Baldwin, "Tory 'action man' scales the heights," *The Times*, April 24, 2000; Andrew Sparrow, "Hague's 14 pints a day boast falls flat in his home town," *Daily Telegraph*, August 9, 2000; Andrew Rawnsley, "Prime Minister Hague? I think not," *Observer* August 6, 2000.

[16] British Election Campaign Study, wave 1 (1996).

evidence is pored over by commentators and the parties themselves when selecting their leader. Responses to such questions influenced the decision of Conservative MPs to replace Margaret Thatcher with John Major in November, 1990.[17] In the autumn of 1999 similar evidence was used to suggest that the Conservatives could not improve their standing with the electorate by the simple expedient of replacing William Hague with Michael Portillo.[18]

Although findings like these suggest that leaders' personalities can have an effect on political preferences, such evidence must be treated with caution. For one thing, the questions are hypothetical: the respondents have no stake in the outcome and cannot necessarily predict their own behavior. For another, such questions rarely provide any indication of the magnitude, as distinct from direction, of any shift in voting behavior. Knowing that "if Charles replaces David then voters are more likely to support party Y" indicates that support for Y is likely to rise, but not necessarily by how much. Finally, it is far from clear what thought-processes go through respondents' minds when responding to such a question. One process might be, "If Alice rather than Bernard leads party X, but nothing else changes, then I would vote for X." However, another process might be, "If Alice rather than Bernard leads party X, then she will change its policies on tax, trade unions, and defense. If these things happen then I will vote X." This second thought process presupposes the sort of indirect effects discussed in Chapter 1, and so the question does not help us to isolate the unique effect of the leader's personality. In short, it is difficult to extract meaning from responses to seemingly simple survey questions.[19] From the perspective of, say, a member of Parliament deciding whether or not to support the incumbent leader, the sorts of hypothetical survey questions outlined above can be informative and provide possible guides to action. Yet from the perspective of a political scientist trying to estimate the direction and magnitude of leadership effects, such evidence is of more dubious value.

The consensus that leaders' personalities matter is often self-reinforcing. Journalists assume that personalities matter and concentrate on them when reporting politics. What is more, they commission opinion polls on voters' evaluations of the leaders. Because so much media coverage is devoted to leaders' personalities and polls, voters, politicians, and commentators alike assume that personalities must matter. This consensus, however, excludes academic political scientists. The long-established view in British political

---

[17] See Alan Watkins, *A Conservative Coup: The Fall of Margaret Thatcher*, 2nd edn (London: Duckworth, 1992), pp. 182–93.

[18] See Alan Travis and Michael White, "Tories worse off with Portillo," *Guardian*, October 4, 1999.

[19] See John R. Zaller, *The Nature and Origins of Mass Opinion* (Cambridge: Cambridge University Press, 1992); Howard Schuman and Stanley Presser, *Questions & Answers in Attitude Surveys: Experiments on Question Form, Wording, and Context* (Thousand Oaks, Calif.: Sage, 1996).

science was that leaders counted for little in elections: what mattered was what the parties stood for, not who stood for the parties. Analysts of voting behavior emphasized the formation and impact of party loyalty. Most voters, they argued, coped with the complexity and remoteness of politics by forming an enduring psychological attachment to a particular party.[20] This party identification was rooted in the enduring features of their everyday lives and, once established, rarely changed. Party identification heavily conditioned voters' responses to politics in general, such that most voters rarely formed attitudes or made judgments at odds with their long-established identification. Labour identifiers, for example, overwhelmingly preferred Harold Wilson to Sir Alec Douglas-Home as prospective prime minister in 1964 simply because he was "their" leader. The causal arrows, it was assumed, ran from parties to leader evaluations rather than the other way round. Moreover, in those rare instances where preferences relating to party and leader diverged, party usually trumped leader. The small minority of Conservative identifiers who happened to prefer the Labour leader overwhelmingly voted Conservative; similarly, the small minority of Labour identifiers who happened to prefer the Conservative leader overwhelmingly voted Labour.[21] Party identification, rooted in enduring group loyalties, was a far more reliable guide to voting behavior than the ephemeral appeal or nonappeal of the current party leader.

To ram the point home, political scientists often cited those elections when the party with the more popular leader nonetheless lost the election—those of 1945, 1970, and 1979—as evidence that leaders counted for next to nought alongside the records, policies, and images of their parties.

Until the 1980s political scientists regarded the issue as settled and proceeded to ignore it.[22] This assumption in turn limited the data that were collected on voters' assessments of leadership traits. Indeed, the main vehicle for research on voting behavior in Britain, the British Election Study, contained very few items that specifically referred to the party leaders. Little attempt was made to determine which personality traits or broad categories of traits were

[20] David Butler and Donald Stokes, *Political Change in Britain: The Evolution of Electoral Choice*, 2nd edn (London: Macmillan, 1974).

[21] In the 1980s and early 1990s about a fifth of all voters preferred the policies of one party but the leader of another and their vote split by five to one in favour of the first. See Ivor Crewe, "How to Win a Landslide Without Really Trying: Why the Conservatives Won in 1983," in Austin Ranney, ed., *Britain at the Polls, 1983* (Durham, N.C.: Duke University Press for the American Enterprise Institute, 1984), pp. 155–96; "A New Class of Politics" and "Tories Prosper from a Paradox," in David Denver and Gordon Hands, eds., *Issues and Controversies in British Electoral Behaviour* (Hemel Hempstead, Herts.: Harvester Wheatsheaf, 1992), pp. 343–54; and "Why did Labour Lose (Yet Again)," *Politics Review*, 2 (1992), 2–11.

[22] The one major exception occurred in *Political Change in Britain*, where Butler and Stokes devoted a whole chapter to "The Pull of the Leaders." They concluded that voters' clear preference for Harold Wilson over Sir Alec Douglas-Home may have contributed to Labour's slim margin of victory over the Conservatives in the closely fought election of 1964. See Butler and Stokes, *Political Change in Britain*, pp. 367–8.

of greatest theoretical relevance.[23] "The popular lore about the role of party leaders in British elections and the bulk of the political science literature on the subject [were] thus like ships that [passed] in the night."[24] The main corpus of work on voting behavior simply ignored an explanation of voting behavior that those who were not political scientists regarded as being obvious.

However, by the mid 1980s the conventional academic wisdom about the electoral insignificance of party leaders began to wane. More studies, adopting a variety of analytic strategies, were undertaken. Bean and Mughan formulated a thought experiment strategy ("How would people have voted if the Labour and Conservative parties exchanged leaders but everything else about them remained the same?") to estimate the effect of leaders' personalities on voting behavior and concluded that leaders' personalities could have a very considerable effect on vote decisions.[25] Yet research by Crewe and King based on a similar approach produced far more modest effects.[26] The formal popularity functions approach has produced similarly discrepant results. For example, Clarke and Stewart concluded from their analysis of monthly opinion poll data that leader evaluations are a primary determinant of party choice,[27] whereas Sanders and his colleagues, using the same data, claim that the impact of a change of party leader on that party's electoral support rarely lasts more than a month or two.[28] Improved-prediction strategies, based on

[23] See Ivor Crewe and Bo Särlvik, *Decade of Dealignment; The Conservative Victory of 1979 and Electoral Trends in the 1970s* (Cambridge: Cambridge University Press, 1983). This book, based on the 1979 general election study, contained a mere three pages on leaders, despite the widespread speculation about how a female leader would influence voting behavior. This pattern was repeated in Anthony Heath, Roger Jowell, and John Curtice, *How Britain Votes* (Oxford: Pergamon, 1985), the book resulting from the 1983 election study. In this case the authors thought it scarcely necessary to refer to the party leaders at all, despite the fact that Margaret Thatcher and Michael Foot represented the two most divisive leaders in Britain since World War II. The pattern was repeated again in Anthony Heath, Roger Jowell, and John Curtice, *Understanding Political Change: The British Voter 1964–1987* (Oxford: Pergamon, 1991). The book analyses electoral change over the quarter century from 1964 to 1987, but contains nothing on leadership effects.

[24] Ivor Crewe and Anthony King, "Did Major Win? Did Kinnock Lose? Leadership Effects in the 1992 Election," in Anthony Heath, Roger Jowell, and John Curtice, eds., *Labour's Last Chance? The 1992 Election and Beyond* (Aldershot, Hants.: Dartmouth, 1994), p. 126.

[25] Clive Bean and Anthony Mughan, "Leadership Effects in Parliamentary Elections in Australia and Britain," *American Political Science Review*, 83 (1989), 1165–79.

[26] Ivor Crewe and Anthony King, "Are British Elections Becoming More 'Presidential'?" in M. Kent Jennings and Thomas E. Mann, eds., *Elections at Home and Abroad: Essays in Honor of Warren E. Miller* (Ann Arbor: University of Michigan Press, 1994), pp. 181–206; Crewe and King, "Did Major Win? Did Kinnock Lose?" Philip Jones and John Hudson, "The Quality of Political Leadership: A Case Study of John Major," *British Journal of Political Science*, 26 (1996), 229–44.

[27] See Harold D. Clarke and Marianne C. Stewart, "Economic Evaluations, Prime Ministerial Approval and Governing Party Support: Rival Models Reconsidered," *British Journal of Political Science*, 25 (1995), 145–70.

[28] David Sanders, "Forecasting the 1992 British General Election Outcome: The Performance of an 'Economic' Model," in David Denver, Pippa Norris, David Broughton, and Colin Rallings, eds., *British Elections and Parties Yearbook 1993* (Hemel Hempstead, Herts.: Harvester Wheatsheaf, 1993), pp. 100–15.

regression analysis of single surveys, have similarly failed to produce a consensus: Stewart and Clarke concluded that in the 1987 election "public reactions to the leaders had sizeable effects on electoral choice," [29] whereas Bartle, Crewe, and King, found that "the addition of further information about voters' evaluations of specific leadership traits adds little to our ability to predict how any given individual will vote."[30] Anthony King's introduction to this volume provides further detail about the inability of political scientists to agree on the true impact of British party leaders' personalities on voters' party choice.

There is thus nothing like consensus in political science about the role of party leaders in motivating the voting choices of individual electors. Interestingly, however, there is a substantial measure of agreement on the broader—and politically more germane—question of the net effect of individuals' leadership preferences on overall election outcomes. The almost universal view is that, whatever effects party leaders' characteristics may or may not have on individuals, these effects, at least in Britain, are only very seldom both on such a large scale and so skewed in their direction as to determine which party actually wins.

For example, Graetz and McAllister in their study of the October 1974, 1979, and 1983 elections concluded that, although the personalities of the party leaders made some difference to individual voters' decisions in 1983, they made no net difference to the overall outcome of any of the three elections.[31] The contribution of leaders to election outcomes, they say, is typically "more marginal than decisive."[32] Stewart and Clarke do not dispute the same point as regards 1987.[33] As regards 1992, Crewe and King conclude that, if leadership effects helped anyone, it was the losing Labour Party rather than the winning Conservative Party; logic dictates that these effects cannot have been decisive in determining the overall outcome.[34] With respect to the 1997 general election, Bartle, Crewe, and King claim that Blair's personal ascendancy over Major (which undoubtedly existed) made only a modest net contribution to Labour's victory, which was on a prodigious scale.[35]

Only two of the eleven British general elections fought since 1964 (and for which survey data are available) stand out as elections in which leaders'

[29] Marianne C. Stewart and Harold D. Clarke, "The (Un)Importance of Party Leaders: Leader Images and Party Choice in the 1987 British Election," *Journal of Politics*, 54 (1992), 447–70.

[30] See John Bartle, Ivor Crewe, and Anthony King, *Was It Blair Who Won It? Leadership Effects in the 1997 British General Election*. Essex Papers in Politics and Government, No. 128 (Colchester: University of Essex, 1998).

[31] Brian Graetz and Ian McAllister, "Party Leaders and Election Outcomes in Britain 1974–1983," *Comparative Political Studies*, 19 (1987), 484–507.

[32] Graetz and McAllister, "Party Leaders and Election Outcomes in Britain," p. 500.

[33] Stewart and Clarke, "The (Un)Importance of Party Leaders."

[34] Crewe and King, "Did Major Win? Did Kinnock Lose?"

[35] They calculate that it may have tipped six Conservative seats to Labour. Bartle *et al.*, *Was It Blair Who Won It?*, p. 17.

personalities may have been decisive. One was 1964 itself, when the Labour leader, Harold Wilson, was vastly preferred by voters to the Conservative leader, Sir Alec Douglas-Home. The other was the election of February 1974 when the Labour leader, still Harold Wilson, was preferred by a wide margin to the Conservative leader, Edward Heath. Both elections were distinctive for their exceptionally close result. In 1964 only 0.7 percentage points separated the two main parties and Labour secured a majority of just four seats; and in February 1974 a mere 0.8 percentage points separated the two parties, and neither secured a parliamentary majority. Crewe and King are not alone in suggesting that, at these two unusually close elections, leadership preferences on their own may well have tipped the balance; but they are not alone either in concluding that "while leadership effects exist and may on occasion be electorally decisive, they are seldom on a large scale and are not decisive very often."[36]

British political science has been slow to assess the influence of leaders' personalities on voting choice and election outcomes and has generally, although not always, reached negative conclusions. In the following section, we revisit the issue by examining the apparent influence of leaders' personalities in a recent general election: that of 1997. We focus on this general election for several reasons. First, the 1997 British Election Study comprised three separate studies: the cross-sectional study (XBES), the campaign study (BECS), and the British Election Panel Study (BEPS). We can, therefore, use these studies to gauge just how sensitive our estimates of the impact of leadership traits are to different data-sources. Second, our experience suggests that many people had strong intuitive beliefs about the effect of leaders at that election; clearly many people strongly believed that comparative evaluations of Major and Blair played a major role. Third, preliminary experiments with vote models for earlier elections have highlighted major data omissions in earlier studies.

The Effect of Leaders' Personalities in 1997

The Vote Models

In this section we use the improved-prediction strategy to disentangle the effect of leaders' personalities from all those other factors that may have influenced vote decisions in 1997. We construct a series of vote models based on the "funnel of causality" device that was first deployed in *The American Voter*,[37] developed in a series of articles in the *British Journal of Political*

---

[36] Crewe and King, "Did Major Win? Did Kinnock Lose?", p. 144.

[37] Angus Campbell, Philip E. Converse, Warren E. Miller, and Donald E. Stokes, *The American Voter* (New York: John Wiley, 1960).

Science,[38] and then fully expounded in *The New American Voter*.[39] These models assume that there is considerable continuity in voters' political preferences, such that they approach an election already predisposed to support one party rather than another. These predispositions are based either on broad agreement with the party's longstanding values (their ideological positions) or on an emotional attachment to a party (their party identification). They are rooted in the enduring features of peoples' lives: their social class, religion, ethnic group, types of neighborhood, and so on. During the campaign, voters are exposed to a flurry of political communications and form opinions on a wide variety of contemporary issues. These are heavily influenced by voters' prior predispositions but are also influenced by the debate itself and the way the issues are dealt with in the media.

The multistage models of voting outlined here are designed to simulate this causal process. The first task is to group variables into blocs containing variables of a similar type or those that influence voting behavior in similar ways. These blocs are then arranged in a sequence according to their long-term stability and distance from the vote decision. Figure 3.1 displays the assumed causal order in our vote models. It assumes that variables in later blocs are, potentially at least, caused by all those variables located in prior blocs. Voters' partisan predispositions are partly a function of their socioeconomic characteristics; their evaluations of national economic and social conditions are partly a function of both their socioeconomic characteristics and partisan predispositions; and so on. The vote decision is itself a function of all the explanatory variables. Before proceeding to the statistical analysis, however, we need to explain the characteristics of our model and to assess its potential weaknesses.

Caveats: The Importance of the Models' Assumptions

The models outlined in Figure 3.1 are used to estimate the effect of a wide range of variables both on individual vote decisions and on the aggregate election outcome in 1997. However, all the estimates derived from such models are subject to a degree of uncertainty that arises from the models' assumptions.[40] By far the most important of these assumptions is the imputed causal order

[38] Warren E. Miller and J. Merrill Shanks, "Policy Directions and Presidential Leadership: Alternative Explanations of the 1980 Presidential Election," *British Journal of Political Science*, 12 (1982), 299–356; J. Merrill Shanks and Warren E. Miller, "Policy Direction and Performance Evaluation: Complementary Explanations of the Reagan Election," *British Journal of Political Science*, 20 (1990), 143–235; J. Merrill Shanks and Warren E. Miller, "Partisanship, Policy and Performance: The Reagan Legacy in the 1988 Election," *British Journal of Political Science*, 21 (1991), 129–97.

[39] Warren E. Miller and J. Merrill Shanks, *The New American Voter* (Cambridge, Mass.: Harvard University Press, 1996), chap. 7.

[40] See Gary King, Robert O. Keohane, and Sidney Verba, *Designing Social Inquiry: Scientific Inference in Qualitative Research* (Princeton, N.J.: Princeton University Press, 1994), pp. 31–2.

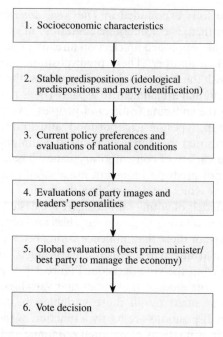

Fig. 3.1 Assumed casual order in vote models

among the explanatory variables. Those variables that are assumed to be located early in the causal sequence will be allocated some explanatory credit for their assumed effect on other explanatory variables located between them and the vote decision.[41] It follows that, if these assumptions are violated, then the assumed prior variable will have allocated to it some explanatory credit that properly belongs to something else. The models outlined in Figure 3.1 contain two important assumptions: (1) that the causal arrows flow from long-term predispositions (party identification and ideological positions) to short-term or contemporary political preferences (policy preferences and evaluations of political objects), and (2) that, while party and leadership images are caused by the same variables, they do not in turn "cause" each other.

Early studies of voting behavior suggested that most voters formed a psychological attachment to a party. It was assumed that this identification was enduring and was modified only in response to large social changes or slowly accumulating political experiences. However, there is increasing evidence that party identification—at least as traditionally measured in Britain by the BES—is itself responsive to many of the very short-term factors, such

[41] See James A. Davis, *The Logic of Causal Order* Series on Quantitative Applications in the Social Sciences, No. 55 (Beverley Hills, Calif.: Sage Publications, 1985); John Bartle, "Left–Right Matters, But Does Social Class? Causal Models of the 1992 British General Election," *British Journal of Political Science*, 28 (1998), 501–29.

as evaluations of the economy, that it was hitherto assumed to cause.[42] Controlling for party identification when assessing the effect of these variables may, therefore, conceal part of their causal impact, since party identification has already changed in response to that variable. We are concerned that the traditional measure of party identification may well conceal some effect of contemporary political variables, and so we engage in some sensitivity testing to assess the apparent effect of leadership evaluations controlling for ideological positions only and omitting the—potentially flawed—measure of party identification. These findings are then reported in footnotes to this chapter in order not to distract from the main lines of the argument.

Similarly, the relationship between party images and leadership images is an ambiguous one. It could be argued that voters largely view the world in terms of partisan stereotypes and, therefore, that party image causes leadership image. This assumption is challengeable since we find that party and leadership images do diverge. Alternatively, it could be argued that because party leaders represent relatively enduring elements in the political environment (typically remaining in place for between seven and ten years) and because they have extensive influence over party organization, party images bear the imprint of their leaders. Our own view, for what it is worth, is that the precise relationship between leadership and party images cannot be fully determined given the limited data available. This is why we prefer, as the Americans say, to "take the fifth" on this issue. Our bloc recursive model assumes that party and leader images are located at the same stage within our model. However, we again engage in some sensitivity testing to assess any potential biases. These, too, are reported in the footnotes to this chapter.

Apart from concerns about causal structure, we are also exercised by the problem of omitted-variable bias. Ideally our data sets need to be as comprehensive as possible if we are to arrive at valid estimates of the effect of leadership traits. However, all three surveys omit a number of theoretically important prior variables, such as voters' ideological positions, perceptions of policy differences between the parties, retrospective evaluations of governmental performance or prospective evaluations of the parties' likely performance in office.[43] Unfortunately, not one of the three BES data sets contains

---

[42] See Harold D. Clarke, Marianne C. Stewart, and Paul Whiteley, "Tory Trends: Party Identification and the Dynamics of Conservative Support Since 1992," *British Journal of Political Science*, 27 (1997), 299–319; John Bartle, "Improving The Measurement of Party Identification," in Justin Fisher, Philip Cowley, David Denver, and Andrew Russell, eds., *British Elections & Parties Review, Vol. 9* (London: Frank Cass, 1999), pp. 119–35.

[43] In addition, the specific questions posed about the leaders are not entirely satisfactory for at least four reasons. First, they do not appear to be based on any recognizable theory of personality effects. Second, the questions also lack an empirical basis, since they are not based on any prior qualitative work to establish which traits are of particular importance to voters. Third, many of the questions seem just as—or possibly more—appropriate to parties than leaders, thus blurring the conceptual differences between leader and party images. Fourth, the number of questions is limited to six: hardly sufficient to tap the multidimensional aspects of personality.

items that record voters' evaluations of the Conservatives' performance in office—variables that might be thought to condition evaluations of both John Major and Tony Blair. It is obvious that the omission of variables like these means that we run some risk of omitted-variable bias. Yet by using all available component parts of the BES we should be able to provide an indication of the likely magnitude of leadership effects in 1997.[44]

Another element of uncertainty in our analysis is the assumption that the effect of explanatory variables is uniform across the various subgroups of the electorate. In reality, the effect of leadership traits may well vary between, say, those with high and low levels of political awareness or between those with extreme and moderate ideological positions.[45] While these issues are interesting, we regard them as being of somewhat secondary importance to our main goals and we do not explore them here. A final source of uncertainty relates to our use of ordinary least squares (OLS) rather than logistic or probit models.[46] Again, although we recognize that the statistical assumptions embedded within OLS models are problematic, we regard these issues as being of somewhat secondary importance compared with the problems of causal order.

Having briefly examined the inherent limitations of our models, we proceed to estimate the effect of leadership traits in 1997 using all the data available to us from the British Election Study.

[44] Respondents to the 1995 BEPS questionnaire were asked a battery of questions about the leaders. They were asked whether they agreed or disagreed that the leader "is willing to change with the times," "inspires hope for Britain"s future," "is concerned about all groups in society," "means what he says," "gets a lot out of a team," "has a lot of common sense," "knows how to solve Britain's problems," "has a clear view of where Britain should be going," "understands ordinary people's problems," "keeps his word," "is a born leader," "sticks to his principles," "will prove a great prime minister," "will get Britain on the move," "increases respect for Britain abroad," "can unite the nation behind him," and "makes the world look up to Britain." Unfortunately, this battery was not repeated in later surveys. Since evaluations of party leaders are exactly the sorts of short-term variables we would expect to change in the run-up to an election, we hesitate to use such variables to predict the vote in 1997. However, a preliminary analysis suggests that only three of the seventeen variables were significant predictors of vote in 1995.

[45] See Hans Dieter Klingemann, "Measuring ideological conceptualization," in S. H. Barnes and M. Kasse, eds., *Political Action* (Beverly Hills, Calif.: Sage, 1979), pp. 215–54. Klingemann found that the highly educated placed less importance on candidates' personal qualities. Also see Douglas Rivers, "Heterogeneity in Models of Electoral Choice," *American Journal of Political Science*, 35 (1991), 737–57.

[46] See R. Michael Alvarez and Jonathan Nagler, "Economics, Issues and the Perot Candidacy: Voter Choice in the 1992 Presidential Elections," *American Journal of Political Science*, 39 (1995), 714–44, and Guy D. Whitten and Harvey D. Palmer, "Heightening Comparativists' Concern for Model Choice: Voting Behavior in Great Britain and the Netherlands," *American Journal of Political Science*, 40 (1996), 231–60; R. Michael Alvarez, Jonathan Nagler, and Shaun Bowler, "Issues, Economics and the Dynamics of Multiparty Elections: The British 1987 General Election," *American Political Science Review*, 94 (2000), 131–50.

The Relationship between Leaders' Personalities and Vote in 1997

By the time of the 1997 general election John Major and Tony Blair had been leaders of their parties for seven and three years respectively. The Conservatives' surprising victory in April 1992 was attributed to voters' doubts about Labour's taxation policies and overall economic competence but also to the personal appeal of Major, the then new Conservative leader, and to deep-seated skepticism about Neil Kinnock's qualifications to be prime minister.[47] Six months later, the standing of both the Conservative government and Major as prime minister had plummeted. Formal econometric modeling of aggregate opinion poll data suggests that two events contributed above all to the massive lead that Labour established and sustained through to the 1997 election (and after).[48] The first was "Black Wednesday" in September 1992, when Britain hurriedly withdrew from the Exchange Rate Mechanism (ERM). The humiliating circumstances and manner of Britain's withdrawal destroyed the Conservatives' reputation for economic competence and reopened their internal divisions on Europe, which then dominated the rest of the parliament.[49] In the wake of the ERM disaster Labour enjoyed a clear lead in the polls of around 17–20 percent, having been level-pegging with the Conservatives before. The second crucial event was the election of Blair as leader of the Labour Party in July 1994. In the following five months, Labour's lead over the Conservatives leapt to an unprecedented 33 points and barely subsided from that level until shortly before the election.

The electoral impact of Blair's election as Labour leader could be thought of as powerful evidence of a leadership effect. However, as Anthony King stresses in Chapter 1, Blair's assumption of the Labour leadership produced other consequences: the abolition of Clause 4 of the Labour Party constitution, which ditched Labour's commitment to public ownership; the further weakening of Labour's links with the trade unions; renewed and strenuous efforts to shed its tax-and-spend image; and a much tougher position on crime.[50] All these changes, but in particular the abolition of Clause 4, represented the abandonment of conventional socialism, and all were pushed by Blair against considerable opposition within his party. These changes had a major indirect effect on the outcome of the election but are not what most

[47] Crewe and King, "Did Major Win? Did Kinnock Lose?" pp. 125–7.

[48] See David Sanders, "Conservative Incompetence, Labour Responsibility and the Feelgood Factor: Why the Economy Failed to Save the Conservatives in 1997," *Electoral Studies*, 18 (1999), 251–70.

[49] See David Denver, "The Government That Could Do No Right," in Anthony King, ed., *New Labour Triumphs: Britain at the Polls* (Chatham N.J.: Chatham House, 1998), pp. 15–48.

[50] See Anthony King, "Why Labour Won—At Last," in King, *New Labour Triumphs*, pp. 177–208.

commentators mean when they talk about Blair's impact on the vote. The remainder of this chapter therefore focuses exclusively on the direct effects that can be uniquely attributed to the rival leaders' personalities.

The British Election Cross-Section Study (XBES)

The XBES offers the best evidence currently available on leadership effects. It comprises a large sample ($N = 2,906$), asks more questions than any other survey, and has particularly good coverage of voters' partisan predispositions.[51] However, as a postelection survey it may be subject to a degree of pro-Labour rationalization. It has other quirks too. It does not contain any retrospective evaluations of governmental performance, nor prospective evaluations of party performance. These variables may influence both evaluations of leaders' personalities and the vote. Their omission is likely to inflate estimates of the effect of leadership traits on the vote.

Moreover, most theories of leadership effects suggest that it is comparisons of the rival party leaders' traits that matter.[52] Unfortunately, in 1997 respondents were asked to evaluate the specific traits of only one leader, Tony Blair. This omission is slightly mitigated by the inclusion of two general evaluations of party leaders. In the first question respondents were asked: "Who would make the best prime minister, Tony Blair, John Major, or Paddy Ashdown?" In the second, respondents were asked: "How good a job do you think that [John Major/Tony Blair] is doing/would do as Prime Minister?" We constructed a simple synoptic measure of the two leaders by subtracting evaluations of Blair from those of Major. We assume that responses to both these general questions are influenced by voters' assessments of specific leadership traits. Our models allocate these variables to the penultimate bloc preceding the actual vote decision.[53]

---

[51] The data are weighted to be representative. The actual N in the vote models ($N = 1,137$) is far smaller, since it includes only those Conservative and Labour voters who gave responses to all the items used in the vote models and returned the self-completion questionnaire. Controls were included for age, race, gender, social class, education, various wealth variables (car, share, and home ownership), region, religion, ideological positions (socialist–laissez faire, liberal–authoritarian, ideological self-position), party identification, policy preferences (European social chapter, minimum wage, tax, and spending), evaluations of national conditions (unemployment, quality of the National Health Service and the general standard of living), and party images (whether good for one class or all classes, will keep promises, and stand up for Britain abroad).

[52] Nadeau *et al.*, "Prospective and Comparative or Retrospective and Individual?"

[53] We regard the "best prime minister" and "synoptic leaders" evaluation as *alternative* measures of leadership effects. This decision is influenced by a number of considerations. First, the two measures appear to represent a conclusion, virtually tautologically determining the vote—they appear to be measuring the same thing. Second, including both measures will inevitably lead to some bias since the BES cross-section does not include equivalent questions on the parties (e.g., which party is best at running the economy or country). It should be noted that a small portion of those who voted either Conservative or Labour chose Paddy Ashdown as the "best prime minister."

Table 3.1 displays respondents' evaluations of Blair across six individual traits in the summer of 1997. It can readily be seen that evaluations of the young Labour leader were almost uniformly positive. Over 80 percent rated him favorably in terms of strength, caring, decisiveness, and the ability to listen to reason. The only slight question marks against him related to whether he stuck to his principles and would keep his promises. However, even here many respondents merely raised a question mark by responding "don't know" rather than by giving a negative response. On the "best prime minister" question, Blair enjoyed a massive 42-point lead over Major (60 points to 18 points).[54] On the face of it, therefore, Blair's overwhelming popularity at the time of the 1997 election must have contributed something to the result. But did it?

We answer this question by presenting a series of tables that outline the effect of leadership traits on both individual voters and the aggregate election outcome. In our models, the vote is scored $+1$ if Conservative and -1 if Labour. All the explanatory variables are scored from $+1$ (the most pro-Conservative opinion) to -1 (the most pro-Labour opinion), with 0 representing a neutral or balanced opinion. In the following tables, we focus on the effect of leadership traits alone in order to avoid unnecessary distractions.

Table 3.2 reports our findings from the cross-sectional data and suggests that not one of the six specific traits outlined in Table 3.1 had a visible impact on the vote in 1997. All the p-values exceed our—statistically generous—$p < 0.1$ criteria and are statistically insignificant. Only the general evaluations of party leaders—the "best prime minister" and the "synoptic evaluation" item—distinguish Conservative and Labour voters, once controls are applied for prior variables. However, in both cases, the strong bivariate relationships documented in the first column are severely reduced once controls are applied

Table 3.1. Evaluations of Tony Blair, 1997

	Positive	Negative	Balance
Capable of being a strong leader/ Not capable of being a strong leader	84.0	8.0	+76.0
Caring/Not caring	86.0	5.0	+81.0
Decisive/Not decisive	81.8	7.2	+74.6
Someone who sticks to his principles/ Does not stick to his principles	69.3	10.6	+59.7
Keeps his promises/Breaks his promises	59.6	8.7	+50.9
Listens to reason/Does not listen to reason	80.2	5.4	+74.8

Source: British Election Study, cross-section survey 1997. All voters.

[54] It should be noted that part of this advantage probably arose from the fact that many of the interviews occurred in the summer of 1997 when Major had resigned as Conservative leader and people had already had actual experience of Tony Blair as prime minister.

for prior variables. In Model 1, for example, the effect of the "best prime minister" item falls from 0.78 to 0.09. This suggests that evaluations of who would make the best prime minister were strongly influenced by (and therefore predictable from) voters' prior predispositions: their party identification and their ideological positions.

The coefficient of 0.09 reported in Table 3.2 for the "best prime minister" item represents the effect of a one-unit movement in this explanatory variable on the vote. We designate this the apparent total effect (ATE) for that variable. Thus, controlling for prior variables, the effect of moving two units—or preferring Major $(+1)$ to Blair (-1)—is to increase the predicted vote by 0.18 (2×0.09) and to make a Conservative vote more likely. The ATEs for party identification (0.83) and socialist *laissez faire* positions (0.27) are substantially larger.[55] This suggests that, once we know a voter's social characteristics, enduring partisan predispositions, policy preferences, retrospective evaluations of national conditions, and assessments of the parties, the addition of further information about their judgments of the party leaders adds little to our ability to predict how any given individual will vote.

What effect, if any, did those judgments have on the overall election result? To estimate the scale of the effect we need to combine information about the effect of the "best prime minister" items on individual voters with additional information about the extent to which opinion about the "best prime minister" is skewed in one party's favor. In 1997 voters overwhelmingly thought that Tony Blair would make the best prime minister. This pro-Labour advantage is reflected by the mean of -0.37 for this variable in Table 3.2. However, our adoption of a multistage model implies that some portion of this mean value may be attributable to the already pro-Labour rather than pro-Conservative score on prior variables. This raw mean must, therefore, be adjusted to assess just how much more (or less) pro-Labour it was than we could have expected given our knowledge of prior variables. This implies that

Table 3.2. Estimated impact of leadership qualities in Britain, 1997 (XBES)

	Bivariate	Apparent total effect	Mean score	Adjusted mean score	Contribution to aggregate outcome
Model 1 (controlling for party identification)					
Best prime minister	0.78	0.09	-0.37	-0.09	-0.0081
Model 2					
Synoptic evaluations of Blair and Major	1.46	0.12	-0.32	-0.20	-0.0240
Average vote					-0.1900

---

[55] The ATE for party identification here is identical with that reported in our previous study that relied on Gallup data. The ATE for socialist–laissez faire positions is slightly higher in this case (0.27 compared with 0.23). See Bartle *et al.*, *Was It Blair Who Won It?* p. 49.

we need to remove the portion of that variable's mean that is predictable from our knowledge of prior variables. We achieve this by calculating a modified residual.[56] Once this adjustment is performed, the substantial pro-Labour advantage is reduced from −0.37 to −0.09. It appears that a substantial portion of the pro-Labour opinion was predictable from prior variables.

To estimate the impact of people's judgments of who would make the best prime minister on the election result, we multiply the ATE (0.09) by the adjusted mean score for the variable (−0.09). The resulting figure (−0.0081) represents our estimate of that variable's contribution to the aggregate election outcome.[57] Among Conservative and Labour voters in the XBES, 19 percent more claimed to have voted Labour than Conservative in the election (hence the mean score of −0.19). Since Labour received some 3.9 million more votes than the Conservatives and enjoyed what was in fact an 11.9 percentage point lead on election day itself we can calculate precisely how many votes Labour gained as a result of favorable evaluations of Blair. Our model suggests that Labour gained an additional 166,263 votes or just 0.5 percentage points as a result of direct leadership effects.[58] This amounts to 262 votes per constituency, enough to have tipped only four Conservative seats into Labour's hands.

However, Model 2 in Table 3.2 shows that, if we prefer the synoptic evaluation of leadership (which compares separate judgments of Blair and Major) as our summary indicator of leaders, it has a slightly stronger effect on the election result. Both the ATE (0.12) and the adjusted mean (−0.20) for this variable are larger and so make a bigger contribution—of −0.0240—to the overall result. In this case, therefore, our model suggests that Labour gained an additional 492,631 votes or 1.5 percentage points because of more favorable evaluations of Blair. This is equivalent to 777 votes per constituency, sufficient to deliver fourteen Conservative seats to Labour. Had Major and Blair been evaluated equally favorably, Labour's lead would have been cut from 11.9 to 10.4 points. These effects are significant but far from enough to alter the election result. It appears that the source of Labour's victory lies somewhere other than in evaluations of leaders' personalities.

It must be noted, however, that sensitivity testing suggested that omitting party identification makes an appreciable difference to our findings. When this

---

[56] This modified residual represents the difference between the actual (or measured) score on the explanatory variable and the score that could have been predicted on the basis of the prior variables. The mean of this modified residual represents the true measure of party advantage on that variable.

[57] It should be noted that this estimate is very similar to that produced in our earlier paper. See Bartle *et al.*, *Was It Blair Who Won It?* p. 49, although in that case we were able to include variables measuring leaders' comparative traits.

[58] The number of votes is calculated simply by multiplying the proportion of the mean score accounted for by leadership effects (0.0081/0.19) by the plurality 3,900,000. The effect on Labour's lead is calculated by multiplying the proportion of the mean score attributable to leadership effects (0.0081/0.19) by the percentage point lead (11.9) = 0.51.

is done, one of the specific leadership traits (keeping promises) becomes statistically significant. The ATE of 0.05, when combined with the adjusted mean of 0.63, makes a substantial contribution of −0.0265 toward Labour's plurality.[59] Equally, assuming that leader images were causally prior to party images also substantially alters our findings. When we do not control for party image, the "sticks to principles" item becomes statistically significant and makes a substantial (−0.0315) contribution to Labour's plurality.[60] These findings emphasize the sensitivity of our findings to specific assumptions about both measurement and causal order. However, we believe that—on the whole—the estimates contained in Table 3.2 are more plausible. Although others will undoubtedly disagree, we take the results of our sensitivity tests as representing the extreme upper-limit estimate of leadership effects.[61]

The British Election Campaign Study (BECS)

However, relying on cross-sectional data alone to estimate the effect of leaders' personalities would clearly be foolhardy, particularly when we have only noncomparative evaluations of the personality traits of one leader. To confirm our results, we examine evidence contained in the second wave of the BECS, which asked respondents about both party leaders. This study is far smaller ($N = 1,592$) than the cross-section and unfortunately contains only one measure of voters' prior partisan predispositions: party identification as measured in 1996.[62] It does not measure retrospective evaluations of the

[59] Omitting party identification and controlling for ideological positions alone has two effects. First, one of the specific trait (keeps promises) becomes statistically significant and contributes to Labour's plurality. The ATE for this variable is 0.05 and the adjusted mean is −0.53. This variable therefore contributes −0.0265 to Labour's plurality. Second, while the ATE for the "best prime minister" variable remains unchanged at 0.19, the adjusted mean is reduced to just −0.01, presumably because some portion of the mean score in Table 3.2 was attributable to this variable and this variable, therefore, now contributes just −0.0019 to Labour's plurality. However, if the synoptic measure replaces the best prime minister item, then the aggregate effect is much greater (−0.0352).

[60] If leadership evaluations are assumed to be causally prior to party images, this again results in slightly different conclusions. If we do not control for party images, the ATE of the "sticks to principles" item is 0.05 and the adjusted mean −0.63. This variable therefore contributes −0.0315 to the plurality. The ATE for the best prime minister item is 0.08 and the adjusted mean is −0.03. The best prime minister variable therefore contributes −0.0024 to Labour's plurality. This is again much smaller than the estimate derived from the synoptic evaluation measure (an ATE of 0.12 and adjusted mean of −0.18 resulting in an aggregate contribution of −0.0198).

[61] We have previously expressed reservations about the current measure of party identification. See Ivor Crewe, "Party Identification Theory and Political Change in Britain," in Ian Budge, Ivor Crewe, and Dennis Farlie, eds., *Party Identification and Beyond: Representations of Voting and Party Competition* (London: John Wiley, 1976), pp. 33–62; Bartle, "Improving The Measurement of Party Identification." However, we believe that it is unsatisfactory to omit the theoretical concept of party identification altogether from our models.

[62] The N in this case is for those who gave a vote preference in the second wave and voted in 1997. The N for the vote models ($N = 880$) is far smaller, since it includes only those Conservative and Labour voters who gave responses to all the items used in the vote models.

Conservative government's performance and contains few measures of respondents' policy preferences. However, unlike the cross-section, it does include items on prospective party competence. Moreover, voters were asked to evaluate the party leaders before they voted, so the risk of postelection rationalization is reduced.

Table 3.3 displays respondents' evaluations of both Blair and Major as reported in the second wave of the BECS study for all voters. The figures for Blair are not wildly out of line with those in Table 3.1 but are a little less impressive. The slight differences suggest that the postelection XBES study did capture both some degree of rationalization and something of the honeymoon that invariably follows an opposition election victory. The figures for Major suggest that he, too, was regarded as caring and as a man who stuck to his principles, although his net scores were considerably less favorable than Blair's. Moreover, the majority of respondents considered Major "not capable of being a strong leader" and "not decisive"—judgments that are easy to understand given the evident divisions within the Conservative Party during his premiership. Blair's lead over Major in terms of these traits ranged from 24 points for "sticking to principles" to as much as 72 points for "decisiveness."

Table 3.4 summarizes the effect of the leadership traits and best prime minister item on the choice between Conservative and Labour using the BECS data. In this case, the bivariate (uncontrolled) relationships between specific traits and the vote are even stronger, presumably because BECS data capture the fact that in this survey the measure of personality traits is a product of judgments of both party leaders, not just Blair.

Again, however, the relationship between evaluations of the party leaders and vote is markedly reduced once controls are applied for prior variables. The traits "capable of being a strong leader," "caring," and "decisive" all achieve statistical significance at the $p < 0.1$ level, but the fourth trait "sticks/does not stick to his principles" did not achieve significance and was dropped from Table 3.4. However, the ATEs are, once again, small when compared with that for party identification (0.83 even though this latter variable is measured one

Table 3.3. Evaluations of party leaders in Britain, 1997 (BECS)

	Blair			Major			
	Pos.	Neg.	Blair balance	Pos.	Neg.	Major balance	Leader balance*
Capable of being a strong leader/ Not capable of being a strong leader	66.3	21.2	+45.1	39.6	54.1	−14.5	(+59.6)
Caring/Not caring	76.9	11.0	+65.9	57.6	33.3	+24.3	(+41.6)
Decisive/Not decisive	63.5	22.7	+40.8	29.8	61.2	−31.4	(+72.2)
Sticks to his principles/ Does not stick to his principles	57.3	26.7	+30.6	48.2	40.0	+8.2	(+24.4)

*Leader balance = Blair balance − Major balance.
Source: British Election Campaign Study, 1996–97 wave 2. All voters.

Table 3.4. Estimated impact of leadership qualities in Britain, 1997 (BECS)

Model 3 (controlling for party identification)	Bivariate	Apparent total effect	Mean score	Adjusted mean score	Contribution to aggregate outcome
Strong leader	0.84	0.06	−0.36	−0.27	−0.0162
Caring	0.93	0.09	−0.15	−0.04	−0.0036
Decisive	0.80	0.09	−0.35	−0.29	−0.0261
Best prime minister	0.84	0.19	−0.16	0.15	+0.0285
Total leadership effects					−0.0174
Average vote					−0.2200

Source: British Election Campaign Study, 1996–97.

year earlier!). Knowledge of evaluations of specific traits adds relatively little to our ability to predict an individual's vote, although the ATE for the "best prime minister" (0.19) is quite impressive. Each of the three specific traits is skewed in a pro-Labour direction, but, once this is adjusted to take account of prior variables, the magnitudes of their pro-Labour bias are much reduced. Together they contribute −0.0459 to Labour's plurality of −0.22—in other words 4.6 percentage points out of the 22 percentage point plurality recorded among the BECS respondents.[63]

Yet, intriguingly, our findings suggest that—once allowance is made for the already pro-Labour distribution of prior variables—voters' general evaluations of who would make the best prime minister actually result in a pro-Conservative advantage (+0.15). This reduces the contribution of leadership effects to the aggregate outcome by +0.0285, suggesting that, although many voters thought Blair caring, decisive, and strong, assessments of John Major's ability to do the job of prime minister continued to benefit the Conservatives![64] Leadership effects as a whole thus contributed 0.0174 or 1.7 percentage points to Labour's recorded plurality of 22 percentage points.[65] Yet again, leadership effects cannot be ignored in the 1997 general election, but they were hardly decisive. Had Major and Blair been evaluated equally favorably, Labour's majority would have been cut from 11.9 to 11.0 points, altering the outcome in just four seats.

The British Election Panel Study (BEPS)

Our final parcel of evidence comes from the 1992–97 BEPS. This data set contains evidence on voters' evaluations of prospective party performance and—

[63] BECS overstates Labour's plurality. The mean on the dependent variable ought to be −0.17, since Labour obtained 44.3 percent of the vote in 1997, compared to the Conservatives 31.4 percent (43.3 −31.4/43.3 + 31.4 = −0.17).

[64] This repeats the finding in Bartle *et al.*, *Was It Blair Who Won It?*

[65] If the best prime minister item is replaced by synoptic measures of leaders item, the ATE is 0.23 and the adjusted mean −0.03, suggesting that it contributed −0.0069 to Labour's plurality.

at least in principle—can be used to unravel complex issues of cause and effect.[66] Yet, like most panel studies, it suffers from serious problems of panel attrition. Indeed, the final sample we have at our disposal has an N of just 1,573, compared with one of 2,855 for the first wave in 1992, and the sample underestimates Labour's actual plurality in 1997. Moreover, the BEPS survey contained the least number of relevant policy items of any of the three surveys, raising strong concerns about omitted variable bias. Added to that, there is an unknown element of panel conditioning that—if present—can distort the estimates of causal impact.

These caveats should be borne in mind when interpreting Tables 3.5 and 3.6, which analyze voters' evaluations of Blair and Major in the BEPS final wave. In this case, respondents were asked to judge the two leaders in terms of their "extremeness" or "moderation" and whether they were "good for one class" or "good for all classes" as well as in terms of their capacity for "strong leadership" and for "keeping promises." Blair's lead on the "capable of being a strong leader" item is far higher here than in the case of BECS. The reason for this is not clear, but it may be partly the result of rationalization, since the 1997 interview took place after the election.

Only two variables are statistically significant: whether the leaders "keep their promises" and general evaluations of the leaders (in this case measured by the synoptic item, since BEPS did not include the "best prime minister" question). In both cases, the strong bivariate associations are substantially reduced once controls are added for prior variables; once again, the pro-Labour bias is considerably smaller. Nevertheless, this analysis suggests that leadership effects contributed −0.0621 to Labour's plurality of −0.15. In other words, in the absence of voters' evaluations of the two party leaders, Labour would have lost 1,600,000 votes and its lead would have been cut by as much as 6.9 percentage points.

Table 3.5. Evaluations of party leaders in Britain, 1997 (BEPS)

	Blair			Major			
	Pos.	Neg.	Blair balance	Pos.	Neg.	Major balance	Leader balance*
Extreme/Moderate	64.9	18.2	+46.7	68.5	14.6	+53.9	+7.2
Looks after one class/ Good for all classes	69.1	9.0	+60.1	39.7	44.3	−4.6	−65.7
Capable of being a strong leader/ Not capable of being a strong leader	77.3	3.8	+73.5	23.6	62.3	−38.7	−112.2
Keeps promises/Does not keep promises	52.3	6.4	+45.9	32.2	49.3	−17.1	−63.0

*Leader balance = Blair balance − Major balance.
Source: British Election Panel Study 1992–97. All voters.

[66] Larry M. Bartels, "Panel Effects in the American National Election Studies," *Political Analysis*, 8 (2000), 1–20.

Table 3.6. Estimated impact of leadership qualities in Britain, 1997 (BEPS)

Model 4 (controlling for party identification)	Bivariate	Apparent total effect	Mean score	Adjusted mean score	Contribution to aggregate outcome
Keeps promises	1.15	0.21	−0.35	−0.25	−0.0525
Synoptic evaluations of Blair and Major	1.71	0.24	−0.23	−0.04	−0.0096
Total leadership effects					−0.0621
Average vote					−0.1500

These are the strongest aggregate effects that we find. However, it is worth underlining that the BEPS is the least comprehensive data set available and the omission of causally relevant variables almost certainly inflates the effect of evaluations of leaders' personalities on the vote. On balance, therefore, we are more comfortable with estimates from the two other surveys, especially as they are in line with previous studies of the 1997 general election.[67]

Summary and Conclusions

The idea that many voters are influenced by their impressions of leaders' human qualities is profoundly important. It influences whom parties select to be their leaders, how they campaign, and the very nature of government itself. Leaders who are thought to be an electoral asset are likely to have more authority than those thought to be a liability. In the wake of New Labour's 1997 landslide, Hugo Young, for example, wrote:

This is a government in thrall to its own disproportionate triumph on May 1st and to the leader who produced it. Its collective membership permits him to run it as a personal fiefdom, consulting here and there with selected colleagues, running the show through an inner cabinet, not all of whose members belong to the real thing or have any other base than a Blair familiar. The Cabinet has taken further giant strides into the desert of irrelevance towards which Mrs. Thatcher propelled it. Nobody these days even talks about the Cabinet as a centre of power, or its meetings as occasions where difficult matters are thrashed out between people whose convictions matter to them.[68]

But is voting behavior influenced by voters' impressions of the party leaders? Given the large number of assumptions required to estimate these effects, together with the data limitations explored above, our answer must necessarily be cautious. However, we believe that the best evidence from 1997 is that the

[67] See Bartle *et al.*, *Was It Blair Who Won it?*
[68] Bill Jones and Dennis Kavanagh, *British Politics Today* (Manchester: Manchester University Press, 1998), p. 166.

effects of the party leaders' perceived personal traits were small. Given our information about a voter's social background, partisan predispositions, policy preferences, and evaluations of national conditions, their assessments of the attributes of party leaders added very little to our ability to predict how they voted. The seeds of Labour's landslide victory in 1997 were to be found much further back in the "funnel of causality": in the events of September 1992 and the creation of New Labour. Similarly, preliminary analysis suggests that Labour's second landslide victory in 2001 was the result of a buoyant economy and the Conservative Party's failure to reassure voters that they would look after the public services rather than voters' markedly more favorable evaluations of Tony Blair than William Hague.[69] This is not to deny that the two party leaders—Blair in particular—had substantial indirect effects on the vote, indirect effects that can be partly attributed to aspects of their personalities.

The belief that leaders' personalities influence voters is deeply ingrained in British politics. Journalists believe it. Politicians believe it. Even voters themselves believe it—at least of other voters.[70] Unfortunately, no one cares what political scientists *believe*—only what they can *demonstrate*.[71] Those who have adopted an improved-prediction strategy have demonstrated that, in Britain at least, leaders have not had much of an impact on election outcomes net of prior variables. These conclusions are supported by evidence from other research that has adopted the alternative thought-experiment strategy discussed in the introduction. The findings, summarized in Table 3.7, suggest that there have been only two recent general elections in Britain (1979 and 1983) where the aggregate vote shares received by the parties were more than marginally influenced by evaluations of the party leaders.[72] And there are only three instances (the knife-edge elections of 1964, February 1974, and 1992) where evaluations of party leaders may have "decided" the outcome, in the sense that the impact of party leaders was greater than the winning margin.[73] Moreover, the estimates on which Table 3.7 is based represent the upper limits of leadership effects since the researchers were unable to apply sufficient controls for other variables. Leadership effects may well matter, but not by very much and not very often. Our analysis of the 1997 election,

---

[69] See John Bartle, "Why Labour Won—Again," in Anthony King, ed., *Britain at the Polls, 2001* (New York: Chatham House, 2001).

[70] We have regularly asked our students whether they believe that people are influenced by leaders' personalities. They overwhelmingly say yes. However, when asked whether they themselves are influenced in this way, most deny that they are. From our informal observations we believe this tendency to ascribe to leaders' great influence over others is quite widespread.

[71] See King, Keohane, and Verba, *Designing Social Inquiry*, p. 15.

[72] The estimates for 1983 produced by Bean and Mughan, together with their methodology have been criticized. See Jones and Hudson, "The Quality of Political Leadership: A Case Study of John Major."

[73] In Table 3.7 we define a very limited impact as a case where the estimated impact is 1 percent or less, a limited impact as being a case where the estimated impact is between 1.1 and 2 percent, a moderate impact as being a case where the impact is between 2 and 3 percent and a substantial impact greater than 3 percent.

thus perpetuates the long and persistent tradition of skepticism among British political scientists about the actual difference that party leaders' personalities make to the way people vote and to the outcomes of elections. Moreover, nothing revealed so far about the 2001 election gives us grounds for changing our view.

There will doubtless be some readers who remain convinced that leaders must have more direct effects than we suggest and who will assert this in the teeth of the evidence we offer. We have experienced at first hand the stunned disbelief, bordering on hostility, of a non-academic audience on being told that the impact of Blair's and Major's personalities on the 1997 election was negligible.[74] We believe, however, that it is for others to demonstrate, rather than merely to assert, that the image of party leaders exerts a powerful and direct effect on voting.

Our conclusions hold only for the election we have studied, although they broadly repeat the conclusions of studies of previous British elections using different analytic strategies. These conclusions are radical and counter-intuitive. By and large, and with relatively few exceptions, the personal appeal to the voters that some democratic politicians are said to possess does not in fact lead to the success of themselves or their party; the success of themselves or their party leads to their appearing to have personal appeal to the voters.

Table 3.7. Influence of evaluations of leaders on election outcomes in Britain, 1964–92

	Which party won?	How much influence did the balance of individuals' assessments have on the overall election outcome?	Which party benefited from any balance of individuals' assessments in his/her favor?	Did individuals' assessments of party leaders determine the election outcome?
1964	Labour	Very limited	Labour/Wilson	Possibly
1966	Labour	Very limited	Labour/Wilson	No
1970	Conservative	Very limited	Con/Heath	No
1974 (Feb.)	Labour*	Very limited	Labour/Wilson	Possibly
1974 (Oct.)	Labour	Very limited	Labour/Wilson	No
1979	Conservative	Moderate	Con/Thatcher	No
1983	Conservative	Substantial†	Con/Thatcher	No
1987	Conservative	Very limited	Con/Thatcher	No
1992	Conservative	Very limited	Labour/Kinnock	No
1997	Labour	Very limited	Labour/Blair	No
2001	Labour	Very limited	Labour/Blair	No

* In February 1974 Labour gained more seats than the Conservatives on a slightly smaller vote share.
† The 1983 estimates are based on Bean and Mughan, "Leadership Effects in Parliamentary Elections in Australia and Britain," Table 6, p. 1174.
Sources: Crewe and King, "Are British Elections Becoming More 'Presidential'?" Table 12, p. 203; and Crewe and King, "Did Major Win? Did Kinnock Lose?", Table 8.8, p. 139. The estimates for 1966, October 1974, 1997, and 2001 are the authors' own.

[74] The authors can vouch for this from experience. A previous paper, which arrived at similar conclusions to those outlined here, was met with stunned disbelief at the Elections Public Opinion and Parties (EPOP) conference held at Essex University in 1997. See Bartle *et al.*, *Was It Blair Who Won It?*

Winners look good. Losers look bad. But their winning or losing seldom has anything to do with their looks.

We do not declare that leaders' personalities have no effect on aggregate election outcomes at any time. It is quite possible to imagine circumstances in which leaders' personalities might be crucial in determining both individual vote decisions and the aggregate outcome. We can easily imagine a future election in which partisan loyalties and clear differences of policy and values between the major parties are much weaker and where the perceived personalities of the party leaders do play a much larger role in determining the outcome. But Britain does not appear to have reached that point yet.

4

Candidate Evaluations and Presidential Electoral Choices in France

ROY PIERCE

France, where the president is directly elected by the voters, is a particularly interesting and challenging site for an examination of the effects of leadership qualities and personal attributes on electoral outcomes.

The origins and nature of the French presidency, as well as the way in which the president is elected, would appear to enhance the potential importance of leadership attributes in presidential selection. Like the U.S. presidency in 1789, the French presidency was established constitutionally in 1958 by people who sought energy (read "leadership") in the executive and who were secure in the knowledge of who the first person to hold the office would be. The U.S. constitutional convention tailored the presidency to fit George Washington; the drafters of the Constitution of the Fifth French Republic tailored the presidency to fit Charles de Gaulle. Neither the United States in 1789 nor France in 1958 chose the president by universal suffrage, but their first incumbencies were virtually assigned in advance to particular persons because they had been victorious generals with remarkable gifts of political leadership.

Beginning with the presidential election of 1965, France proceeded to select its president by direct, universal suffrage. The electoral system employed, which we will describe in more detail below, is candidate-centered in ways that create multiple opportunities for aspirants to the office to try to exploit whatever leadership attributes they may possess.

At the same time, despite the comparative rarity of French presidential elections (there were only six during the thirty-year span between 1965 and 1995), there has been considerable variation in the extent to which the candidates' leadership attributes might have contributed to the voters' choices and affected the electoral outcomes.[1] And during that same period, there has been

---

[1] See Table 4.1 on pp. 102–3 for the main candidates at and the results of the French presidential elections from 1965 to 1995.

an unusual degree of constancy in the nature and strength of the kind of underlying social and political forces that can militate against personal break-throughs.

The collision between these two forces, transient candidate qualities and long-term electoral forces, is the underlying theme of this chapter. Before we can deal with the issue head-on, however, we must lay the groundwork, by setting out in brief compass the main contours of the problem as it applies to France, by describing how presidential elections are conducted in that country and then by looking at the highlights of the French experience in this domain.

Characteristics of French Presidential Elections

The first French popular presidential election of the twentieth century, held in December 1965, pitted an extraordinarily popular political leader—Charles de Gaulle—against a comparatively unknown leftist challenger—François Mitterrand. More than any other political leader in a Western democracy, de Gaulle was the epitome of what most people have in mind when they refer to a candidate's distinctive style of leadership and personal appeal as a source of electoral support.

The 1965 election, however, was not the norm. Nor indeed was the following one, in 1969. After those early experiences, informal rules of presidential candidate recruitment developed in France that tended to bring to the fore seasoned and experienced party leaders whose visibility is normally very high and whose capacity to withstand the demands of a presidential campaign has been repeatedly tested. This means that a French presidential election is likely to pit two or more political heavyweights against one another in circumstances that reduce the likelihood that any of them will enjoy a commanding electoral advantage based on familiarity, personality traits, perceived character, or leadership attributes.

In addition, electoral conflict in France has—at least through 1995—been so firmly anchored in the class structure, religion and religious practice, and broad ideological orientations (that are customarily expressed in left–right terms) that there is little room in the French electoral equation for all but the most striking personal idiosyncrasies. The partisan consistency between electoral choices for presidential candidates and for legislative candidates displayed in France, at least in comparison with what one finds in the United States, where ticket splitting often reaches high levels,[2] further suggests that the personal attributes of presidential candidates are likely to play only minimal roles in affecting how the electorate casts its votes.

---

[2] Roy Pierce, *Choosing the Chief: Presidential Elections in France and the United States* (Ann Arbor: University of Michigan Press, 1995), chap. 10.

These three characteristics of French presidential elections: the early prominence of a "heroic leader" in the person of Charles de Gaulle,[3] the more common pattern of competition between more or less equally endowed partisan contenders, and an enduring set of powerful attitudinal and demographic vote determinants could serve as an almost ideal backdrop against which to measure the independent effects of personal candidate attributes in mass electoral behavior. How much variance in the 1965 presidential vote was due to de Gaulle's personal appeal, as compared with the more prosaic factors in the French vote? Did personal appeal play a role in the outcome of the more orthodox French presidential elections of 1974 and 1981, both of which saw the same two competing candidates, Valéry Giscard d'Estaing (the 1974 winner) and François Mitterrand (who won in 1981)? And so on.

Alas! We have the frame but not the canvas, the potential but not the actual; in short, we do not have the kind of data we need to answer those and related questions with the precision and confidence one always prefers. There is no French equivalent to the various series of national sample survey election studies, under academic sponsorship, that have been conducted in other (mainly northern) European countries and the United States.[4] These studies

---

[3] Stanley Hoffmann, "The Rulers: Heroic Leadership in Modern France," in *Decline or Renewal: France Since the 1930s* (New York: Viking, 1974), chap. 4.

[4] The first major incursion in France was the ambitious panel study conducted by the Institut Français d'Opinion Publique (IFOP) for the Association Française de Science Politique in connection with the referendum of September 1958 that ratified the constitution of the Fifth Republic and the November elections for the first legislature of the new Republic (see Association Française de Science Politique, *L'Etablissement de la Cinquième République: Le Référendum de septembre et les élections de novembre 1958*, Cahiers de la Fondation Nationale des Sciences Politiques 109 (Paris: Armand Colin, 1960).

Three eminent French scholars were associated with that project: Jean Stoetzel, a social psychologist, Alain Girard, a demographer, and Georges Dupeux, a young historian attracted to electoral research. Stoetzel was the president and one of the founders of IFOP, Girard was the director of *Sondages*, the quarterly journal that published the results of various IFOP surveys.

Dupeux, who was the general supervisor of the 1958 survey, was working on a fine, more or less traditional history of a French *départment* for his major doctoral thesis (*Aspects de l'histoire sociale et politique du Loir-et-Cher, 1848–1914* (Paris: Mouton, 1962)), as well as a detailed account of the Popular Front election of 1936 for his minor thesis, which later appeared in a series of volumes published by the political science establishment in Paris (*Le Front Populaire et les élections de 1936* (Paris: Armand Colin, 1959)). He also spent time both at the Institute for Social Research in Oslo, Norway, and at the Survey Research Center of the Institute for Social Research of the University of Michigan, in Ann Arbor, Michigan, where he broadened and deepened his familiarity with sample survey research.

The history of survey-based electoral research in France might well have been different if those three men, or any subset of them, had chosen to enlist the cooperation and support of other French social scientists in converting the 1958 study into the cornerstone of a sustained, continuing program of survey-based research into French political behavior. At the time, the study of electoral behavior in France was dominated by electoral geography, of which François Goguel— after André Siegfried, the doyen of political science in France—was the most prominent practitioner. Goguel's support for such an initiative would probably have been essential, but even though his preferred methodology was electoral geography, there is no reason to think he would have been opposed to such a development. In fact, Goguel had a high opinion of Dupeux and

have shaped, enriched, and given continuity to efforts, both national in emphasis and comparative in inspiration, to trace the unfolding of electoral developments and test potentially promising theoretical propositions.

This is not to say that scholars interested in understanding French politics have no data based on sample surveys with which to work. Commercial polling agencies increasingly publish electoral surveys in the French press. These reports, however, normally present only univariate analyses, fail to report relevant case numbers, rarely refer to missing data, and—so far as I know—are not archived and conveniently accessible for secondary analysis. Nor do we mean to suggest that other, academically sponsored research, in France or elsewhere, necessarily contains convincing answers to our preoccupation in this book. Unless a study, of whatever kind, is primarily directed toward trying to answer our central question, it is not likely to provide much more than tentative answers to it.

The unfortunate fact remains, however, that there are no academically sponsored sample surveys for the French presidential elections prior to 1988, and those conducted in 1988 and 1995 that are easily accessible were not aimed at capturing the strength of what might be called the leadership factor.[5] We must, therefore, try to tease as much information as we can from various scattered data sources that touch on our subject. Among the French national presidential sample surveys available, we will rely principally on one dealing with the "cohabitation" election of 1988,[6] which saw the prime minister (Jacques Chirac) unsuccessfully challenge the incumbent president (François Mitterrand) with whom he had served for two years.

went out of his way to help him make a success of his visit to the University of Michigan. It is more likely that other young social scientists at the time did not recognize the potential value of trying to build on the 1958 study.

The three early French "behavioralists" associated with the 1958 study went their separate ways and pursued careers that only incidentally intersected with electoral research. At that time, political science lacked the legitimacy within the French academy of the older, established disciplines such as history, and there were virtually no university openings for such specialists. Dupeux became a Professor of Modern History at the University of Bordeaux and his research priorities altered accordingly, but not before he had collaborated with Philip Converse on two classic articles in comparative politics (Philip E. Converse and Georges Dupeux, "Politicization of the Electorate in France and the United States," and "De Gaulle and Eisenhower: The Public Image of the Victorious General," both in Angus Campbell, Philip E. Converse, Warren E. Miller, and Donald E. Stokes, *Elections and the Political Order* (New York: Wiley, 1966). Dupeux's choice removed from the Parisian political science community the person who was most temperamentally sympathetic to and academically prepared for planning a long-term program of French survey research on the basis of the foundation laid by the 1958 French study.

The study itself has been archived by the Inter-university Consortium for Political and Social Research (ICPSR); see *French Election Study, 1958* [computer file], conducted by Institut Français d'Opinion Publique (IFOP), Paris, 2nd edn., 1974.

[5] Two French presidential election studies that are easily accessible, because archived at the ICPSR, are Roy Pierce, *French Presidential Election Survey, 1988* [computer file], and Michael S. Lewis-Beck, Nonna Mayer, and Daniel Boy *et al.*, *French National Election Study, 1995* [computer file](Ann Arbor: ICPSR [distributor], 1996).

[6] Pierce, *French Presidential Election Survey, 1988*.

The Organization of French Presidential Elections

France operates under a mixed presidential and parliamentary system in which the president is directly elected by the voters. There is a direct and immediate connection between the candidates for the presidency and the electorate. Whatever likes or dislikes the voters may feel for one or another candidate on grounds of leadership or personality, as opposed to other factors, such as partisanship, ideology, issues and the like, can be expressed directly and easily by the way they cast their votes.

Furthermore, the French constitution provides incentives for media attention and popular participation by making the presidency a powerful office in its own right. The operational weight of the French president's powers naturally varies with political circumstances, but the French presidency is not a mere figurehead position. The importance of the office enhances public interest in presidential selection at both elite and mass levels. Turnout at presidential elections is normally higher than at elections for any other office. Despite the heroic precedent of Emile Zola's "J'accuse . . . ," which led to the eventual exoneration of Alfred Dreyfus, who had been falsely accused of treason by an antisemitic French high command, French media elites do not normally engage in investigative reporting or give penetrating scrutiny to political contenders. The centrality of the presidency, however, ensures widespread if not necessarily probing media coverage of at least the leading candidates for the office.[7]

The electoral system that France employs at presidential elections also serves to make them highly candidate-centered. France (like Russia) employs a two-ballot, majority-rule electoral system for presidential elections. Any candidate may run who satisfies the comparatively lenient requirements for nominating petitions, and this produces a multiplicity of candidates. If a candidate receives a majority of the votes at the first ballot, that candidate is elected, but that has never happened at any French popular presidential election.[8]

In the absence of a first-ballot majority, the two front-runners compete two weeks later at a decisive runoff. Because there can be only two candidates at

---

[7] One paper, *Le Canard enchaîné*, helped to undermine the presidential prospects of Gaullist Jacques Chaban-Delmas in 1974 by publishing his tax forms, which showed that—albeit perfectly legally—he paid no income tax. By contrast, the public was blissfully unaware that President Mitterrand had a mistress and an illegitimate daughter until they appeared at his funeral. In recent years, courageous (and often female) judges have widened the depth and range of media attention by their investigations of political corruption.

[8] The first presidential election of the Fifth Republic, in December 1958, was not by direct popular vote. Instead, the president was elected by an electoral college consisting of some 80,000 electors including or selected by local elected officials. De Gaulle won that election overwhelmingly, at the first ballot, against only token opposition.

the runoff, the president is necessarily elected by a majority of the valid votes cast. The relevance of this electoral system for our purposes here is that it contributes toward focusing media attention on a diminishing number of individual candidates. Partisan, programmatic, and strategic considerations are always present, of course, but public interest normally first generates around which candidates will run, then narrows to which two first-ballot candidates will survive into the runoff and, finally, concentrates on which of the two survivors will win.

Furthermore, in France (again, as in Russia) a presidential election is exclusive, in the sense that no other office is filled at the same time. The only candidates in the spotlight are the presidential candidates; there are no legislative or regional candidates or referendum items on the ballot, as there are in the United States, to compete—however feebly—for the public's attention.[9]

Candidate Visibility and Information Flow

Probably the most important problem associated with the conduct of French presidential elections is how to convey information about all the candidates to the voters. At the six presidential elections held between 1965 and 1995, fifty-three candidates threw their hats into the ring—an average of almost nine candidates per election. Those candidates were far from equal in political stature. At three of those elections only the two front-runners were credible candidates in the sense that most informed observers considered them the only likely winners; at the other three elections, there were only three credible candidates. Among the remaining candidates, more than half (twenty-seven) received less than 5 percent of the votes at the first ballot. None of the remaining eleven won more than 16 percent of the votes (see Table 4.1 for details).

---

[9] There is no constitutional requirement that French presidential elections be held separately from legislative or other kinds of election. The practice is partly the result of the desire of de Gaulle and the Gaullists who created the Fifth Republic to emphasize the centrality of the presidency, and partly the by-product of differences in the lengths of the presidential and legislative terms of office since 1965.

France does not have fixed presidential or legislative election dates as the United States does. The normal presidential term has been seven years, now reduced to five, beginning with the presidential election following that of 1995. However, there is no vice-presidency, and if a president resigns (as Charles de Gaulle did in 1969) or dies in office (as Georges Pompidou did in 1974) a new presidential election must be held within only a few weeks. The popularly elected chamber of the national legislature, called the National Assembly, can sit no longer than until April of the fifth year following its election, but it can be dissolved by the president before that limiting date is reached (with some limitations). The National Assembly has been dissolved well before its term limit on several occasions, notably by de Gaulle in 1962, by François Mitterrand in 1981 and 1988, and by Jacques Chirac in 1997.

Table 4.1. French presidential election results, 1965–95

	Dec. 5, 1965		Dec. 19, 1965		June 1, 1969		June 15, 1969	
Registered voters	28,223		28,233		28,774		28,762	
Abstentions	4,231	(15.0%)	4,360	(15.5%)	6,282	(21.8%)	8,907	(31.0%)
Invalid ballots	244	(1.0%)	665	(2.4%)	287	(1.0%)	1,295	(4.5%)
Charles de Gaulle	10,387	(43.7%)	12,644	(54.5%)				
François Mitterrand (Leftist)	7,659	(32.2%)	10,554	(45.5%)				
Jean Lecanuet (Centrist)	3,767	(15.9%)						
Three others	1,945	(8.2%)						
Georges Pompidou (Gaullist)					9,761	(43.9%)	10,688	(57.6%)
Alain Poher (Centrist)					5,201	(23.4%)	7,871	(42.4%)
Jacques Duclos (Communist)					4,780	(21.5%)		
Four others					2,463	(11.2%)		

	May 5, 1974		May 19, 1974		April 26, 1981		May 10, 1981	
Registered voters	29,779		29,774		35,459		35,459	
Abstentions	4,493	(15.1%)	3,606	(12.1%)	6,487	(18.3%)	4,810	(13.6%)
Invalid ballots	228	(0.8%)	349	(1.2%)	467	(1.3%)	888	(2.5%)
Valéry Giscard d'Estaing (Conservative)	8,254	(32.9%)	13,082	(50.7%)				
François Mitterrand (Leftist)	10,863	(43.4%)	12,738	(49.3%)				
Jacques Chaban-Delmas (Gaullist)	3,646	(14.6%)						
Nine others	2,294	(9.2%)						
François Mitterrand (Socialist)					7,437	(26.1%)	15,542	(52.2%)
Valéry Giscard d'Estaing (Conservative)					7,930	(28.0%)	14,219	(47.8%)
Jacques Chirac (Gaullist)					5,139	(18.0%)		
Georges Marchais (Communist)					4,413	(15.5%)		
Six others					3,586	(12.4%)		

	April 24, 1988	May 8, 1988	April 23, 1995	May 7, 1995
Registered voters	37,049	37,039	38,558	38,549
Abstentions	6,667 (18.0%)	5,690 (15.4%)	7,934 (20.6%)	7,514 (19.5%)
Invalid ballots	602 (1.6%)	1,145 (31.%)	851 (2.8%)	1,864 (6.0%)
François Mitterrand (Leftist)	10,094 (34.0%)	16,304 (54.0%)		
Jacques Chirac (Gaullist)	5,884 (19.8%)	13,900 (46.0%)		
Raymond Barre (Conservative)	4,915 (16.5%)			
Jean-Marie Le Pen (Extreme Rightist)	4,352 (14.6%)			
André Lajoinie (Communist)	2,042 (6.9%)			
Four others	2,493 (8.2%)			
Jacques Chirac (Gaullist)			6,094 (20.5%)	15,367 (52.7%)
Lionel Jospin (Socialist)			6,909 (23.2%)	13,804 (47.3%)
Edouard Balladur (Gaullist-Conservative)			5,520 (18.5%)	
Jean-Marie Le Pen (Extreme-Rightist)			4,545 (15.3%)	
Robert Hue (Communist)			2,598 (8.7%)	
Four others			4,106 (13.8%)	

Note: The results are given in thousands and refer to metropolitan France only.
Sources: Recueil des Décisions du Conseil Constitutionnel (Paris: Imprimerie National, 1965, 1969, 1974, 1981, and 1988). *L'Election Présidentielle de 1965,* Numero Spécial des Dossiers et Documents du Monde (Paris: May 1995), pp. 36 and 62.

Presidential candidates and their supporting parties or pressure groups are prohibited by law from purchasing press, radio or television advertising.[10] Instead, an official body, the Conseil Supérieur de l'Audiovisuel (CSA), allocates free television and radio time to each of the candidates in a manner designed both to reflect past attainment of high public standing and to ensure a minimum degree of equality among all the officially designated candidates. A distinction is made between a preelectoral period (in the case of the presidential election of April 23 and May 7, 1995, from January 1 to April 6) and the official campaign period (from April 7 to May 7). During the preelectoral period, all would-be candidates must depend for radio and television coverage on routine news and discussion programs. These are officially monitored by the CSA and allocated in principle to serve the dual goals of equity and equality of broadcast exposure. This system inevitably advantages the people who are already well known because of the media attention they have received as a result of their positions, roles, and behavior prior to the preelectoral period. It can also result in overexposure of politicians who eventually decide not to run as well as underexposure of candidates who decide to run late in the game.[11]

During the official campaign, equal but limited radio and television time is allocated to all the candidates before the first ballot as well as to the two front runners between the two ballots. The number of slots allocated depends on the number of candidates, but they normally take the form of varied five-minute and fifteen-minute broadcasts. Since 1974 there has also been a televised debate between the two finalists. Journalists participate in order to stimulate the flow of the debate, but this rarely flags as, unlike the situation at

---

[10] There are numerous useful works on political campaigning in France. I have relied particularly on: Roland Cayrol, "The Electoral Campaign and the Decision-Making Process of French Voters," in Howard R. Penniman, ed., *France at the Polls, 1981 and 1988: Three National Elections* (Durham, N.C.: Duke University Press, 1988); Jean Charlot and Monica Charlot, "France," in David Butler and Austin Ranney, *Electioneering: A Comparative Study of Continuity and Change* (Oxford: Clarendon Press, 1992); Monica Charlot, "The Language of Television Campaigning," and Alfred Grosser, "The Role of the Press, Radio, and Television in French Political Life," both in Howard R. Penniman, ed., *France at the Polls: The Presidential Election of 1974* (Washington, D.C.: American Enterprise Institute for Public Policy Research, 1975); Susan Hayward, "Television and the Presidential Elections April–May 1988," in John Gaffney, ed., *The French Presidential Elections of 1988: Ideology and Leadership in Contemporary France* (Aldershot, Hants.: Dartmouth, 1989); Anne Johnston and Jacques Gerstlé, "The Role of Television Broadcasts in Promoting French Presidential Candidates," in Lynda Lee Kaid and Christina Holtz-Bacha, eds., *Political Advertising in Western Democracies: Parties and Candidates on Television* (Thousand Oaks, Calif.: Sage Publications, 1995); Lynda Lee Kaid, Jacques Gerstlé, and Keith R. Sanders, *Mediated Politics in Two Cultures: Presidential Campaigning in the United States and France* (New York: Praeger, 1991); Howard Machin, "The 1995 Presidential Election Campaign," in Robert Elgie, ed., *Electing the French President: The 1995 Presidential Election* (London: Macmillan, 1996); and Pamela M. Moores and Christophe Texier, "The Campaign and the Media," in John Gaffney and Lorna Milne, eds., *French Presidentialism and the Election of 1995* (Aldershot, Hants.: Ashgate, 1997).

[11] Moores and Texier, "The Campaign and the Media," p. 194.

presidential-candidate debates in the United States, the two French rivals confront each other face-to-face.[12]

1965: De Gaulle's Election

The 1965 presidential election presents us with a paradox.[13] De Gaulle was, by any measure, one of the most popular political leaders within any Western democracy. His personal popularity in France in 1958 was higher than that of Dwight D. Eisenhower had been in the United States in either 1952 or 1956.[14] De Gaulle's position prevailed at a 1958 referendum on the adoption of the Constitution of the Fifth French Republic with almost 80 percent of the votes. His policy concerning Algeria was similarly upheld at two national referendums, in 1961 and 1962, with more than 75 percent and 90 percent of the votes respectively.

In 1962, de Gaulle took the initiative in amending the Constitution to provide for election of the president by direct popular vote, and at a referendum his proposal was supported by more than 60 percent of the voters, in the face of fierce opposition by all the old-guard political parties. De Gaulle's referendum victory was confirmed the following month at legislative elections, called in the midst of bitter conflict between de Gaulle's supporters and the parties that had opposed his constitutional amendment concerning popular election of the president. Gaullist candidates won almost 36 percent of the votes, more than any other single party had won at a postwar French legislative election.

Yet at the presidential election of 1965, when de Gaulle was a candidate at a national popular election for the first and only time, he failed to win a majority of the votes at the first ballot. He easily outdistanced his main challenger, the much less well-known François Mitterrand, who was jointly supported by the Communist and Socialist parties, but a centrist candidate named Jean Lecanuet, who was associated with the movement for European integration, with which de Gaulle was hardly sympathetic, won some 15 percent of the votes, forcing a runoff. At the runoff, de Gaulle won with less than 55 percent of the votes. That was a larger margin of victory than any other French president has enjoyed in a left–right contest since that date. (As we will see in a moment, Georges Pompidou defeated Alain Poher by a larger

---

[12] Speaking of flagging, U.S. readers may be interested to know that during the official campaign in France candidates may neither exhibit the French flag in their television broadcasts nor appear surrounded by the trappings of whatever political office they may hold.

[13] The principal account of the French presidential election of 1965 is Fondation Nationale de Sciences Politiques, Centre d'Etude de la Vie Politique Française, *L'Élection présidentielle de décembre 1965*, Cahiers de la Fondation Nationale des Sciences Politiques 169 (Paris: Armand Colin, 1970).

[14] Converse and Dupeux, "De Gaulle and Eisenhower."

margin in 1969, but not in a straight left–right duel.) It was, however, a slimmer margin than had been enjoyed by the winning candidate at nine of the seventeen U.S. presidential elections held between 1900 and 1964, including not only Theodore Roosevelt's victory in 1904, Franklin D. Roosevelt's first three elections, and the Eisenhower victories of 1952 and 1956, but even Harding's and Hoover's elections during the 1920s. Indeed, in 1964, one year before the French election of 1965, Lyndon Johnson triumphed over Barry Goldwater with more than 60 percent of the votes. How could such a commanding national leader as de Gaulle achieve what appears in comparative perspective to be only a mediocre electoral victory?

The solution to the puzzle appears to rest on several considerations: (1) De Gaulle's supporters surely included many voters who were drawn to him primarily because of perceived personal traits and his record of leadership, and (2) the overall level of his support was higher than it would have been for any other candidate, but (3) the conditions of a presidential election gave expression to countervailing political forces that de Gaulle had been able to circumvent in his earlier moments of triumph but could not wholly escape in the new electoral framework.

De Gaulle's great referendum victories, cited above, were all won in the context of his role as the founder of a new regime, the adoption of a new constitution, the solution of the Algerian problem that had brought down the previous regime and whose removal was essential for peaceful French political development, and the provision for the direct popular election of the president. These issues all aroused partisan controversy, of course, but their substance nevertheless permitted de Gaulle to cast himself and project his positions as being "above parties."

Converse and Dupeux have shown that the only really successful force in limiting the popularity of a victorious general is political, and in democratic societies political forces are normally expressed by parties.[15] To be above parties is to acquire immunity from the most important force that can limit a leader's personal appeal. But a presidential election, which inevitably mobilizes partisan sentiments and directs national attention to the clash of partisan interests, is less well suited than a popular referendum as a platform for above-party pronouncements. The issue at the 1965 election was not only whether one was for or against de Gaulle but also whether one sympathized with the political left. In the arena of a presidential election, de Gaulle could not convincingly claim to be above parties. A preelectoral survey conducted by the Institut Français d'Opinion Publique (IFOP) found that, while more than half their sample thought that the French president should remain above partisanship, only a third of the sample, including less than half of the people

---

[15] Converse and Depeux, "De Gaulle and Eisenhower."

who preferred a nonpartisan president, thought that de Gaulle had acted in a nonpartisan fashion during the previous seven years.[16]

The level of de Gaulle's popular support at the 1965 presidential election probably approximated and reflected the impact that de Gaulle had already had on the balance of French political forces in the immediate context of partisan conflict before 1965. That impact had been considerable, even if it was not enough to give de Gaulle either a first-ballot victory or a runoff landslide.

In addition to being the catalyst for the referendum victories to which we have already referred, de Gaulle was both the inspiration for a new major political party and the pole of attraction for enough voters to shift the majority of the electorate from left to right.

There were Gaullist parties prior to 1958, but the most durable (albeit under a succession of names) and the strongest, because it was associated in the public's mind with de Gaulle, was the Union for the New Republic (Union pour la nouvelle république—UNR), which was founded in 1958 to support and profit from de Gaulle's efforts to establish a new regime. The current incarnation of the old UNR is the increasingly fractious Rally for the Republic (Rassemblement pour la république—RPR), which tries to exploit the Gaullist heritage and was the main instrument on which Jacques Chirac relied in his pursuit of the presidency.

François Goguel, writing in 1967, called attention to the shift in the balance of electoral support between the leftist parties, on the one hand, and all the others, on the other hand, between the Fourth Republic (1947–58), which de Gaulle opposed, and the Fifth Republic, which de Gaulle and his supporters founded in 1958.[17] During the early postwar years, from 1945 through 1956, the traditional leftist parties, the Communist Party, the Socialist Party, and the Radical Socialists, had together won a majority of the votes at every legislative election. At the first three elections of the Fifth Republic, in 1958, 1962, and 1967, those same three partisan groups did not win as much as 44 percent of the vote in comparable conditions. Indeed, it was not until 1978 that the leftist parties together regained the majority of the votes—barely— that they had last won in 1956.

Although it is not systematic or uniform in character, all the evidence available indicates that it was the electoral appeal of de Gaulle that produced and sustained that electoral shift from left to right. Dupeux showed that virtually everyone who voted for the UNR in 1958 did so in order to support de Gaulle.[18] A scale of attitudes toward de Gaulle, pro and con, constructed by

[16] Michel Brulé, "Les français et le mandat présidentiel," *Sondages: Revue française de l'opinion publique*, 4 (1965), pp. 39–49.

[17] François Goguel, *Chroniques électorales. Vol. 2. La cinquième république du général de Gaulle* (Paris: Presses de la Fondation Nationale des Sciences Politiques, 1983).

[18] Georges Dupeux, "D'une consultation à l'autre: Les réactions du corps électoral," in Association Française de Science Politique, *L'Etablissement de la cinquième Republique: Le Référendum de septembre et les élections de novembre 1958*. Cahiers de la Fondation Nationale des Sciences Politiques 109 (Paris: Armand Colin, 1960), pp. 143–9, 159.

Michelat correlated with partisan choices at the legislative elections of 1962.[19] Goguel plausibly estimated, on the basis of aggregate electoral returns and census estimates of mortality, that de Gaulle won about 3 million votes at the first ballot of the presidential election of 1965 from people who had voted for leftist parties at the legislative elections of 1956.[20] Converse and Pierce showed that attitudes toward de Gaulle were as powerful an electoral force in 1967 as attitudes toward religion or self-assigned left–right placement (to be discussed more fully below).[21] There can be little doubt of de Gaulle's effect on the disposition of partisan forces in postwar France. But much if not most of his accomplishments in that domain took place before he was personally tested in the crucible of the 1965 presidential election.

1969: Left–Right Polarization Suspended

The presidential election of 1969 ushered in the post-Gaullist era in French politics.[22] De Gaulle's public image and political standing suffered from a staggering wave of student demonstrations and near-general strikes in May 1968. While he and his supporters were vindicated by a landslide victory at legislative elections in June of that year, de Gaulle's authority among the political elites and his capacity for initiative had been diminished. Ostensibly in an effort to respond to the discontents expressed in the May upheaval, in April 1969 de Gaulle submitted a complicated and obscure plan for regionalism and senatorial reorganization to a popular referendum. The proposal was defeated. De Gaulle promptly resigned the presidency after this repudiation at the polls, and a new election was held.

The 1965 presidential election, as well as the legislative elections of 1967, had been organized around two main electoral blocs: a left supported by the Communists, Socialists and various splinter groups, and a right consisting of the Gaullists and various non-Gaullist conservative groups. Conditions at the time of the 1969 presidential election, however, were not conducive to a renewal of this pattern of political competition. The invasion of Czechoslovakia by Soviet and Warsaw Pact troops in August 1968 made it impossible for the Socialists to ally electorally with the Communists, and the leftist parties approached the 1969 election in total disarray.

---

[19] Guy Michelat, "Attitudes et comportements politiques à l'automne 1962," in François Goguel, ed., *Le Référendum d'octobre et les élections de novembre 1962.* Cahiers de la Fondation Nationale des Sciences Politiques 142 (Paris: Armand Colin, 1965), pp. 242–54.

[20] Goguel, *Chroniques électorales*, pp. 453–8.

[21] Philip E. Converse and Roy Pierce, *Political Representation in France* (Cambridge, Mass.: Harvard University Press, 1986), pp. 318–22.

[22] A brief account of the 1969 election appears in Roy Pierce, "Presidential Selection in France: The Historical Background," in Penniman, ed., *France at the Polls: The Presidential Election of 1974*, pp. 29–40.

The main candidates at that election were Georges Pompidou, who had been de Gaulle's prime minister from the spring of 1962 to the summer of 1968, and Alain Poher. Poher was a centrist and, to the public, a virtually unknown politician who was president of the Senate and, as a result, the acting president of the Republic during the interim between de Gaulle's resignation and his replacement at the 1969 election. These two roles catapulted him into an unaccustomed limelight. As de Gaulle's referendum initiative was designed in part to weaken the Senate over which Poher presided, Poher became a leading opponent of de Gaulle during the referendum campaign, and after de Gaulle's resignation he tried to project some aura of presidential authority via his position as acting president.

Pompidou easily outdistanced Poher at a low turnout first ballot, but Poher ran second, ahead of both the Socialist and Communist candidates. The runoff was, therefore, not a left–right contest, but rather a muddled Gaullist–anti-Gaullist one. The Socialist Party supported Poher, but the Communist Party could see little difference between Pompidou and Poher and advised its supporters to abstain. The result was a large Pompidou victory on the lowest turnout for a presidential election on the French record.

There is, to my knowledge, no study of the voters' motivations at the 1969 election, but it would not be unreasonable to believe that favorable perceptions of his leadership qualities at least contributed to Pompidou's electoral victory. Ordinary people became aware of who Poher was by the time of the election, but he was outdistanced in public familiarity by Pompidou, who had not only been prime minister for six years but had also been virtually the only Gaullist leader who played a prominent public role in the government's effort to control the dangerous situation during the May 1968 upheaval.

At the same time, however, in the absence of a leftist candidate at the runoff, there was virtually no mobilization of the traditional leftist forces, slogans and symbols that could blunt the appeal of a popular Gaullist leader (as happened, within limits, at the election of 1965). Pompidou enjoyed the support of both Gaullist and traditionally conservative voters, in the absence of any massive leftist opposition. He probably profited from an image that projected leadership qualities, but his supporters also did not lack other, time-honored reasons to vote for him.

1974: Leadership by a Nose?

The personal standing and background of the leading candidates at the 1965 French presidential election were highly asymmetrical—as at, to a lesser extent, the atypical election of 1969. De Gaulle was a heroic leader and the incumbent president. Mitterrand was a comparatively obscure politician who was acceptable to the Socialist and Communist parties, neither of which wanted to put forward a candidate of its own in the face of what was

considered beforehand to be an inevitable defeat for the left at the hands of
de Gaulle. Georges Pompidou had been a highly visible and experienced
prime minister. His opponent, Alain Poher, was a newcomer to the national
scene who was almost accidentally propelled into a short-lived limelight.

The 1965 and 1969 elections, however, took place under exceptional circumstances. These included the establishment of new institutions (among them the
popularly elected presidency itself), the greatest mass upheaval in a postwar
democracy, the repudiation of the regime's founder at a referendum over an
almost trivial issue, and uncertainly and instability in the party system.

With Pompidou's election in 1969, however, French politics became less
dramatic and moved toward a new pattern of normality, defined principally
by the left–right, two-bloc competition that had characterized the 1967
legislative elections. In this post-Gaullist era, there might still be marked
differentials in the personal popularity of presidential candidates, but they
could not be expected to express the drama or match the combined effects
on both electoral behavior and electoral outcomes that occurred during
the extraordinary period when de Gaulle personally challenged the entire
traditional French political leadership.

Furthermore, beginning in 1974 the recruitment of major French presidential candidates started to acquire characteristics that went a long way toward
ensuring that there would be rough parity of experience, standing and visibility among the major contenders. This development elevated the electoral
importance of the traditional, long-term electoral forces, such as ideology,
partisanship, religion, and socioeconomic status, with which each of the
competing candidates was associated. It did not necessarily rule out a decisive
role for leadership attributes or personality in electoral appeal. What it did do
was to confine the operative effect of those factors to the margins. There was
(and is) always the possibility that personal traits might account for the winning margin between two otherwise closely matched opponents. This may
well have happened at the presidential election of 1974.

The 1974 election, like the 1969 election, took place before the incumbent
president had completed his term of office.[23] De Gaulle resigned in 1969;
Georges Pompidou, who succeeded him within a month, died in office in
April 1974. Neither occasion allowed much time for aspiring candidates to
plan their strategies or build support. As in 1969, the principal candidates in
1974 were well-placed top-tier politicians, although unlike the situation in
1969, when only one runoff candidate was highly visible to the public, both of
them were in 1974.

There were three main candidates at the first ballot. One, who did not survive to the runoff, was Jacques Chaban-Delmas, a Resistance hero and a
Gaullist who had been mayor of Bordeaux since 1947, president of the

---

[23] A good overall account of the 1974 French election is Penniman, ed., *France at the Polls:
The Presidential Election of 1974.*

National Assembly (France's popularly elected national legislative chamber) from 1958 until 1969, and President Pompidou's first prime minister from 1969 to 1972. The two other major candidates were François Mitterrand and Valéry Giscard d'Estaing.

Mitterrand was becoming a familiar figure on the political stage. People with long memories could recall him as the presidential candidate who had given de Gaulle a stiffer fight in 1965 than many observers had expected. Younger voters probably knew him better as the leader of the Socialist Party and the most prominent leader of an alliance of left-wing parties that jointly contested the legislative elections of 1967 and 1973 (but not 1968).

Giscard d'Estaing was a younger man, but he was the founder and leader of a small conservative party that remained independent of the Gaullists but usually allied with them electorally and in parliament. He had been a comparatively high-profile minister of finance early in the 1960s and again after the presidential election of 1969. He was also the first presidential candidate after de Gaulle for whom there is some direct evidence that he was appreciated highly for his personal qualities.

Chaban-Delmas sought to retain the presidency within the Gaullist family, but he was undermined by other Gaullist leaders (including Jacques Chirac) who believed that despite his credentials he could not win the election, mainly because he was more liberal than the Gaullist electorate. Chaban's initial standing waned as the campaign for the first ballot proceeded, and Giscard and Mitterrand became the two finalists.[24]

Giscard won the election with a razor-thin majority of the votes. To a considerable extent, the close outcome reflected an even division between traditionally leftist and traditionally rightist voters. But one particular analysis makes a plausible, if not an iron-clad, case that Giscard's margin of victory came from people who perceived him to be a potentially better leader than Mitterrand.[25]

Throughout the 1974 campaign, sample surveys were conducted in order to measure the public's perceptions of the personal qualities and leadership capacity of the main candidates.[26] It is difficult to interpret the results of these surveys if only because the published results do not indicate how much importance the voters attributed to the various factors on which they were asked to rate the candidates. For example, Giscard was rated very high on intelligence, but did that win him more votes than Mitterrand won because the latter was rated almost as high on being close to people's problems?

---

[24] Chaban-Delmas also suffered from personal attacks relating to his tax status (see fn.7) and innuendo concerning his private life (see Charlot, "The Language of Television").

[25] Denis Lindon and Pierre Weill, "Autopsie d'une campagne: Pourquoi M. Giscard d'Estaing a-t-il gagné?" *Le Monde*, May 22, 1974; see also Alain Lancelot, "Opinion Polls and the Presidential Election, May 1974," in Penniman, ed., *France at the Polls: The Presidential Election of 1974*, pp. 196–206.

[26] Lancelot, "Opinion Polls and the Presidential Election, May 1974," pp. 187–8.

Overall, the public seems to have rated Giscard more highly than Mitterrand on personal traits, but we cannot tell from the summary findings whether and how closely these personal judgments correlated with other conventional electoral forces.

Lindon and Weill, however, argue that Giscard won the election because, after the televised debate between the two candidates, one "critical group" of voters thought that Giscard, more than Mitterrand, was "made of presidential material" (*avait l'étoffe d'un président de la République*).[27] Prior to the runoff ballot, the electorate was divided into three groups: one, consisting of about 43 percent of the voters, that was "firmly and practically irreversibly" committed to Mitterrand and another, of equal size, that was equally committed to Giscard. The remaining 14 percent of the voters were undecided until the last minute. These people had divided their votes at the first ballot between the two runoff candidates and not voting at all. They were mainly apolitical, of modest social status, and presumably unattached to any particular policy objectives or political orientation.

At the runoff ballot, this "critical group" divided by eight to six in favor of Giscard, and the only factor that distinguished the Giscard supporters from the Mitterrand voters was that they gave Giscard the edge on presidential stature. If this analysis is correct, it suggests that Giscard's narrow electoral victory was produced, at the margin, by his similarly slight advantage in perceived leadership qualities.

Clashing Heavyweights: 1981 and 1988

The runoff of the 1981 election was a virtual replay of the 1974 election, although with a different outcome.[28] Giscard was defeated in his bid for a second term by Mitterrand, who—now successfully—was making his third try for the big prize. As in 1974, there was also a Gaullist candidate among the also-rans at the first ballot, Jacques Chirac. Chirac, it will be recalled, had failed to support Chaban-Delmas, his fellow-Gaullist, in 1974. He was duly rewarded by Giscard, who, after his election, appointed Chirac prime minister. There was a falling out between the two men, however, and Chirac unsuccessfully challenged his former boss at the 1981 election, winning less than 20 percent of the votes. In addition to those three, Georges Marchais, the leader of the French Communist Party, also threw his hat into the first-ballot ring.

This array of leading candidates illustrates the kind of accumulated political weight and experience that has regularly surfaced at French presidential elections since 1974. It also stood de Gaulle's efforts to reshape the French presidency on their head. De Gaulle had wanted to wrest the

[27] Lindon and Weill, "Autopsie d'une campagne."
[28] See Howard R. Penniman, ed., *France at the Polls, 1981 and 1988: Three National Elections* (Durham, N.C.: Duke University Press, 1988).

presidency from partisan control, and the ease with which one can become a candidate is a vestigial reminder of that objective.[29] In 1981, however, the principal candidates were all partisan heavyweights who had either created their own political party or captured an existing one.[30] Giscard, the incumbent, had created his own party a decade earlier; Chirac, the mayor of Paris and a former prime minister, had become leader of the now neo-Gaullists, after Giscard (with Chirac's help) had wrested the presidency from the old Gaullist dynasty; Mitterrand, now running for the third time, had become the leader of the Socialist Party in 1971; and Marchais was the boss of the Communist Party.

As in 1974, Giscard's personal image was more favorable than that of Mitterrand, although again it is not possible to tell how closely the judgments involved correlated with other relevant factors.[31] It appears, however, that this time—contrary to what Lindon and Weill found for the previous election[32]—Mitterrand's victory was based on political and programmatic considerations rather than perceived leadership ability.

Jaffré performed an analysis on a 1981 postelectoral SOFRES survey that is analogous to, although not identical with, the one performed for the 1974 election by Lindon and Weill.[33] The 1981 survey asked the voters why they thought Mitterrand had defeated Giscard. Jaffré treats the 18 percent of the voters who had voted for Chirac at the first ballot, but who contributed to Mitterrand's victory by voting for him rather than for Giscard at the runoff, as the counterpart of the Lindon and Weill "critical group." Of Jaffré's group, only 2 percent thought that Mitterrand had won because he "was better presidential material" (*avait davantage que M. Giscard d'Estaing l'étoffe d'un président de la République*). Many more of those contributors to Mitterrand's winning margin cited Mitterrand's desire for change or their desire to get rid of Giscard. The respondents were asked only why they thought Mitterrand had won, and not why they had voted for him, but Jaffré concludes that perceptions of Mitterrand's presidential stature had little to do with his victory.

We will discuss the 1988 election in detail in a separate section below; here we will emphasize only how it exemplified to near perfection the developing pattern of matched heavyweight competition that emerged in 1974 and reappeared in 1981. The 1988 presidential election was the cohabitation election, which produced the ultimate in top-tier political competition. The 1988 contest

---

[29] To be nominated, a candidate must submit a petition signed by at least 500 of France's some 40,000 locally elected officials, from at least thirty of the some hundred French departments or overseas territories (with no more than 10 percent of the signatures from any one of them).

[30] Charlot and Charlot, "France," pp. 137–9.

[31] Cayrol, "The Electoral Campaign," pp. 139–45.

[32] Lindon and Weill, "Autopsie d'une campagne."

[33] Jérôme Jaffré, "De Valéry Giscard d'Estaing à François Mitterrand: France de gauche, vote à gauche," in *Pouvoirs*, No.20, pp. 16–19; Lindon and Weill, "Autopsie d'une campagne."

pitted the incumbent president—François Mitterrand—against his own prime minister—neo-Gaullist Jacques Chirac.[34]

A brief recapitulation is in order here. Jacques Chirac, who had supported Giscard d'Estaing's bid for the presidency in 1974 and who served as prime minister from 1974 to 1976, unsuccessfully challenged Giscard at the election of 1981, which was won by François Mitterrand. In 1986, Mitterrand's leftist supporters in the legislature lost their parliamentary majority, and Mitterrand had no choice but to appoint rightist Chirac, the leader of the Gaullist party, as prime minister. The 1988 election, therefore, was a contest between the incumbent president, now running for the fourth time, and a party leader who had twice been prime minister, who had already tried his luck once before as a presidential candidate, and who was the high-profile mayor of Paris to boot.

This fifteen-year period, from 1974 to 1988, during which only three top-drawer politicians emerged to compete at the second, decisive ballot of France's presidential elections, is quite extraordinary when placed in a comparative perspective. Only Franklin D. Roosevelt's unprecedented four electoral victories in the United States surpasses Mitterrand's four runs in France (although the U.S. elective vice-presidency gave Richard Nixon the opportunity to appear on the presidential ballot five times, twice as Dwight Eisenhower's running mate, and three times as the presidential candidate). Before World War I, former U.S. presidents ran again for the top office (Cleveland in 1892, Theodore Roosevelt in 1912), but that practice has vanished. Even in Britain, which is not a presidential system but where there is no legal limit to the terms of party leaders and, hence, of potential prime ministers, the days are long gone since the pendulum could swing between a Gladstone and a Disraeli, or even a MacDonald and a Baldwin. Recurrent competition between familiar pairs of high-profile national leaders is a thing of the past in the United States and Britain; between 1965 and 1995 it was the prevailing mode in France.

1995: The Return of Asymmetry

The presidential election of 1995 was probably the only left–right contest since 1974 where mass perceptions of leadership attributes may have played a significant role in determining the outcome.[35] There were three main candidates

[34] There are several book-length studies of the 1988 French presidential election: Daniel Boy and Nonna Mayer, eds., *L'Electeur français en questions* (Paris: Presses de la Fondation Nationale des Sciences Politiques, 1990: English translation—*The French Voter Decides* (Ann Arbor: University of Michigan Press, 1993); Gaffney, ed., *The French Presidential Elections of 1988*; and Pierce, *Choosing the Chief*.

[35] On the 1995 French presidential election, see Daniel Boy and Nonna Mayer, *L'Electeur a ses raisons* (Paris: Presses de Sciences Po, 1997); Robert Elgie, ed., *Electing the French President: The 1995 Presidential Election* (London: Macmillan, 1996); and John Gaffney and Lorna Milne, eds., *French Presidentialism and the Election of 1995* (Aldershot, Hants.: Ashgate, 1997).

at that election: two conservatives (Jacques Chirac and the incumbent prime minister Edouard Balladur) and Lionel Jospin, the recently elected (but not uncontested) leader of the Socialist Party.

Most preelectoral press speculation, which was not notably perceptive or accurate during the 1995 campaign centered on the rivalry between Chirac and Balladur.[36] The two men had been close friends and political colleagues since the late 1960s. Balladur had been Chirac's chief minister and right-hand man during the latter's term as cohabitation prime minister from 1986 to 1988, and Balladur became prime minister during a second period of cohabitation under President Mitterrand, from 1993 to 1995, when the leftist president was again faced with a rightist majority in the National Assembly. It was widely believed that Balladur was serving as a stand-in for Chirac and that he would step aside and let Chirac have the leading role for the presidential election of 1995, but Balladur became very popular with right-wing voters and chose to contest the election himself.

Jospin had enjoyed a reputation as a favorite of Mitterrand and a potential prime minister during the early Mitterrand era, when he served as first secretary of the Socialist Party. He later served for a while as minister of education, but his stern moralism in the face of his leader's Machiavellian tendencies caused him to lose favor with some of his peers within the Socialist Party. After legislative elections in 1993 gave the rightist parties an overwhelming parliamentary majority, in part because of charges of corruption in Socialist Party fund-raising, Jospin withdrew temporarily from elective politics. Before long, however, his stock rose again within his party. It was widely expected and, by most Socialists, hoped that the Socialist candidate for president in 1995 would be Jacques Delors, a former minister of finance and popular president of the Commission of the European Community. Delors, however, decided not to run, and Jospin was nominated in an internal Socialist Party contest comparatively late in the run-up to the formal election campaign.

Jospin's standing with the electorate was uncertain, and few commentators gave him much of a chance to defeat either of the two main conservative contenders, both of whom surpassed him in national prominence and executive experience. There was even much preelectoral press speculation over the possibility that Jospin would be eliminated from the presidential race at the first ballot and that the decisive ballot would be a choice between the two conservative rivals.

There was, therefore, some considerable surprise when Jospin emerged in first place at the first ballot, ahead of both of his top-level conservative opponents. Chirac nosed out his old friend Balladur by fewer votes than Jospin ran ahead of Chirac, so the runoff was between Chirac, twice prime

---

[36] Jean Charlot, "The Polls and the 1995 Election;" and Catherine Pradeilles, "Politics as Narrative: The Media, the Polls and Public Opinion," both in Gaffney and Milne, eds., *French Presidentialism.*

minister, mayor of Paris, and a long-time party leader, now competing at a presidential election for the third time, and the relative newcomer Jospin.

Chirac defeated Jospin at the runoff, with less than 53 percent of the votes, and it is likely that his reputation as a *présidentiable*, buttressed by his pursuit of the office for almost two decades, contributed some portion of his margin of victory, not only over Jospin at the decisive ballot but also over Balladur at the first ballot. Several sample surveys conducted in connection with the 1995 presidential election made efforts to sort out the relative roles of personal and leadership attributes in accounting for the distribution of the popular vote. We have relied primarily on reports from two BVA exit polls, each with large samples, conducted on April 23 and May 7, the dates of the two presidential ballots.[37]

At the first survey, only 6 percent of Jospin's supporters, compared with more than 30 percent of Balladur's and almost 40 percent of Chirac's, selected as the main reason for their vote their man's having "the stature of a chief of state".[38] This imbalance on that one item, however, did not prevent Jospin from winning more votes at the first ballot than either of his two more "presidential" opponents. Of course, Jospin might have done even better if more people had thought more highly of his presidential qualities. But other considerations—perhaps the fact that three times as many of his voters as those of Balladur or Chirac gave as the main reason for their vote that their choice of a candidate was "close to my concerns"—were enough to give him the early lead.

The BVA exit poll for the runoff ballot produced similar results. Some 40 percent of Chirac's voters (virtually without any variation depending on whom they had voted for at the first ballot) picked him primarily because they thought he had the stature of a chief of state, while only some 5 percent of Jospin's voters picked him mainly for that same reason. Jospin's voters again gave top priority to his perceived closeness to their own concerns (45 percent). And Jospin improved his image during the short campaign between the two ballots on another dimension: that of inspiring confidence. Some 23 percent of his first-ballot supporters cited that as the main reason for their votes, while 28 percent of his runoff ballot supporters did so.

This large imbalance in the extent to which Chirac's and Jospin's voters in 1995 cited the two candidates' presidential stature as the main reason for their support certainly means that leadership attributes contributed, and probably heavily, to Chirac's electoral victory. It does not, however, necessarily mean that other forces were not equally or even more important as factors in accounting for Chirac's votes. Nor does it necessarily mean that despite its importance, it alone accounted for the outcome (witness the situation,

---

[37] *L'Élection présidentielle 23 avril–5 mai 1995* (Special issue of *Les Dossiers et Documents du Monde*, May 1995), pp. 47–50, 72–4.

[38] The respondents were asked to choose among four responses: He inspires confidence; he has the stature of a chief of state; he is close to my concerns; he represents change.

described above, at the first ballot). The reason for this is that there are several well-established sets of considerations that have traditionally affected electoral behavior in France. Candidate appeal is only one factor among several.

We have just faithfully reported the results of the most complete and relevant sample survey relating to the 1995 French election. Those results, however, are based on univariate analysis. The distribution of votes at the two ballots is analyzed one factor at a time. We have no means of performing the kind of multivariate analyses that might help us measure the simultaneous contributions of several potentially explanatory variables to the overall electoral outcome. Such an analysis might well show that perceptions of presidential stature outstripped other factors in the vote. It also might not.

Constraints on Personal Candidate Appeal

Candidate appeal, whether based on personality or leadership attributes, is normally a short-term force among the various factors that collectively account for electoral outcomes. One likely exception to that general rule is the case of differing attitudes toward de Gaulle, whose centrality and prominence shaped the French political agenda for a generation.[39]

Whether one is considering acknowledged historic figures or more prosaic political leaders, however, it remains true that personal appeal is distinct from, and must compete with, other determining factors in the distribution of causal influence on electoral outcomes. Assuming that we know all the factors, and assuming that all the factors apply to all the people in our sample, determination of the vote is a zero-sum game; if one factor accounts for more, the others must account for less. It follows that the more firmly electoral behavior is rooted in comparatively stable long-term political and social forces, the less likely short-term personality considerations are to affect electoral choices.

A multivariate analysis (in the form of a logistic regression) of the attitudinal bases of the second ballot vote at the French presidential election of 1988 found that the single most important factor in the voters' choices of a candidate was a generalized measure of candidate evaluations, followed by ideological orientations (expressed in terms of self-locations on a left–right scale) and partisan identifications.[40] Candidate evaluations were measured on a conventional "thermometer" scale, ranging from 0 (no sympathy at all) to 100 (a great deal of sympathy). This measure is content-free; the respondent may like or dislike a candidate for any reason or reasons (including perceptions of his

---

[39] Converse and Pierce, *Political Representation in France*, pp. 174–8, 318–22, treat attitudes pro and con de Gaulle as a long-term force, on a par with party identification, left–right locations, and the clerical–anticlerical dimension.

[40] Pierce, *Choosing the Chief*, chap. 7.

stature as a president), but these cannot be identified from the candidate evaluations alone.

On the face of it, this 1988 result suggests that, given the importance of candidate evaluations as a factor in the vote, the kind of imbalance we find in the perceived presidential stature of Jacques Chirac and Lionel Jospin in 1995 must have accounted greatly for Chirac's overall vote and perhaps even been decisive in determining the outcome of the election. Perhaps it did one thing or the other or even both. But in 1988 we also find that candidate evaluations are very closely associated with ideological positions and partisan attachments! These two variables did not individually affect the distribution of votes as much as candidate evaluations did, but together they counted very heavily in producing those very candidate evaluations.

Ideology and partisanship, as well as attitudes toward the Catholic Church and subjective class perceptions, regularly and tightly constrain the popular vote in France. Leadership attributes and personal traits may overcome those traditional forces. We know that happened in the case of de Gaulle, and it may well have happened in the case of Giscard in 1974 and/or Chirac in 1995, but the evidence that it happened in those latter years is fugitive.

The amount of variation in the vote produced by short-term forces such as perceptions of leadership qualities is normally limited. A heroic leader such as de Gaulle, or war, depression, or mass unrest (such as that in France in 1968) among social events, can override the impact of traditional vote determinants. But these normally dominate electoral outcomes. Without these factors making for long-term stability in electoral behavior it would be difficult to account for the tremendous inertia that characterizes the electoral results in democratic societies with established party systems. Witness the comparative narrowness even of de Gaulle's 1965 electoral victory.

It is not possible to measure precisely how limited the space for the play of leadership factors actually has been across the entire series of French presidential elections since 1965 because of the lack of accessible and consistently formulated measures. However, thanks to Deutsch, Lindon, and Weill, and to a succession of SOFRES electoral reports, as well as other independent studies, the critically important measure of left–right locations is available to us in association with the voters' second-ballot choices for each presidential election.[41] While we are, therefore, unable to estimate how much causal power is exercised by ideology, partisanship, religion and socioeconomic class combined for each of the elections we are considering, we can at least estimate how potent left–right locations were, at each election, in their own right.

---

[41] Eméric Deutsch, Denis Lindon, and Pierre Weill, *Les Familles politiques: Aujourd'hui en France* (Paris: Editions de Minuit, 1966); SOFRES, *Les Intentions de vote des français après le 1er tour de l'élection présidentielle* (Paris: 1969); *Comment ont voté les français* (Montrouge: 1974); *Les Français et l'élection présidentielle: Sondage post-électoral* (Montrouge: 1981); *L'Élection présidentielle de mai 1995: Sondage post-électoral* (Montrouge: 1995).

The left–right dimension, which ranges across a varying number of categories from the extreme-left to the extreme-right, is one of the more enduring products of the French Revolution. In the semicircular French parliamentary chambers of that era, the advocates of radical change sat on the left (facing the speaker) while the conservatives or reactionaries sat on the right. The accompanying terminology not only survived as an ideological shorthand but also spread across continental Europe. It has an irresistible appeal for continental European politicians, pundits, and scholars (nowhere more so than in France), with the result that they, as well as (although to a lesser extent) the more politically involved citizens, share a common if imprecise vocabulary for classifying the shades of radicalism and conservatism that are presumably expressed by political parties and their voters.[42]

Since the publication of Deutsch, Lindon, and Weill's pioneering work on the left–right dimension, *Les Familles politiques*, in 1966, the polling organization SOFRES has regularly reported the proportions of sample voters who voted for one candidate or the other within each of five left–right categories (extreme-left, left, center, right, and extreme-right), plus the category of the Marais.

The Marais, a term that literally means "swamp" and which can also be translated as "morass," is a very important but still often overlooked category relating to the left–right dimension. Deutsch, Lindon, and Weill discovered that, when asked to place themselves within one of the five left–right categories listed above, some 10 percent of the respondents could not make a choice and by far the largest proportion of respondents (more than 30 percent) chose the center. Further analysis revealed that, like the respondents who could not place themselves on the scale, two-thirds of the self-described centrists had little or no interest in politics and, presumably, little or no understanding of what the left–right dimension itself signified. Deutsch, Lindon, and Weill baptized the joint group of people who could not place themselves on the left–right scale, or who placed themselves in the center of it without being involved politically, the "Marais." They did so, they tell us, because "it evokes well the fluidity, the inconsistency, the absence of mental structures and of stable tendencies that characterizes this group of voters."[43]

SOFRES (like virtually all the French survey agencies) normally reports its results in the form of proportions without including the actual frequencies. In

---

[42] For the differential policy content of left–right locations among masses and elite in France, see Converse and Pierce, *Political Representation in France*, chap. 7; for the French electorate alone, see Deutsch, Lindon, and Weill, *Les Familles politiques*, chaps. 2–4; for an early comparative analysis at the mass level alone, see Ronald Inglehart and Hans Klingemann, "Party Identification, Ideological Preference and the Left–Right Dimension among Western Mass Publics," in Ian Budge, Ivor Crewe, and Dennis Farlie, eds., *Party Identification and Beyond: Representations of Voting and Party Competition* (New York: Wiley, 1976).

[43] Deutsch, Lindon, and Weill, *Les Familles politiques*, p. 21. Readers familiar with Paris will know that the Marais is also the name of the marvelous old neighborhood roughly bounded by the Bastille, the Hôtel de Ville (City Hall), and the Place des Vosges.

Table 4.2. Relationship between left–right locations (Marais excluded) and the presidential vote (2nd ballot), France, 1965–95

Election Year	Measure	
	Tau-*b*	Gamma
1965	0.60	0.84
1969	0.44	0.69
1974	0.72	0.96
1981	0.71	0.95
1988	0.73	0.95
1995	0.68	0.91

Sources: For 1965: Eméric Deutsch, Denis Lindon, and Pierre Weill, *Les Familles politiques: Aujourd'hui en France* (Paris: Editions de Minuit, 1966); for 1969: Unpublished data collected for Philip E. Converse and Roy Pierce, *Political Representation in France* (Cambridge, Mass.: Harvard University Press, 1986); for 1974: SOFRES, *Comment ont voté les français* (Montrouge, 1974); for 1981; SOFRES, *Les Français et l'élection présidentielle: Sondage post-électoral* (Montrouge, 1981); for 1988: Roy Pierce, *French Presidential Election Survey, 1988* [computer file] ICPSR version (Ann Arbor, Michigan, 1996); for 1995: SOFRES, *L'Éléction présidentielle de mai 1995: Sondage post-électoral* (Montrouge, 1995).

SOFRES studies these can usually be estimated from other internal data with a reasonable degree of confidence. The reader should keep in mind, however, that what we present in Table 4.2 for the years other than 1969 and 1988, for which we have relied on complete individual-level data sets, are estimates not only in the usual statistical sense but in the more elementary arithmetical sense as well.

Table 4.2 reports two common measures of the degree of association between left–right locations (in five categories, excluding the Marais) and the second-ballot vote at all six French presidential elections. Both measures of association tell the same story, which conveys three main messages.

The first message is that the degree of association between left–right locations and the vote is very high by conventional social science standards and fully matches the degree of association between party identification (in seven categories) and the two-candidate vote at recent U.S. presidential elections. The mean tau-*b* measure of 0.71 from our estimates for the three French elections since 1981 surpasses the mean tau-*b* estimate of 0.62 that obtains for the association between the U.S. two-candidate presidential vote and party identification at the five elections from 1980 to 1996.

The second message of Table 4.2 is that left–right considerations operate strongly only when the runoff ballot pits a leftist candidate against a rightist candidate. The election where the voters' left–right locations counted the least was the 1969 contest between Gaullist Georges Pompidou and centrist Alain Poher, and there was no leftist candidate to attract leftist voters. But it would be excessive to insist that, because traditional ideological considerations played only a modest role in 1969, the outcome of the election necessarily turned primarily on personality or leadership factors. We have indicated above that the element of leadership may well have given Pompidou a major advantage, but there is little or no hard data to demonstrate that proposition.

The third and final message of Table 4.2 is that the election where the personal vote surely counted the most, that of 1965, when de Gaulle defeated Mitterrand, shows the smallest impact of left–right locations of any of the five elections where they played a significant role (that is, other than 1969). That is, of course, exactly what we would expect.

Left–right locations counted the most, at a more or less equally high level, at the election of 1974 (at which Giscard's personal image of leadership may well have produced his narrow margin of victory), and the elections of 1981 and 1988, where we doubt that leadership attributes played a decisive role. The 1995 election displays the second least degree of importance of the effects of left–right locations, although by such a narrow margin that we can hardly infer that the personal factor must, therefore, have played a major role in the outcome.

Of course, the data reported in Table 4.2 reflect only those voters who assigned themselves a valid left–right location at the same time as they reported their presidential vote. The Marais are necessarily excluded from the analysis. The Marais, however, is very important electorally. The size of the Marais at any given election, and how it divides its votes, can be (and has been) decisive for French electoral outcomes.[44]

Unfortunately, there is not enough longitudinal consistency in the relative size of the Marais to permit us to produce fine measures. Across our array of presidential elections, the estimated size of the Marais ranged from some 12 percent of the voters (in 1974 and 1981) to more than 30 percent of them (in 1965). But, as fragile as some of our measures may be, it seems clear that in 1965 Charles de Gaulle won a larger proportion of his votes from the Marais (37 percent) than any other presidential candidate has done since, and it is probably also the case that a larger proportion of the Marais (72 percent) voted for de Gaulle than has voted for any other candidate.

According to SOFRES estimates, neither de Gaulle in 1965 nor Giscard d'Estaing in 1974 won a clear majority of the votes among people who had a left–right location; their second-ballot majorities were due to the commanding leads they enjoyed among the voters of the Marais. De Gaulle's and Giscard's preponderance of support among the Marais necessarily derived from factors other than left–right sympathies. We have seen that in the case of de Gaulle there is ample reason to believe that his leadership qualities and personality were decisive, not only in accounting for the outcome but also in accounting for a large proportion of his overall electoral support. There is no evidence that Giscard's personal image was independently responsible for the bulk of his votes at the 1974 election, although we have seen that it is possible that, for him too, his perceived presidential stature among unengaged voters from the Marais enabled him to carry the day.

---

[44] Pierce, *Choosing the Chief*, pp. 64–5.

1988: The Chairman of the Board versus the C.E.O.

The 1988 French presidential election was fought between two candidates, François Mitterrand and Jacques Chirac, who were as equally matched in electoral experience, political standing, and national visibility as one is likely to find in any system at any time.

As Table 4.2 suggests, it would be difficult to find an election at which the classic ideological, religious, and socioeconomic forces that normally shape electoral choices in France were more conspicuously deployed.[45] Not only did the rough experiential equality of the two candidates minimize the extent to which leadership factors might give a major advantage to either candidate. The extent to which any such differential might emerge was also severely constrained by the near-pervasive dominance of long-term, socially rooted electoral forces.

The two candidates did, of course, project different public personalities, but one would be hard put to insist that one of them was the more generally appealing on those grounds alone. Both were confident, forceful and—like virtually all high-profile French politicians—solemn. The public naturally perceived them differentially on various personal attributes, but both were regarded as "competent" by roughly equal proportions (one-third) of the electorate.[46]

The two rivals were distinguished by anchorage in different constitutional bases of support, which defined their fields of maneuver and shaped their campaign opportunities. Mitterrand was the incumbent president, and this gave him the edge in protocol and considerable latitude in deciding whether and when to intervene in affairs that might be turned to his advantage. Chirac was the prime minister, which enabled him to range across the entire spectrum of policy alternatives and gave him vast bureaucratic resources on which both to draw for information and to rely for execution. In those senses, the contest was rather like a conflict between a chairman of the board and a chief executive officer.

Fortunately, we are in a position to test the extent to which the deep-seated and more or less permanent features of the French political landscape can be distinguished from the shorter-term public assessments of the candidates' leadership capacity as factors in the voters' electoral choices in 1988. We have summary indicators of the electorate's estimates of the leadership qualities of President Mitterrand and Prime Minister Chirac, as these were displayed in the constitutional roles the two men had conspicuously occupied (and, from 1986 to the date of the election in 1988, simultaneously).

Two relevant questions were asked of the respondents at a 1988 post-electoral survey.[47] One question asked how satisfied the respondents were with

---

[45] Pierce, *Choosing the Chief*, chaps. 7 and 8.   [46] *Le Monde*, April 29, 1988.

[47] Roy Pierce, *French Presidential Election Survey, 1988* [computer file] ICPSR version (Ann Arbor, Michigan, 1996).

Mitterrand's activity as president of the Republic; the other asked how satisfied they were with Chirac's activity as prime minister. Four ordered response categories were designated for each question, two each pro and con, to which a fifth category was added at the center for repondents with no opinion.

With these two variables in hand, we can compute a hard measure of how much those two leadership factors contributed to the voting public's electoral choices at the 1988 French runoff ballot over and above the contribution of ideology alone in the form of self-assessments on the left–right scale. Regressing the second-ballot vote on left–right locations (exclusive of the Marais) shows that these alone account for 68 percent of the variance in the runoff vote. Adding our two "leadership" variables to the equation increases the proportion of the variance accounted for to 79 percent.

That differential of about 10 percent may serve as an estimate of how much one can reasonably expect leadership factors to contribute to the outcome in the case of a more or less evenly matched pair of candidates, within the portion of the electorate that has a valid left–right location. In order to specify the impact of leadership factors across the entire electorate, however, we need also to take the Marais into account.

To gain a sense of the extent to which the Marais, as compared with each of the various valid segments of the left–right dimension, was sensitive to leadership in 1988, we also regressed the second-ballot vote on our two leadership measures within each valid left–right category, as well as within the Marais.

Table 4.3 reports the results of this series of regressions. The results are consistent with our earlier, more general formulations. There was inadequate variance in electoral choice among the pure leftists for the analysis to register, but among the center-left, the center-right, and the right our leadership factors played a significant but not particularly commanding role. Not more

Table 4.3. Effects of executive job performance on the presidential vote (2nd ballot) France, 1988

Left–right category	Job performance	Coefficient	Probability	Adj. R^2	(N)
Left	(Inadequate variance)				(116)
Center-left	*FM as president	0.089	0.000	0.192	(285)
	*JC as prime minister	0.025	0.007		
Center	FM as president	0.140	0.001	0.548	(54)
	JC as prime minister	0.203	0.000		
Center-right	FM as president	0.066	0.000	0.187	(162)
	JC as prime minister	0.074	0.000		
Right	FM as president	0.114	0.000	0.266	(113)
	JC as prime minister	0.049	0.028		
Marais	FM as president	0.144	0.000	0.441	(156)
	JC as prime minister	0.202	0.000		

*FM = François Mitterrand; JC = Jacques Chirac.
Source: Roy Pierce, *French Presidential Election Survey, 1988* [computer file] ICPSR version (Ann Arbor, Michigan, 1996).

than about a quarter of the variance in the vote was accounted for by executive job performance ratings within those groups of voters.

The role of leadership was much more prominent among the Marais and the (comparatively few) genuine centrists. These are the voters who are electorally unguided by some sense of ideological location and the social forces related to it. Leadership considerations were not irrelevant for any left–right group except the unqualified leftists, but they approached major importance only for those voters who were not already anchored to one or another location along the opposing segments of the left–right dimension.

Conclusions

The main theme of this chapter has been that candidate-centered variables, such as personality or leadership capacity, constitute one factor among several that together contribute toward the outcome being analyzed, whether this be an electoral choice or the overall electoral outcome. The implicit logic is that the more that the outcome is "caused" by one factor, the less it must be "caused" by the other (assuming that the two factors are independent of each other).

Applying this logic to the six French presidential elections since 1965, we have focused on the extent to which the traditional left–right dimension, which has long been associated with stubborn religious and socioeconomic forces, can be shown to have affected both the electorate's behavior and the electoral outcome. We sought further to see whether there were elections at which it can be reasonably claimed that one candidate had a clear advantage over the other in personal popularity or perceived leadership attributes. The objective was to determine whether the left–right factor was weaker at elections where personal qualities were presumably stronger.

Such an analysis may have been foolhardy with so few cases, but the hypothesis received some support. Despite the operation of a full panoply of left–right forces, the left–right dimension was weaker in 1965 than in any other year except 1969, when there was no leftist candidate at the runoff ballot. The 1981 and 1988 elections, at which personal leadership qualities were highly symmetrical, were more or less equally and overwhelmingly affected by left–right considerations. The two post-Gaullist elections at which perceptions of leadership attributes may have been decisive, those of 1974 and 1995, register as inconclusive in Table 4.2, which shows them to be as affected by traditional left–right considerations as the elections of 1981 and 1988.

Of course, it is not always true that if one factor is strong the others must be weak (even if they are independent). That proposition requires that every voter register a position on every variable. In the case of left–right locations, that is not possible, because there are large numbers of voters (the Marais) for whom the left–right dimension has no meaning. A country could be highly polarized on a left–right basis at the same time as one candidate enjoyed a large personal advantage among the Marais. To a considerable extent, that is what appears to have happened in France in 1965. Left–right polarization was less high than at any other election except that of 1969, but it was still quite robust. It is probably also what happened in 1974 when, as we have reported, Lindon and Weill found Giscard's critical support to be localized among the Marais.[48] It is possible that the same phenomenon occurred in 1995. That line of reasoning is clearly supported by our analysis of the effects of assessments of executive performance on electoral choices in 1988 (see Table 4.3).

It will perhaps be helpful at this point if, consistent with Table 1.2 of Chapter 1 of this book, we summarize systematically our conclusions concerning the role of candidate evaluations at the series of French presidential elections we have examined (see Table 4.4). The main characteristic of Table 4.4 is the sharp difference between our findings for the elections of 1965 and 1969, on the one hand, and those for all the later elections, on the other hand. De Gaulle in 1965 surely, and Pompidou in 1969 probably, benefited from public perceptions of their leadership qualities compared with those of their much less prominent opponents. There are no surprises there.

Readers may not find any surprises in the remaining judgments in Table 4.4 either, especially as they have been couched with considerable caution. There is one sense, however, in which the generally low importance attributed to leadership perceptions might be unexpected. We spent considerable time, early in this chapter, outlining the extent which the constitutional standing of the French presidency was aimed at promoting strong leadership and how the

Table 4.4. Influence of candidate assessments on presidential election outcomes, France, 1965–95

Winner	Assessments of candidates' personality influences on voters' decisions	Balance of assessments influences outcome	Candidate who benefited from balance of assessments	Assessments of candidates determine the outcome
De Gaulle (1965)	Very much	Very much	De Gaulle	Yes
Pompidou (1969)	Probably much	Very much	Pompidou	Probably
Giscard d'Estaing (1974)	Some	Possibly very much	Giscard d'Estaing	Possibly
Mitterrand (1981)	Limited	Negligible	Neither	Probably not
Mitterrand (1988)	Limited	Negligible	Mitterrand	Probably not
Chirac (1995)	Probably some	Possibly some	Chirac	Possibly

[48] Lindon and Weill, "Autopsie d'une campagne."

method of electing the French president proceeds through clearly defined stages that increasingly and exclusively focus on individual candidates. Given that constitutional and electoral context, one might reasonably expect that candidates would make special efforts to project whatever leadership talents they have and that those efforts might meet with a noticeable public response. Our assessments suggest that this has not been the general case.

We have tried to show why. The public's evaluations of candidates is constrained by long-term forces that are activated in the electoral context. It requires a large imbalance in perceptions of leadership attributes to attract people away from a candidate whom they are predisposed to support on grounds of established political orientations. Such an imbalance existed in France in 1965. People who are not anchored in such orientations are those most likely to be affected by such perceptual imbalances. In a close race, those unanchored voters can supply the margin of victory for one candidate or another. That may well have occurred in 1974 and 1995.

None of this means that candidate images, built on personality, leadership skills, experience, energy, or other attributes that might spark a connection between the candidate and the public, count for nothing except in the rare cases of heroic leadership or probably more common cases of tight races. Candidate evaluations interact with other forces that also motivate the voters and affect the electoral outcome. But insofar as we have been able to distinguish perceptions of leadership ability from traditional left–right orientations in France, we have identified the circumstances and conditions under which leadership has had a decisive effect on individuals' voting decisions and electoral outcomes.

5

The Nonpersonalization of Voting Behavior in Germany

FRANK BRETTSCHNEIDER AND OSCAR W. GABRIEL

Leadership Qualities in Germany

Apart from telling a good story, the movie released in Germany as *Hello Mr. President* offers some intriguing insights into how the personality and life circumstances of political leaders can find their way onto the political agenda. Andrew Shepherd, played by Michael Douglas, is running as a candidate for the American presidency. His campaign managers take advantage of the fact that his wife died shortly before the campaign began. After he has been in office a while, he falls in love with a political consultant, Sidney Ellen Wade (Annette Bening), engaged in lobbying for an environmental organization. Since Sidney Ellen had formerly been a militant anti-war activist, President Shepherd is attacked by his opponent, Senator Bob Rumson (Richard Dreyfuss), for not behaving in a manner appropriate to his office. A debate on the president's character is planned as the centerpiece of Rumson's campaign. As opinion poll findings indicate, putting "the Sidney question" on the political agenda seems to be a successful strategy. As least initially, President Shepherd's popularity is seriously damaged. However, as so often in American movies, our hero triumphs. President Shepherd convinces the public that his liaison with Sidney is not at all inappropriate and, moreover, that Senator Rumson and his managers are playing a dirty game.

What message is conveyed by this story? If the movie is true to real political life, it suggests that the personal circumstances of political leaders as well as their personalities can play a crucial role in the electorate's evaluations of political leaders, at least in the United States. And, needless to say, debates about the character of political leaders are not confined to the movies: they went on more or less continuously during Bill Clinton's two terms in office. Numerous other examples could be given of political careers that were suddenly terminated, or did not even start, when questions were raised about the individual's character or personal behavior. Whether or not the "personalization" of politics is really a recent phenomenon is open to question, but without doubt the phenomenon has become a topic of political research during the last few years.

The many institutional and cultural differences between Germany and the United States mean, of course, that the two countries cannot be equated. Germany has a far stronger and more disciplined party system than the United States has ever had. Moreover, German voters, at least formally, choose between competing parties rather than competing chancellor-candidates. At first glance, these differences might indicate that the personalization of politics is not particularly relevant to voting behavior in Germany. It is possible that German voters have always held strong opinions about the personal qualities of their political leaders but that, until recently, they did not attach much weight to these opinions when casting their ballots on election day. German election campaigns have accorded only a minor role to the personalities and circumstances of candidates for the chancellorship. Unlike in the United States, the chancellor-candidates' families have not played any part in campaigns. Television advertisements and posters have always referred primarily to the candidates' performance rather than to their personal qualities. The minor role played by the voters' assessments of candidates' personal characteristics in determining election outcomes is strongly suggested by the fact that, although former chancellor Helmut Kohl was never particularly popular (except during the year of German reunification), he remained in office for considerably longer than several of his more charismatic and popular predecessors, notably Ludwig Erhard and Willy Brandt.

During the federal elections of 1998, however, the notions of personalization, presidentialization and Americanization were, for the first time, discussed at length. The mass media focused their reporting and comments on the competition between the long-serving Christian Democrat chancellor Helmut Kohl and his Social Democratic challenger Gerhard Schröder, and the same applied to the political parties' campaign strategies. Although German election campaigns have always been to some extent candidate-centered, this increased emphasis on the two chancellor-candidates in 1998 could clearly be attributed to the strategic role that the parties now believed was being played by potential switch-voters among the electorate. Every element in the increased personalization of the 1998 campaign—the devotion of more time to the selling of the candidates' personalities than to their performance, incorporating the logic of media campaign reporting into the planning of the two campaigns and the way in which the two campaign staffs came to be professionalized—evidently relied on a single rationale: the campaign strategists regarded the increasing number of switch-voters as a decisive target group. Appealing to them became a crucial complement to the more traditional German strategy of mobilizing the main parties' core electorates— the true believers.

Despite the overwhelming evidence of personalization in the 1998 election campaign, the question of whether this personalization actually affected the individual choices made by voters is still unanswered. No empirical analysis has been made. In addition, there is considerable ambiguity in the very notion of "personalization." It could refer to the fact (if it is a fact) that voters in making their individual decisions pay more attention than in the past to the parties' chancellor-candidates, irrespective of which attributes of the candidates they are paying attention to. Alternatively, the notion of personalization could be interpreted more narrowly to refer to an increasing emphasis on the chancellor-candidates' personalities as distinct from their performance as political leaders. It is said, for example, that being perceived as likeable and charming, having great personal appeal and having an attractive family are becoming more important criteria in the evaluation of chancellor-candidates than, for instance, their competence in handling economic and social affairs and their leadership qualities.[1] Wattenberg has observed a "rise of candidate-centered politics" in the United States.[2] As far as parliamentary systems are concerned, a tendency for such systems to become more presidential in character has been attributed to the increasing personalization of national electoral politics.[3]

Statements like these look plausible at first glance, but they have not so far been convincingly supported by empirical analyses. Moreover, since personalization implies a dynamic rather than a static process, it can be examined thoroughly only by means of time-series data covering a long historical period. Fortunately, some questions on German voters' orientations toward the various chancellor-candidates have invariably been included in the German election studies since 1961, with the result that the role of candidate orientations in the broad context of voters' choices can be examined quite comfortably on the basis of longitudinal data. Unfortunately, the questions that have been asked lack continuity, with the result that it is more difficult to assess the roles played by specific components of the candidates' images. In the present context, therefore, our more detailed analyses will be based on the data gathered in surveys conducted solely in connection with the 1998 elections.[4]

---

[1] Jürgen Lass, *Vorstellungsbilder über Kanzlerkandidaten: Zur Diskussion um die Personalisierung von Politik* (Wiesbaden: Deutscher Universitäts-Verlag, 1995).

[2] Martin P. Wattenberg, *The Rise of Candidate-Centered Politics: Presidential Elections of the 1980s* (Cambridge, Mass.: Harvard University Press, 1991).

[3] See, among others, Peter Radunski, *Wahlkämpfe: Moderne Wahlkampfführung als politische Kommunikation* (Munich: Olzog, 1980), p. 22, and Ulrich Sarcinelli, "Im Kampf um öffentliche Aufmerksamkeit: Wie sich politische Parteien in der Mediendemokratie verändern," *Frankfurter Allgemeine Zeitung*, September 24, 1998, p. 15.

[4] In connection with the 1998 election, a differentiated inventory of the evaluation of particular attributes of the candidates was developed, consisting of open-ended as well as different types of closed questions on various of Gerhard Schröder's and Helmut Kohl's attributes. These data are part of the 1997 EMNID Science Award, granted to Angelika Vetter and Frank Brettschneider for their research project "Personalization of Politics: Images and Image Agenda Setting Through the Mass Media" (ZA 3095). The fieldwork was conducted, by means of computer-aided personal interviewing (CAPI), in November 1997. A total of 953 respondents were interviewed, 754 West Germans and 199 East Germans.

The first part of the analysis that follows refers to the role that voters' orientations toward the chancellor-candidates plays in the broad context of electoral choice. Particular attention will be paid to the influence of candidate orientations on the voting choices of people lacking any long-term party identification. This part of the analysis is based on data pertaining to all the electoral contests fought in Germany since 1961.[5]

The second part of the analysis deals with the various components of the chancellor-candidates' images. Does the way in which voters evaluate the candidates simply reflect existing patterns of party identification, or do the voters construct their own candidate orientations by fitting into a pattern separate pieces, each of which refers to specific attributes of the candidates as perceived and evaluated by them? Are the proponents of the personalization thesis right in assuming that the candidates' images are largely determined by the voters' perceptions of the candidates' personalities rather than by their performance? These questions will be answered with specific reference to data collected by the 1998 German Election Study.[6]

The Impact of Candidate Orientations on Electoral Choice

We examine in this section whether or not, as a general proposition, evaluations of chancellor-candidates determine individuals' votes. Personalization here refers, statically, to whether or not candidates' personal characteristics count for a great deal in determining how voters cast their ballots and, dynamically, to whether or not any such influence has tended to increase over time. At least implicitly, the notion of personalization entails the dynamic hypothesis that the impact of issue orientations and party identification, as compared with the impact of chancellor-candidate orientations, has declined over the years.

Although there are many empirical analyses of issue voting, studies of the role of candidate voting are relatively rare and most of those that do exist are not based on long-term trend data. Moreover, if the small numbers of extant empirical analyses permit any conclusion at all, they do not support the personalization thesis. Instead of showing a clear trend toward an

---

[5] The following data were analyzed: preelection survey, "Cologne Election Study 1961" (ZA 0055); preelection survey, "Federal Parliament Election 1965" (ZA 05567); first panel wave (preelection) of survey, "Federal Parliament Election 1969" (ZA 0426); first panel wave (preelection) of "Election Study 1972" (ZA 0635); first panel wave (preelection) of "Election Study 1976" (ZA 0823); preelection survey, "Election Study September 1980" (ZA 1053); first panel wave (preelection) of "Election Study 1983" (ZA 1276); first panel wave (preelection) of "Election Study 1987" (ZA 1533); first panel wave (preelection) of "Election Study 1990" (ZA 1919); preelection survey, "Election Study October 1994" (ZA 2599); pre- and postelection surveys, "German Election Study 1998" (ZA 3064). Details of the surveys can be found at http://www.za.uni-koeln.de.

[6] The data analyzed are from the surveys numbered ZA 3095 (see fn. 1 above) and ZA 3064 (see fn. 2 above). Details of these two surveys can be found on the website cited at the end of fn. 5.

increase in candidate orientation in voting, they show that the relative impact of attitudes toward the candidates has been very different from one election to the next and that the impact of candidate-related variables differs strongly from one electoral race to another.[7]

Conditions of Candidate Voting

According to the socio-psychological explanation of voting behavior promoted by Campbell and his colleagues, the voter's ultimate decision is the product of a combination of short-term and long-term influences.[8] For most voters, the most important long-term influence is their party identification, which usually develops as a result of individuals' membership of particular social groups and is transmitted from generation to generation by the process of socialization. Party identification tends to be reinforced as individuals repeatedly vote for the same party. Nevertheless, even a strong party identification does not necessarily lead the individual to vote in conformity with that identification. From time to time, attitudes toward candidates and issues may induce voters to deviate from their standing party loyalty. However, according to this school of thought, long-term influences usually reinforce short-term influences among party identifiers and lead to consistency between long-term party identification and short-term attitudes toward candidates and issues. People holding such consistent attitudes will generally vote for the party with which they identify. The logic of this kind of explanation implies a rather weak *independent* influence on the vote at any given election of attitudes toward the candidates.

However, a completely different situation may obtain among non-identifiers and, to a lesser extent, among weak identifiers. Non-identifiers simply lack party identification as a cue or shortcut device simplifying the complexity of political

---

[7] See, among others, Oscar W. Gabriel and Angelika Vetter, "Bundestagswahlen als Kanzlerwahlen? Kandidatenorientierungen und Wahlentscheidungen im parteienstaatlichen Parlamentarismus," in Max Kaase and Hans-Dieter Klingemann, eds., *Wahlen und Wähler: Analysen aus Anlass der Bundestagswahl 1994* (Opladen: Westdeutscher Verlag, 1998); Wolfgang Jagodzinski and Steffen M. Kühnel, "Zur Schätzung der relativen Effekte von Issueorientierungen, Kandidatenpräferenz und der langfristiger Parteibindung auf die Wahlabsicht," in Karl Schmidt, ed., *Wahlen, Parteien, politische Einstellungen* (Frankfurt am Main: Peter Lang, 1990); Max Kaase, "Is There Personalization in Politics? Candidates and Voting Behavior in Germany," *International Political Science Review*, 15 (1994), 211–30; Lass, *Vorstellungsbilder über Kanzlerkandidaten*; Angelika Vetter and Oscar W. Gabriel, "Candidate Evaluations and Party Choice in Germany, 1972–94: Do Candidates Matter?" in Christopher J. Anderson and Carsten Zelle, eds., *Stability and Change in German Elections: How Electorates Merge, Converge, or Collide* (Westport, Conn.: Praeger, 1998); and Frank Brettschneider, "Candidate-Voting: Die Bedeutung von Spitzenkandidaten für das Wählerverhalten in Deutschland, Grossbritannien und den USA von 1960 bis 1998," in Hans-Dieter Klingemann and Max Kaase, eds., *Wahlen und Wähler: Analysen aus Anlass der Bundestagswahl 1998* (Opladen: Westdeutscher Verlag, 2001).

[8] Angus Campbell, Philip E. Converse, Warren E. Miller, and Donald E. Stokes, *The American Voter* (New York: John Wiley, 1960).

life. Among weak identifiers, inconsistencies between an individual's long-term party identification and his or her short-term attitudes may emerge more easily. The attitude–behavior chains in the cases of strong identifiers, non-identifiers and weak identifiers will differ accordingly. The non-identifiers—independents—make short-term influences such as candidate and issue orientations serve as the most important, indeed almost the sole, basis for decision making. It follows that candidate-centered voting is likely to occur if non-identifiers perceive few policy differences between the parties and if, at the same time, they strongly prefer one party's leaders to those of the other parties.

Weak identifiers are, of course, exposed to the same influences as strong identifiers; but, by definition, party identification plays a smaller role in influencing their vote decisions. More room is left for the effects of attitudes toward candidates and issues. In practice, and especially given the fact that modern politics is more about the details of problem solving than about broad issues of ideology, there is a good chance that issue attitudes will largely neutralize each other. Candidate-centered voting will then become highly probable among weak identifiers under the following two conditions:

(1) If they strongly prefer their own party's candidate and therefore vote for that party rather than either abstaining or switching to another party; i.e. they vote in a way that is consistent with their party identification;

(2) If they think badly of their own party's candidate and think well of another party's candidate and decide either to abstain or to vote for that other party; i.e. they either do not vote at all or vote in a way that is inconsistent with their party identification.

People holding inconsistent political attitudes often abstain or switch votes, with the result that they—as well as independents—are natural target groups for personalized election campaigns. Additionally, of course, personalization may be a useful means of mobilizing a party's core voters and consolidating its marginal voters.

Whether or not candidate-centered voting occurs should depend primarily on the existence and strength of party identification among the electorate and, in addition, on the existence and strength of the policy and candidate differentials perceived by voters. It is significant that both levels of party identification and differences between the political parties in policy and ideological terms have declined sharply in Germany in recent years.

Party identification declined in West Germany during the 1970s and 1980s, as it did in all the other Western nations for which empirical data are available.[9] The decline did not continue in West Germany in the 1990s. Even so,

---

[9] See for details Russell J. Dalton, Scott C. Flanagan, and Paul Allen Beck, eds., *Electoral Change in Advanced Industrial Democracies: Realignment or Dealignment?* (Princeton, N.J.: Princeton University Press, 1984) and Hermann Schmitt and Soeren Holmberg, "Political Parties in Decline?" in Hans-Dieter Klingemann and Dieter Fuchs, eds., *Citizens and the State* (Oxford: Oxford University Press, 1995).

by the second half of the 1990s fully one-third of West German voters did not think of themselves as party identifiers. The figure in the former East Germany was even higher (41 percent). Moreover, even those who did continue to identify with a party reported that their identification was relatively weak.[10] It follows that, for many modern German citizens, factors other than party identification must play a decisive role in determining how, and whether, they vote.

In addition to these changes on the "demand side," so to speak, of the political marketplace, there have also been changes on the "supply side," and these changes have likewise contributed to a weakening of long-term party alignments and ideologies in favor, potentially at least, of an orientation toward political leaders as points of reference in the electoral decision. Briefly, the main German political parties, like the parties in many other countries, have moved in the direction of what Otto Kirchheimer famously called "catchall" parties and William E. Wright later called "rational-efficient" parties:[11] that is, parties that appeal to the broad mass of the electorate rather than to specific social groups and that base their appeals on widely shared values rather than on narrowly conceived policies and ideologies.[12]

Finally, the institutional structures that exist in Germany have long been conducive to candidate-centered voting. Although the German federal chancellor is elected by the Bundestag rather than directly by the voters, the strong position of the chancellor in the German system has long contributed to a presidentialization of election campaigns in Germany.[13] As early as the 1960s, during the period of Konrad Adenauer's "chancellor-democracy," Eschenburg asserted convincingly that "Elections of the Bundestag are in fact elections of a Chancellor."[14] That said, political parties still play a considerably stronger role

[10] For details, see Oscar W. Gabriel, "It's Time for a Change!'—Bestimmungsfaktoren des Wählerverhaltens bei der Bundestagswahl 1998," in Fritz Plasser, Peter A. Ulram, and Franz Sommer, eds., *Das österreichische Wählerverhalten* (Vienna: Signum Verlag, 2000), pp. 357 ff.

[11] Otto Kirchheimer, "The Transformation of Western European Party Systems," in Joseph LaPalombara and Myron Weiner, eds., *Political Parties and Political Development* (Princeton, N.J.: Princeton University Press, 1966) and William E. Wright, "Comparative Party Models: Rational Efficient and Party Democracy," in William E. Wright, ed., *The Comparative Study of Party Organization* (Columbus: Ohio State University Press, 1971).

[12] On the changes in West European party systems generally, see Richard Rose, "The New Labour Government: On the Crest of a Wave," in Pippa Norris and Neil T. Gavin, eds., *Britain Votes 1997* (Oxford: Oxford University Press), p. 243; Richard S. Katz and Peter Mair, "Changing Models of Party Organization and Party Democracy: The Emergence of the Cartel Party," *Party Politics*, 1 (1995), 5–28; and Klaus von Beyme, "Funktionenwandel der Parteien in der Entwicklung von der Massenmitgliederpartei zur Partei der Berufspolitiker," in Oscar W. Gabriel, Oskar Niedermayer, and Richard Stoess, eds., *Parteiendemokratie in Deutschland* (Opladen: Westdeutscher Verlag, 1997).

[13] See Karlheinz Niclauss, "Bestätigung der Kanzlerdemokratie? Kanzler und Regierungen zwischen Verfassung und politischen Konventionenn," in *Aus Politik und Zeitgeschichte*, B20/99 (1999), 27–38, and Vetter and Gabriel, "Candidate Evaluations and Party Choice in Germany."

[14] Theodor Eschenburg, *Zur politischen Praxis in der Bundesrepublik*, Vol. II, *Kritische Betrachtungen 1961–1965* (Munich: Piper, 1966), p. 35.

in Germany than in the United States, with the result that the relationship between party identification and candidate orientation is stronger in Germany than in the United States. Genuine candidate-centered voting might therefore be expected to occur more frequently in the United States.[15]

Long-Term Trends in Candidate-Centered Voting in West Germany

At first glance it might seem easy to identify the separate contributions made by party identification, issue orientations, and candidate orientations toward voting decisions. In practice, however, disentangling the relative contributions made by the three, particularly in exact quantitative terms, is by no means easy. In the first place, these three components, the principal ones identified in the Campbell *et al.* model, are closely interwoven. Every attempt to estimate their exact contributions to the explanation of voting behavior is confronted with the well-known problem of multicollinearity. In addition, variations in the instruments used to measure all three components cause problems for both long-term trend analyses and cross-national comparisons. Some resolution can be achieved by using research strategies that lead to approximate assessments of the impacts of the relevant factors on electoral choice.[16]

In the subsequent sections we will first give a short overview of the development of voters' preferences toward the various politicians who have run for the chancellorship since 1969 (the first year for which the relevant standard question is available). We will then, with a view to sorting out the impact of candidate evaluations on electoral choice, follow an approach developed by Jagodzinski and Kühnel, which involves a two-step estimation of the strength of orientations toward candidates as a determinant of party choice.[17] The upper limit of the presumed impact is set by the simple bivariate correlation coefficient between candidate orientation and voting behavior. The lower limit is set by the increase in explained variance in the voting choice when candidate orientations are included in a multivariate analysis after party identification has been controlled for (see the upper and lower lines in Figure 5.1).

[15] Brettschneider, "Candidate-Voting."

[16] For details, see Jürgen W. Falter and Hans Rattinger, "Parteien, Kandidaten und politische Streitfragen bei der Bundestagswahl 1980: Möglichkeiten und Grenzen der Normal-Vote-Analyse," in Max Kaase and Hans-Dieter Klingemann, eds., *Wahlen und politisches System: Analysen aus Anlass der Bundestagswahl 1980* (Opladen: Westdeutscher Verlag, 1983), p. 332; Jagodzinski and Kühnel, "Zur Schätzung der relativen Effekte;" and Hans-Dieter Klingemann and Charles Lewis Taylor, "Affektive Parteiorientierung, Kanzlerkandidaten und Issues: Einstellungskomponenten der Wahlentscheidung bei Bundestagswahlen in Deutschland," in Max Kaase, ed., *Wahlsoziologie heute: Analysen aus Anlass der Bundestagswahl 1976* (Opladen: Westdeutscher Verlag, 1977).

[17] Jagodzinski and Kühnel, "Zur Schätzung der relativen Effekte."

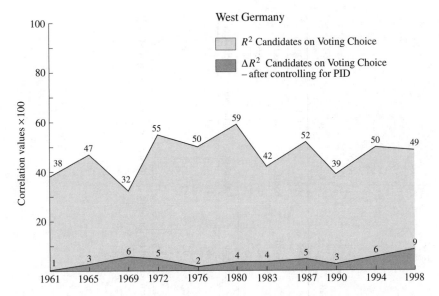

Fig. 5.1 The contribution of candidate orientations to voting choice with and without controlling for party identification in West Germany, 1961–98

On no occasion since 1969 have the two main German parties at two consecutive elections presented to the electorate the same two chancellor candidates.[18] The main reason is that losing candidates, with the solitary exception of Helmut Kohl, who lost in 1976 but ran again in 1983, have never been given a second chance. There has been far greater stability on the winning side. Helmut Schmidt was the SPD's candidate for the chancellorship in 1976 and again in 1980, and Helmut Kohl led the CDU/CSU no fewer than five times between 1983 and 1998. Schmidt held the chancellorship for nearly eight years, Kohl for sixteen. Given the comings and goings (mainly goings) of opposition candidates and given the chancellor's power in the political system and his high visibility to the German electorate, the long periods of incumbency of Schmidt and Kohl might be expected to have left traces in the perceptions and behavior of German voters. It has even been suggested by observers of German politics that there exists a "bonus of chancellorship," an advantage to the incumbent chancellor arising simply out of his high visibility and the resources available to him.

However, the notion of a chancellor bonus is not generally supported by the evidence. As the data in Table 5.1 show, chancellor-candidates invariably ran ahead of their party until the 1980 election, but since then the incumbent

[18] The data used in Table 5.1 are not the same as those employed in the other analyses. Instead of using sympathy ratings, which have been included in all of the election surveys conducted since 1961, we use a question concerning which chancellor-candidate voters would prefer to see become chancellor. This question was not asked before 1969.

Table 5.1. Voters' preferences between candidates and parties in Germany, 1969–98

	1969	1972	1976	1980	1983	1987	1990	1994	1998
	Kiesinger	Barzel	Kohl	Strauss	Kohl	Kohl	Kohl	Kohl	Kohl
CDU/CSU	52	24	39	29	44	44	47	42	36
SPD	28	56	51	61	35	36	32	31	57
	Brandt	Brandt	Schmidt	Schmidt	Vogel	Rau	Lafontaine	Scharping	Schröder
Chancellor's lead	24	32	12	32	9	8	15	11	−21
Gap candidate-party: CDU/CSU	+6	−19	−10	−16	−5	0	+3	0	+1
Gap candidate-party: SPD	−15	+11	+9	+18	−3	−1	−2	−5	+16

Notes: The data recorded are percentage points. The gap is counted as the difference between the voters' preference of the candidate and the share of votes of the CDU/CSU and SPD in the subsequent election. The names of the incumbent chancellors are underlined.

chancellor's advantage has been small, nonexistent or even negative. In all four of the federal elections between 1969 and 1980—that is, the first four elections for which relevant survey data are available—the incumbent chancellor not only ran ahead of his party but ran well ahead of the candidate of the opposition party, who, in turn, ran behind his party. But since the 1983 election the incumbent chancellor's position has become markedly less favorable. German chancellors have not become unpopular, but the gap between them and their main challengers has narrowed significantly. Between 1969 and 1980 the average distance between the incumbent chancellor and his principal rival was 25 percentage points; between 1983 and 1998 the gap was only 11 points. The outlier, as the figures in Table 5.1 make clear, was 1998, when Helmut Kohl, as in 1987 and 1994, was rated little or no better than his party but when in addition, unlike in 1987 and 1994, there was an enormous gap between his approval rating and that of his Social Democratic opponent, Gerhard Schröder.

A first conclusion can be derived from these data: the popularity of chancellors as candidates has varied considerably over time. Some were attractive to the electorate; others were not. Chancellor Kohl's ratings during election years (1983–98) were consistently lower than Willy Brandt's (1972) and Helmut Schmidt's (1976–80). Similarly, Brandt, Schmidt, and Schröder received substantially higher scores than the Social Democratic Party while Kohl was never substantially more popular than the CDU/CSU.

A more important question, however, now needs to be addressed: Given that a chancellor-candidate was popular or unpopular, to what extent did his popularity or lack of it influence the fortunes of his party? The data in Figure 5.1 are based on the Jagodzinski–Kühnel approach described earlier, with the upper line in the graph defining the upper limit of chancellor-candidates' possible influence. As can be seen, the contribution of candidate orientations to voting choice ranges between a minimum of 32 percent in 1969 and a maximum of 59 percent in 1980, the average being 47 percent.

On this initial criterion, the voters' orientations toward the parties' candidates for the chancellorship seem to have had a strong influence on their voting decisions. Moreover, this influence seems to have been stronger in some elections than others. Such influence seems to have been at its greatest in 1972, when the enormously popular Willy Brandt faced Rainer Barzel, and in 1980, when the even more popular Helmut Schmidt faced Franz-Josef Strauss. It seems to have been at its least in the four elections of 1961, 1969, 1983, and 1990. In 1961 the CDU/CSU fared reasonably well despite the declining popularity of the aging Konrad Adenauer. In 1969 the personal popularity of Kurt-Georg Kiesinger seems not to have benefited the CDU/CSU to any considerable extent, probably because Kiesinger was at the head of a coalition comprising both the CDU/CSU and the Social Democrats. In both 1983 and 1990 the electoral contests were dominated by highly salient issues: in 1983 by the way in which the preceding government coalition had been brought down (with the Free Democrats changing sides midway through the previous Bundestag term) and in 1990 by the reunification issue. Whatever else may be the case, the upper line in Figure 5.1 does not support the idea that electoral behavior in Germany has become more personalized over the past four decades. On the contrary, the data indicate fluctuations without any consistent pattern.

The upper line in the figure, however, almost certainly overestimates the importance of candidate orientations in determining German voting behavior because it takes no account of party identification, i.e. of previous party loyalties which themselves affect candidate orientations. The lower line in the figure provides strong evidence of the need to control for party identification. As can be seen, if party identification is controlled, the added variance explained by candidate factors appears to vary between a mere 1 percent (in 1961) and 9 percent (in 1998, when Schröder's popularity so greatly exceeded that of Kohl). Just as, however, the upper line in Figure 5.1 almost certainly overstates of the importance of candidate orientations in determining the vote, the lower line almost certainly understates it, at least to some degree. The lower line rests on the assumption that party identification determines candidate orientations and not the other way round; but of course candidate orientations may, in the case of some voters, have a bearing on their party identification. The rigid assumption underlying the lower line is out of keeping with political reality.

Nevertheless, broad empirical evidence points to the role of party identification as being by far the most important single determinant of voter choices in Germany as well as in other Western democracies.[19] The conclusion therefore seems reasonable that the "true extent" of the influence of candidate orientations in Germany lies somewhere between the extreme poles of the explained variance shown in Figure 5.1 but that it is much closer to the lower line than to the upper. Be that as it may, the lower line in the figure, like the upper line, suggests that German elections, while they may have become more personalized in terms of the way election campaigns are fought, have not shown any consistent tendency to become more personalized in the minds of ordinary voters. Instead, the extent of chancellor-candidates' influence depends, election by election, on the specific individuals involved and the circumstances under which the election is fought.

The analysis presented to this point is augmented by the data set out in Table 5.2. This table presents a conventional multivariate regression analysis which takes into account not merely party identification and candidate orientations but also voters' issue orientations. Once again, we find that there has been no long-term tendency toward personalization: that is, no long-term tendency for candidate orientations to loom larger in voters' decision making. The impact of candidate orientations has, instead, varied from one election to

[19] Brettschneider, "Candidate-Voting."

Table 5.2. Impact of party identification, issue orientations, and candidate orientations on voting behavior in Germany, 1961–98

	1961	1965	1969	1972	1976	1980	1983	1987	1990 West	1994 West	1994 East	1998 West	1998 East
Nonstandardized coefficients													
Party identification	0.69	0.44	0.61	0.60	0.73	0.57	0.67	0.63	0.75	0.57	0.63	0.42	0.48
Candidates	*0.21*	*0.29*	*0.26*	*0.41*	*0.24*	*0.29*	*0.28*	*0.33*	*0.24*	*0.44*	*0.33*	*0.44*	*0.29*
Issues	0.31	0.36	0.47	0.25	0.29	0.38	0.43	0.33	0.28	0.30	0.43	0.30	0.39
Standardized coefficients													
Party identification	0.52	0.38	0.39	0.50	0.59	0.49	0.52	0.50	0.60	0.44	0.40	0.33	0.36
Candidates	*0.11*	*0.18*	*0.17*	*0.26*	*0.12*	*0.18*	*0.14*	*0.19*	*0.13*	*0.26*	*0.19*	*0.28*	*0.17*
Issues	0.29	0.34	0.32	0.17	0.21	0.29	0.26	0.23	0.19	0.30	0.27	0.27	0.36
Adj. $R^2 \times 100$	65	65	59	72	75	81	73	74	75	65	61	65	61
Valid N	1,037	1,225	951	1,696	1,732	1,258	1,422	1,753	1,789	877	986	958	464

Notes: A detailed description of the issue orientations together with the coding rules is given in the Appendix to this chapter.

another. Party identification was the most important single determinant of party choice during the period as a whole, with issue orientations clearly more important than candidate orientations.

That said, two elections do stand out: those of 1972 and 1998. The 1972 election was fought by highly contrasted candidates—the charismatic Willy Brandt and the technocrat-politician Rainer Barzel—and, as the figures in Table 5.2 indicate, candidate orientations played an unusually large part in voting behavior at that election. In 1998, as the figures in the table also indicate, the impact of party identification was smaller than ever before, and in West Germany the influence of preferences for one or other of the two competing candidates was actually roughly equal to the influence of party identification. A record number of voters seem not to have cast their ballot according to their longstanding partisan affiliation, and Schröder's personal ascendancy over Kohl may well have contributed to the overall result. In the context of the personalization debate, it is important to note that one of these two elections took place in the early 1970s while the other took place in the late 1990s, more than a quarter of a century later. Yet again, we see no evidence of a long-term trend.

The point is further reinforced if we look at the long period of Helmut Kohl's ascendancy, from 1982 to 1998. During these sixteen years, spanning five federal elections, Kohl remained Kohl, but voters' views of him changed and so, over this long sweep of time, did political circumstances. As the figures in Table 5.2 show, during this period the weight that voters gave to candidate orientations varied considerably, with a lower threshold of 0.24 in 1990 and an upper, in West Germany, of 0.44 in both 1994 and 1998. With regard to the 1987 and 1994 elections, Kohl was increasingly unpopular, but his two SPD opponents—Johannes Rau in 1987 and Rudolf Scharping in 1994—were far from being attractive alternatives.

Since the proportion of party identifiers in the electorate declined during the 1972–90 period, a separate analysis of the determinants of voting behavior among the nonaligned citizens, who now form a much larger proportion of the electorate, is clearly necessary. The data in Figure 5.2 fit neatly into the results presented so far. Compared with party identifiers, the voting behavior of the unaffiliated is more strongly influenced by their candidate preferences; but, at the same time, the data do not indicate that candidate preferences have become more important since the 1960s. Once again, candidates appear to matter more to the nonaligned in some elections than in others. As we have already seen in connection with the electorate as a whole, the candidate question seems to have been highly salient in 1972—but not in 1980. Other elections in which the candidate factor seems to have had a high impact on the electoral choices of non-identifiers were 1961, 1965, and 1994. In 1961 the "Adenauer question" seems to have been particularly important to non-identifiers, and in 1965 the CDU chancellor Ludwig Erhard campaigned on the basis of a strongly nonpartisan and largely personal appeal. Erhard, who was immensely popular as the former architect of Germany's postwar economic miracle, had the additional advantage of not really being perceived as a party leader. The deviating case of 1994 is hard to explain.

Given the general thrust of our findings so far, Figure 5.2 does show one somewhat surprising trend. Candidate orientations do not seem to have become steadily more important among non-party identifiers; but, as can be seen, there is something of a trend in that direction among party identifiers. There was little evidence of candidate effects among identifiers in 1961, but since then the trend, albeit with interruptions, has been gradually upward— with, again, the greatest impact seeming to come in 1972, 1980, and, of course, 1998. In 1972, the rival candidates appear to have attracted (or repelled) nonpartisan voters and simultaneously to have mobilized the parties' core electorates. In 1980, the rival candidates seem to have had a straightforwardly mobilizing effect. The 1998 election, as always, stands out.

We have seen again and again that the 1998 election was an outlier, unlike any of its predecessors (although, admittedly, we do not have relevant data for the 1949, 1953, and 1957 federal elections). It is time, therefore, to turn to a more detailed analysis of that election.

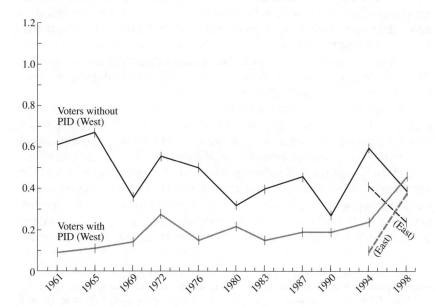

Fig. 5.2 The contribution of candidate orientations to voting choice among party identifiers and the nonaligned in West Germany, 1961–98, and East Germany, 1994–98.

Note: Nonstandardized regression coefficients for candidate orientations on voting decision after controlling for party identification and issue orientations; for coding see Appendix.

How are the Candidates for the Chancellorship Perceived and Evaluated by the German Electorate?

Whether leading political figures are evaluated positively or negatively is generally assumed to be strongly influenced by voters' perceptions of their particular attributes. Voters' perceptions of these attributes depend in turn on the impressions conveyed by the mass media.[20] Needless to say, other political orientations, notably general feelings toward one or more of the political parties, may also impinge on voters' assessments of the parties' leading figures. However, it is far from clear which particular normative standards voters use in forming their attitudes toward candidates and which factors matter most as determinants of their overall candidate orientations.

The lack of good research on candidate images partly results from the lack of an elaborated theory of the formation of relevant political attitudes; but mostly it results from variations in the research strategies that have been employed. Conclusive results are obviously hard to obtain if the measurement instruments that are used vary widely from one survey to another. Open-ended questions have sometimes been asked in German surveys, with respondents asked to name the good and bad points of the various candidates. More commonly, German election studies include batteries of items listing the candidates' possible personal attributes and asking respondents to make their assessments using pre-assigned scale formats. Some questions have forced respondents to choose between the candidates; others have allowed respondents to rate the candidates separately. As Max Kaase notes, "There is still no standard instrument to regularly, validly and reliably assess the core elements of beliefs about political leaders."[21]

The question formats are thus diverse; but there is even greater diversity regarding which possible attributes of leaders are relevant and how voters go about organizing their opinions in order to form overall judgments. People seem to use various information-processing devices—such as cues, shortcuts, and schemata—as ways of reducing the complexity of the environment they find themselves in. Their perceptions and evaluations of particular objects, including politicians, appear to be derived from broad and abstract principles, which, though they may be designed for specifically political purposes, are more often general principles that refer to broad classes of similar

[20] See Frank Brettschneider, "Kohls Niederlage: Kandidatenimages und Medienbericht-erstattung vor der Bundestagswahl 1998" in Peter Winterhoff-Spurk and Michael Jäckel, eds., *Politische Eliten in der Mediengesellschaft: Rekrutierung—Darstellung—Wirkung* (Munich: Verlag Reinhard Fischer, 1999); Klaus Kindelmann, *Kanzlerkandidaten in den Medien: Eine Analyse des Wahljahres 1990* (Opladen: Westdeutscher Verlag, 1994); and Hans Mathias Kepplinger, Hans-Bernd Brosius, and Stefan Dahlem, *Wie das Fernsehen die Wahlen beeinflusst: Theoretische Modelle und empirische Analysen* (Munich: Verlag Reinhard Fischer, 1994).

[21] Kaase, "Is There Personalization in Politics?" p. 221.

objects.[22] Taking this approach assumes that people assess candidates for political office by making use, at least in part, of the same criteria that they use in assessing potential friends, travelling companions, business partners, and so forth.[23] However, the first major study of candidate orientations, *The American Voter*, adopted a simpler approach and merely differentiated between, on the one hand, U.S. presidential candidates' personal (i.e. non-political) attributes (integrity, trustworthiness, good family life) and, on the other, their political performance (experience, strong leadership).[24] Others have used a similar approach.[25] Others go still further and assume an even larger number of separate dimensions of candidate images, such as their problem-solving capacity, leadership qualities, integrity, trustworthiness, and even appearance.[26]

Several of these dimensions are worth pausing over. All the evidence suggests that modern electorates, at least in Europe, are preoccupied with issues such as full employment, economic growth, and social security. To the extent that voters are preoccupied with such issues, it could be expected that the capacity to solve problems would be a quality they would look for in their prospective political leaders. Clearly, however, problem-solving capacity is unlikely to be the only quality they look for. Effective leadership and managerial capacity are also likely to come into play. Likewise, integrity as a crucial quality of political leaders is usually associated with trustworthiness, reliability and a perceived sense of obligation toward the common good.

[22] See Stanley Feldman, "Structure and Consistency in Public Opinion: The Role of Core Beliefs and Values," *American Journal of Political Science*, 32 (1988), 416–40; Susan T. Fiske and Shelley E. Taylor, *Social Cognition*, 2nd edn. (New York: McGraw-Hill, 1991); Paul M. Sniderman, "The New Look in Public Opinion Research," in Ada W. Finifter, ed., *The State of the Discpline II* (Washington, D.C.: American Political Science Association, 1993); Paul M. Sniderman, Richard A. Brody, and Philip E. Tetlock, *Reasoning and Choice: Explorations in Political Psychology* (Cambridge: Cambridge University Press, 1991); and John R. Zaller, *The Nature and Origins of Mass Opinion* (Cambridge: Cambridge University Press, 1992).

[23] Donald R. Kinder, "Presidential Character Revisited," in Richard R. Lau and David O. Sears, eds., *Political Cognition* (Hillsdale, N.J.: Lawrence Erlbaum Associates, 1986).

[24] Campbell, Converse, Miller, and Stokes, *American Voter*.

[25] Lass, *Vorstellungsbilder über Kanzlerkandidaten*; Dan Nimmo and Robert L. Savage, *Candidates and their Images: Concepts, Methods and Findings* (Santa Monica, Calif.: Goodyear, 1976); Roberta S. Sigel, "Effect of Partisanship on the Perception of Political Candidates," *Public Opinion Quarterly*, 28 (1964), 483–96.

[26] See, among others, Brettschneider, "Kohl oder Schröder;" Angelika Vetter and Frank Brettschneider, "Idealmasse für Kanzlerkandidaten," *ZUMA-Nachrichten*, 43 (1998), 90–115; Susan A. Hellweg, "Campaigns and Candidate Images in American Presidential Elections," in Kenneth L. Hacker, ed., *Candidate Images and Presidential Elections* (Westport, Conn.: Praeger, 1995); and, similarly, Markus Klein and Dieter Ohr, "Gerhard oder Helmut?' 'Unpolitische' Kandidateneigeschaften und ihr Einfluss auf die Wahlentscheidung bei der Bundestagswahl 1998," *Politische Vierteljahresschrift*, 41 (2000), 199–224; and Dieter Ohr, "Wird das Wählerverhalten zunehmend personalisierter, oder ist jede Wahl anders? Kandidatenorientierungen und Wahlentscheidung in Deutschland von 1961 bis 1998," in Markus Klein, Wolfgang Jagodzinski, Ekkehard Mochmann, and Dieter Ohr, eds., *50 Jahre empirische Wahlforschung in Deutschland: Entwicklung, Befunde, Perspektiven, Daten* (Wiesbaden: Westdeutscher Verlag, 2000).

Finally, the so-called "role-distant" or nonpolitical attributes include whether or not the candidate is pleasant, likeable, charming, has a good family life, and so on.

Which Attributes Make a Good Leader? And How Did the 1998 Chancellor-candidates Meet These Expectations?

What do Germans associate with the idea of good political leadership? Before answering this question, we need to figure out whether survey respondents can describe the qualities of a political leader at all or whether, instead, they know little about leadership and have highly diffuse expectations. A first indication of the degree of differentiation among people's concepts of political leadership can be gained from the proportion of nonresponses to an open-ended question that was asked in a survey conducted in 1997. The question read: "Regardless of who is running for the chancellorship at the next federal election, what are the most important qualities that an ideal chancellor should have in your opinion?" In the event, only a small proportion of the respondents, roughly 11 percent, were unable to mention any such important qualities. Thirty-two percent mentioned three, 57 percent at least two, and almost 89 percent at least one.

In light of the previous research referred to above, the ideal-chancellor qualities spontaneously mentioned by the 1997 respondents were classified into a number of broad categories: capacity in the handling of particular political issues; general leadership qualities; integrity; and personal appeal. As the figures in Table 5.3 indicate, "integrity" and "general performance as a political leader" were mentioned considerably more frequently than the ideal chancellor's purely personal qualities. These findings are consistent in most respects with the responses to a standardized battery of closed-ended items (the details of which are not reported here). The data in Table 5.3 point to an obvious conclusion. To the extent that German voters in the late 1990s considered the personal characteristics of potential chancellors to be important, the characteristics they had in mind were moral and political rather than nonpolitical and "personal" in the narrow sense of that term. There is no evidence here suggesting that nonpolitical attributes of the kind stressed in the personalization debate were salient to most German voters.

To what extent did Helmut Kohl and Gerhard Schröder, the two men who went on to contest the chancellorship in 1998, live up to the public expectations of an ideal chancellor? Kohl in the preelection year of 1997 evidently did not. Having been in office for the previous fifteen years, Kohl was by then extremely unpopular (and, as we have seen, he had never been particularly popular even in the past). Some of his unpopularity in 1997 was probably no more than the result of his long tenure in office, but by 1997 his reputation as an effective leader had been damaged as well. As the figures in Table 5.4 show, his rating on "strong leadership" alone was still

Table 5.3. The qualities of an ideal German chancellor, 1997

Open-ended question: "Regardless of who is running for chancellor at the next federal election: What are the most important qualities that an ideal chancellor should have in your opinion?" Up to three mentions were possible.

	% of responses (N = 1,751)	% of respondents (N = 953)*
Integrity	**37**	**49**
honest	17	28
trustworthy	9	15
open to the citizens' concerns (caring)	6	11
reliable	3	6
fair	2	3
responsible	1	2
General performance as a political leader	**23**	**42**
leadership qualities; successful	10	18
energetic; active	3	6
decisive	3	5
new ideas; creative; dynamic	2	4
able to compromise	1	2
persistent; steadfast	1	2
looking ahead; has vision	1	2
eloquent	1	2
Issue-related performance	**19**	**34**
issue-related competence	12	19
conception of how to solve problems	5	9
aware of social matters	3	5
Personal appeal	**12**	**18**
strong personality; charismatic; self-confident	8	14
pleasant	2	3
approachable	1	2
young; healthy; fit	1	2

*Because of multiple mentions of qualities that belong to the same dimension, the N of respondents in the overall dimension is greater than the addition of the Ns for the qualities that belong to that dimension.

marginally positive but voters rated him negatively on all the other attributes associated with being an effective leader (for example, decisiveness and being energetic). A majority of respondents, moreover, did not believe that Kohl knew either how to strengthen the economy or how to reduce unemployment. Perhaps most serious of all, the electorate's low opinion of Kohl extended not only to his personal appeal—or, rather, lack of it—but also to his integrity—or, rather, lack of it. Few voters by 1997 believed Kohl was trustworthy or honest or could be counted upon to pursue a responsible policy.

The SPD in 1997 had not yet officially nominated Schröder as Kohl's challenger, but, as the figures in Table 5.4 show, most Germans already had a kinder and friendlier image of him than of Kohl. Whereas Kohl's ratings were negative on all but one of the battery of eleven items, Schröder's were positive on all but three; and on no fewer than ten of the eleven items

Table 5.4. The perception of the leadership qualities of Helmut Kohl and Gerhard Schröder by the German public, 1997–98

"Now, I will list some qualities. Please tell me to what extent these qualities are met by Helmut Kohl and by Gerhard Schröder. −2 means that Helmut Kohl/Gerhard Schröder does not have that quality at all; +2 means that Helmut Kohl/Gerhard Schröder has that quality. You can differentiate your opinion with the values between −2 and +2."

	Kohl			Schröder		
	11/97	9/98	10/98	11/97	9/98	10/98
Integrity						
He is trustworthy.	−0.34	0.26	0.58	−0.02	0.23	0.44
He is honest.	−0.34			−0.14		
He pursues a responsible policy.	−0.41			0.10		
General performance as a political leader						
He is a strong leader.	0.32			0.19		
He is decisive.	−0.12			0.36		
He is energetic.	−0.14	0.39	0.52	0.34	0.67	0.93
Issue-related performance						
He has a good conception of how to strengthen the economy.	−0.74	0.08	0.22	−0.02	0.37	0.50
He has a good conception of how to fight unemployment.	−1.02			0.27		
Personal appeal						
He has good taste.	−0.40			0.24		
He is pleasant.	−0.42	−0.03	0.36	0.14	0.38	0.50
He has charisma.	−0.43			0.25		

Note: The values shown are the means.

Schröder was ahead of Kohl (the only exception being "strong leader," where Kohl was undoubtedly helped by being still in office). One of the findings in Table 5.4 deserves particular attention. Schröder's lead was greatest on the issue that voters regarded as the most urgent problem facing Germany: fighting unemployment.[27] In respondents' eyes, Schröder had some credibility on the issue; Kohl had little or none.

Four of the battery of eleven items included in the 1997 questionnaire were replicated a year later in surveys conducted both before and after the federal election. Some measures of the changes that took place between 1997 and 1998 are therefore available. As Table 5.4 shows, both leaders, especially Kohl, considerably improved their images in the course of the year. Three of Kohl's negative ratings had become positive by the time of the 1998 campaign, and all four were positive by the time of the survey following the election. Schröder's ratings were already quite high in 1997, and there was therefore less room for improvement. Even so, Schröder improved his position on all four of the items

[27] For details, see Wolfram Brunner and Dieter Walz, "Die politische Stimmungslage im Vorfeld der Bundestagswahl," in Gert Pickel, Dieter Walz, and Wolfram Brunner, eds., *Deutschland nach den Wahlen: Befunde zur Bundestagswahl 1998 und zur Zukunft des deutschen Parteiensystems* (Opladen: Leske & Budrich, 2000).

between 1997 and the eve of the election in 1998 and again between the pre- and postelection periods. With regard to his trustworthiness and his ability to strengthen the economy, Schröder's ratings, which had been neutral or ambivalent in 1997, had become strongly positive by 1998. Ironically, in light of the money-laundering scandal that subsequently enveloped Kohl and the CDU, the only item on which Kohl led Schröder at the time of the 1998 election was trustworthiness.

Respondents were not asked in any of the three surveys to assess the importance of particular leadership qualities, and it is therefore not possible to say definitely whether personality-related or performance-related qualities mattered more to them in determining how they evaluated Kohl and Schröder. Nevertheless, it is striking that both Kohl and Schröder were rated most strongly—both before and after the election—on attributes relating to strength of leadership. Schröder enormously improved his standing in the leadership domain between 1997 and 1998. Kohl did well in this area; Schröder did even better.[28] The findings in Table 5.4 point to a first and very preliminary conclusion: that Kohl lost the federal chancellorship in 1998 less because of his perceived failings as a political leader than because of his perceived failings as a problem-solver, especially in connection with the economy. The strong gains he made during the election year were not enough to compensate for the initial weaknesses in his profile. Voters' evaluations of the two men's purely personal characteristics seem to have contributed little to either Kohl's defeat or Schröder's victory.

Do Personal Attributes Form a Separate Dimension in the Evaluation of Candidates?

Differentiating voters' attitudes toward candidates into the four components just described and set out in Table 5.4 is intuitively plausible; but of course whether and how various aspects of voters' attitudes cluster along a limited number of general dimensions is a matter for empirical investigation rather than intuition. Accordingly, we conducted a confirmatory factor analysis to test the goodness of fit between our theoretical assumptions and the data. As the findings in Figure 5.3 indicate, the fit is excellent: Our assumption of the existence of four separate dimensions is clearly supported by the data. Moreover, the four dimensions identified by the factor analysis are the same dimensions as the ones we originally postulated, and the results of other tests, not reported here, showed our four-dimensional model to be superior to a range of alternative solutions. The attitudes of voters assessing Kohl and Schröder in 1997 formed the expected four clusters: competence in solving particular problems, general qualities as political leaders, personal appeal,

---

[28] On Kohl's high ratings in this connection, see Gabriel and Vetter, "Bundestagswahlen als Kanzlerwahlen?" and Vetter and Gabriel, "Candidate Evaluations and Party Choice in Germany."

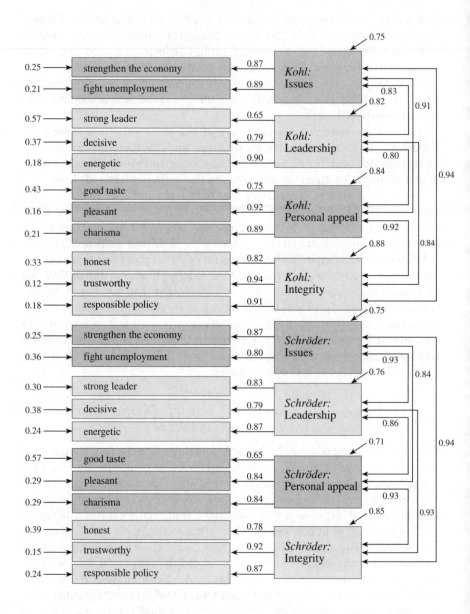

Fig. 5.3 Perceived qualities of Kohl and Schröder, 1997

Notes: Confirmatory factor analysis and standardized path coefficients. Kohl: df = 38; χ^2 = 88; p = 0.0000077; adjusted general fit index. Schröder: df = 38, χ^2 = 92; p = 0.0000021; adjusted general fit index = 0.98 PRELIS 2.03; LISREL 8; WLS after polychoric correlation and asymptotic covariance matrix; N = 676.

and, finally, integrity. The first two of these clusters—problem-solving competence and general leadership qualities—may be regarded as concerning political performance. The third—personal appeal—is clearly the one that the proponents of the personalization thesis have principally in mind. The fourth—integrity—links purely personal characteristics and role-related characteristics since trustworthiness, honesty, and responsibility are clearly relevant to both politics in particular and human relations in general.[29] The four dimensions identified by our factor analysis are, of course, interrelated: for example, people who perceived Kohl as a strong leader in 1997 also expressed confidence in his personal integrity and vice versa. It is also the case that the results are by no means surprising: they tend to confirm current assumptions about the way that people perceive their political leaders.

In view of the ongoing debate about personalization, perhaps the most important result of these analyses is the identification of a separate dimension of candidate attitudes tapping into Kohl's and Schröder's purely personal attributes: whether or not they are likeable and pleasant and whether or not they are of good appearance. As the figure shows, this dimension is most strongly linked to the assessment of politicians' integrity. In the case of Kohl, it is also linked to his perceived problem-solving capacity, suggesting that a favorable affective orientation toward the chancellor produced a strong carryover into the instrumental domain. To put it another way, a good deal of personal sympathy was needed to see Kohl as a problem solver.

It goes without saying that different psychological processes may lead to these patterns of orientation. One possibility is that candidates are perceived in a holistic way which manifests itself in the evaluation of particular attributes. Another is that some respondents are simply exhibiting a response-set, especially respondents who have not yet made up their minds (and may never make up their minds) about the people they are being asked about. Yet another possibility is that the astonishingly consistent evaluation of the candidates may be due to respondents' striving for attitudinal consistency, leading to seemingly coherent orientations. Finally, of course, as the findings of the social-psychological school would lead us to expect, respondents' attitudes toward candidates in general and toward their specific attributes may be influenced by the respondents' prior party identification.

The Impact of Party Identification and the Assessment of Attributes on the General Evaluation of Candidates

The connection between party identification and voters' evaluations of the chancellor-candidates is worth exploring in more detail since, as we have repeatedly seen, the 1998 federal election was a deviating election in many

---

[29] Robert D. Putnam, "Bowling Alone: America's Declining Social Capital," *Journal of Democracy*, (1995), 65–78.

respects. In 1998 it turned out that the connections between party identification, general candidate evaluations and the assessment of specific candidate
attributes were altogether more complicated—and unpredictable—than in
the past. We need to explore more deeply the ways in which party identification and the assessment of particular candidate attributes are linked to voters' overall preferences for one candidate rather than another. Clarifying the
role of particular attitudinal components in forming voters' preferences and
assessments is not only of scientific interest: it is also of practical concern.
Political parties planning election campaigns need to rely not only on generalized data concerning the various candidates' popularity with the electorate:
they also need more detailed information about the specific components of
the candidates' images. A party with a candidate who is perceived by the public as being likeable and trustworthy but not especially competent will want,
or should want, to campaign differently from one whose candidate exhibits
the opposite traits or has a favorable image across the board.

So far we have employed simple bivariate analyses in examining the interrelationships between party identification and voters' assessments of the candidates' attributes. The results now to be presented are based on more
complex data analyses, taking into account the complete set of relevant variables: party identification, straightforward preference for Kohl or Schröder
as federal chancellor, and the indicators on all four of the dimensions that we
identified in the previous section. The standardized path coefficients linking
the variables, along with other relevant data, are displayed in Figure 5.4. As
can be seen, party identification strongly influences perceptions of Kohl's—
and, to a lesser extent, Schröder's—integrity.[30] Party identification also has a
strong influence on the two men's perceived problem-solving capabilities. But
otherwise the connections between party identification and perceived attributes are far from strong. In particular, party identification clearly has little
bearing on voters' assessments of either the two candidates' leadership qualities or the quality of their personal appeal. At least at the time of the 1997 survey, the images of the two competing candidates were only partially colored
by general, longstanding party loyalties. Instead, a good deal of each man's
image was nonpartisan. This was especially so in the case of the personal
characteristics of each.

Some components of the candidates' images are thus largely unaffected by
party identification. These components nevertheless impinge strongly, as can
be seen, on Kohl and Schröder's images overall. Moreover, with regard to
Kohl, the impact of almost every one of these particular components exceeds
the role played by party identification in determining voters' overall evaluation

---

[30] For the coding of the party identification variable and candidate evaluation, see Appendix.
The four dimensions were coded on a five-point scale with the following extremes: -2 = candidate does not have the respective qualities; $+2$ = candidate has the qualities. The chancellor
preference variable was coded on a three-point scale with -1 = preference for Schröder;
0 = preference for neither candidate or both candidates; $+1$ = preference for Kohl.

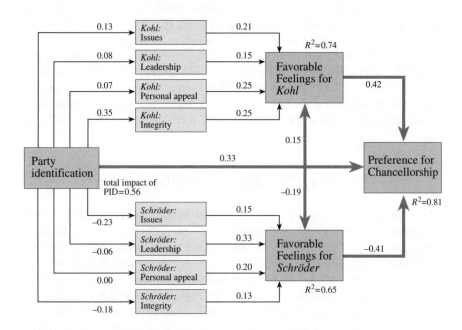

Fig. 5.4 Components of candidate images as determinants of preference for Kohl and Schröder, 1997

Notes: WLS after polychoric correlation and asymptotic covariance matrix; N=453.

of him. The personalization thesis, at least in its static version, finds some support in the fact that perceptions of Kohl's integrity and appreciation of his personal attributes are most closely related to a view of him that is favorable overall. Traces of personalization are also visible in Schröder's overall image. Leadership matters most, but personal appeal also makes a substantial contribution.

As we have already noticed, the images of Kohl and Schröder in the year preceding the 1998 election showed some remarkable differences. Schröder's overall image was clearly dominated by his being perceived as a strong and effective political leader—a perception that played a far stronger role than any other factor, including his perceived personal attributes and even voters' party identification. In making up their minds about his rival, Kohl, voters placed an almost equal emphasis on his personality, integrity, and problem-solving capacity. Party identification and perceptions of Kohl as a strong political leader counted for less. Looking at it another way, Kohl's low standing in the eyes of large numbers of voters was due to unfavorable evaluations of his personality, integrity, and problem-solving capacity. The central point to notice is that the different components in the two men's images were given different weights as voters arrived at their general conclusions about them.

What do these data tell us about the validity of the familiar personalization thesis? If personalization is equated with the idea that a candidate's personality is the predominant element in his overall image, then the data contradict this view. Schröder's image clearly comprises more important components, and in the case of Kohl voters' perceptions of his personality were an important factor but not the most important. However, a less restrictive view of personalization, suggesting that voters accord considerable weight to candidates' personalities in forming their judgments of them, is clearly in line with the data.

Summary, Conclusions, and Discussion

Many observers interpreted the 1998 Bundestag election as signalling a fundamental change in German electoral behavior. As in many other Western democracies, German campaigns and elections were seen as having become more and more candidate-centered. Accordingly, many observers took it for granted that perceptions of the two main chancellor-candidates, Helmut Kohl and Gerhard Schröder, had played an important role, if not the decisive role, in the outcome of the election and the ousting of Kohl. One observer wrote: "The attempt to characterize Kohl as 'yesterday's man' and Schröder as the winner of tomorrow had succeeded. The voters accepted this type of *mise-en-scène*; they even seemed to enjoy it."[31]

As we have shown elsewhere, interpreting the 1998 election as a "plebiscite against Chancellor Kohl" only partly meets the real situation of that year.[32] Many factors—not only voters' unfavorable perceptions of Kohl's quality and performance—contributed to the defeat of the center-right coalition. And, putting the 1998 election into the larger context of Germany's postwar electoral history, there is simply no convincing empirical evidence that, so far as the voters are concerned, the country's electoral politics have become progressively more personalized, whatever meaning is given to the notion of personalization. It is possible, of course, that voters' strong personal preferences for Schröder over Kohl in 1998, and their impact on the outcome of the election, will prove to have been a breakthrough and that in the future chancellor-candidates' personalities and other personal characteristics may weigh more heavily in German voters' minds than they have in the past. But it is much too early to say. Only time will tell.

Needless to say, nothing that has been said in this chapter should be taken to mean that candidates' personal characteristics, and voters' evaluations of

---

[31] Ulrich von Alemann, "Der Wahlsieger von 1998: Politische Achsenverschiebung oder glücklicher Ausreisser?" in Oskar Niedermayer, ed., *Die Parteien nach der Bundestagswahl 1998* (Opladen: Leske & Budrich, 1999).

[32] Gabriel and Brettschneider, "Die Bundestagswahl 1998."

them, never play a part in determining election outcomes. All that is being claimed—in situations in which millions of individual vote decisions are being aggregated—is that the influence of the competing party leaders is strongly mediated by such situational factors as the strength as well as the direction of partisan affiliations, the presence or absence of hotly contested political issues, and, on occasion, as Franz Urban Pappi and Susumu Shikano have shown, by voters' judgments of candidates not running for the chancellorship.[33]

On the question of any growth in personalization over time in Germany, the relevant data concerning the role of candidates' personal appeal in building their general image contradict the idea that personal characteristics—such as being pleasant or attractive, or living in an intact family—are becoming steadily more important in voters' minds. In 1997–98 items like these ranked lowest in the responses to an open-ended question on the ideal characteristics of a good political leader, and they were by no means the most important determinants of the candidates' general images. What counts considerably more is integrity, although of course integrity is not exclusively a political virtue but is central among the attributes of people with whom we generally want to associate. Integrity is also far from being the central topic in the debate on the personalization of politics. Moreover, even if the lack of reliable data requires us to be rather cautious in drawing conclusions about the personalization of elections in Germany, one thing is clear. Since those personal attributes of candidates that are emphasized by the proponents of personalization played such a small role in the late 1990s, any suggestion that personalization had increased would necessarily imply that they were almost completely irrelevant in former times.

Although there is no real evidence that personalization is a useful way of describing recent trends in German voting behavior, the question still remains of why the changes in campaign strategy and media reporting that are certainly evident in Germany have not yet been accompanied by the rise in candidate-centered voting that appears to have taken place in the United States. In our view, the answer lies largely in important differences in the political contexts in which voting takes place in Germany and the United States. Despite the decline in party identification that took place in the 1980s and 1990s, parties still play a far stronger role in Germany than in the United States, notably in the process of recruiting candidates for political office. In the nomination process, German voters tend to play a spectator role, while the U.S. system of primaries gives Americans a direct say in who will run for the presidency. Moreover, the federal chancellor, formally at least, is not

---

[33] Franz Urban Pappi and Susumu Shikano, "Personalisierung der Politik im Mehrparteien-system am Beispiel deutscher Bundestagswahlen seit 1980," *Politische Vierteljahresschrift*, 42 (2001), 355–87.

elected by the voters but by the parliament, and the majority needed to form a government almost invariably presupposes the building of a coalition between two or more parties. As a result, many of the electors treat deciding who is their preferred chancellor-candidate as only one of the factors to be taken into account. Another factor to be taken into account may, for example, be the probable distribution of influence among the parties likely to form the next coalition.

An additional and very important impediment to personalization in Germany is the role played by politicians in everyday life. It is hard to imagine a movie like *Hello Mr President*, dealing with the private life of a political leader, being made in Germany. By contrast, using political figures, real or imagined, as the subjects of entertainment is completely familiar in the United States. Other examples of American fictional political movies are *Emergency*, in which Harrison Ford plays the hero, and *Wag the Dog*, a movie in which a war is invented to distract public attention from the sex affair of an incumbent president. But, even when American movies do deal with real political figures or events, such as the careers of Abraham Lincoln, Richard Nixon, or the Watergate scandal, or in a soap opera like *White House Backstage*, the human-interest element is always more important than historical truth. Only rarely have films dealing with the lives of political leaders in Germany been made, and, when they are made, their topics are the political lives rather than the private lives of distant historical figures such as Bismarck, Frederick the Great, or the Austrian Empress Elisabeth. Political events, moreover, are treated documentary-style and not as light entertainment. A German television film about the life of Konrad Adenauer, for instance, treated its subject wholly seriously.

A deeper examination of the way in which politics presents itself to the public and is presented to the public by the entertainment industry is beyond the scope of this chapter; but the personalization of politics does seem to depend on the linkages that exist between a society's public and private spheres. The more political leaders present themselves to the citizenry as "people like you and me," and the more political leaders become the subject of popular entertainment, the higher, it would seem, is the probability that personalization will become an important factor in people's orientations toward political life. In Germany some political leaders have learned the lesson taught by a former CDU campaign manager, Peter Radunski, that a single successful performance on a television talk show can contribute more to a political leader's popularity than thousands of political speeches. Because talk shows are highly popular on German television, they may in the long run—who knows?—contribute to political leaders' personalities having a greater impact on German electoral behavior than at present. But, so far, no German television or movie producer has shown the slightest interest in making *Hello Mr. Chancellor*. We leave to others the task of speculating why this should be so.

Appendix

Voting Intention

Similar questions with only minor variations: "If there were a general election next Sunday, would you participate in the election?" "As you know, in a German general election you have two votes: one for your constituency candidate and one for the candidate list of your preferred party. Which party would you intend to vote for with your party list vote?" (-5 = voting intention CDU/CSU, 0 = all respondents without voting intention to CDU/CSU or SPD or those giving no answer, $+5$ = voting intention SPD).

Party Identification

1961–69: "What do you think, generally speaking, about the German political parties? Please signify your evaluation with the following scale. The more you choose the white boxes, the more you like the party, the more you choose the black boxes, the more you dislike them. Now please tell me: Generally speaking, what do you think of . . . ?" (-5 = strongest dislike, 0 = no decision, $+5$ = strongest sympathy). The CDU rating was subtracted from the SPD rating. -10 . . . -4 were recoded to -5 (strong ID with CDU/CSU), -2 and -3 were recoded to -3 (weak ID with CDU/CSU), -1 . . . $+1$ were recoded to 0 (independents), $+2$ and $+3$ were recoded to $+3$ (weak SPD ID), $+4$ . . . $+10$ were recoded to $+5$ (strong SPD ID).

Since 1972: "Many people in Germany tend to identify with one party in the long run, even though they may vote differently at times. Do you—generally speaking—identify with a special party? If so, which party do you identify with?" "How strong would you say is your identification with this party: very strong, quite strong, moderate, quite weak, weak?" (-5 = very strong CDU; -3 = weak CDU, 0 = other party or no party ID, $+3$ = weak SPD, $+5$ = very strong SPD).

Candidate Evaluation

All elections except 1969: "Using the following scale, please tell me what you think about some of the following politicians; $+5$ means that you like the politician very much; -5 means, that you dislike him very much. What do you think of . . . ?" The CDU candidate rating was subtracted from the SPD candidate rating; -10 and -9 were recoded to -5 (strong CDU candidate), -8 and -7 to -4, -6 and -5 to -3, -4 and -3 to -2, $-2/-1$ to -1, 0 remained 0, $+1$ and $+2$ to $+1$, $+3$ and $+4$ to $+2$, $+5$ and $+6$ to $+3$, $+7$ and $+8$ to $+4$, $+9$ and $+10$ to $+5$ (strong SPD candidate).

1969: "Thinking about the politicians in Bonn: Which of the politicians in Bonn do you think are able to cope with their duties best?" (open question) "And which of the politicians in Bonn do you like most?" (open question). If a candidate is mentioned twice, he receives the value $+5$; if he is mentioned once, he receives the value $+2$; if he is not mentioned, he receives the value 0. The Kiesinger ratings were subtracted from the Brandt ratings. Finally, -10 was recoded to -5 (strong CDU candidate), -6 to -3, -3 to -2, 0 remained 0, $+3$ to $+2$, $+6$ to $+3$, $+10$ to $+5$ (strong SPD candidate).

Candidate Qualities

1969 and 1987 with only minor variations: "Now I would like to ask you about the good and bad points of the chancellor-candidates of the two big parties in Germany. Is there anything in particular that you like about . . . , the chancellor-candidate of the SPD?" "Anything else?" "Is there anything in particular that you don't like about . . . ?" "Anything else?" "And what about . . . , the chancellor-candidate of the CDU/CSU? Is there anything in particular that you like about . . . ?" "Anything else?" "And is there anything in particular that you don't like about . . . ?" "Anything else?" Up to three answers were possible. From 1972 to 1980 only the supporters of the Social Democratic and the conservative chancellor-candidate were asked: "Why do you prefer . . . to become the next federal chancellor?" In 1972 and 1980 up to three answers were possible, in 1976 no more than two answers. 1997: "Thinking of Helmut Kohl and Gerhard Schröder, which qualities come to your mind? Which qualities come into your mind when you think of Helmut Kohl?" "And which qualities come to your mind when you think of Gerhard Schröder?" Up to three answers were possible.

Issue Competence

1961: First the respondents were asked about the importance they attribute to the following problems (old age pensions, fighting rising prices, German reunification). If the respondents attributed relatively high importance to the problem, they were asked in 1961: "No matter what party you personally like best, which party do you think would be better able to handle this problem: the SPD or the CDU/CSU?" How often the SPD or the CDU/CSU were mentioned as more competent to handle a problem was counted. The number of CDU/CSU problem-solving attributions was subtracted from the number of SPD problem-solving attributions. Finally -3 was recoded to -5 (strong CDU/CSU problem-solving competence); -2 was recoded to -3; -1, 0 and $+1$ remained the same; $+2$ was recoded to $+3$, $+3$ was recoded to $+5$ (strong SPD problem-solving capacity).

1965–94: The following codings of the parties' issue competencies are based on three to five given political problems (1965: old age pensions, inflation, reunification; 1969: economic and social policy making, foreign policy, education; 1972: inflation, law and order, health and social services, fighting terrorism; 1976: inflation, European unification, unemployment, professional education, law and order; 1980: old age pensions, inflation, law and order, environmental policies, unemployment; 1983: inflation, unemployment, environmental policies, old age pensions, national debts; 1987: economic policies, unemployment, environmental policies, old age pensions, inflation; 1990: unemployment, environmental policies, old age pensions, inflation, housing market policies; 1994: unemployment, environmental policies, law and order, housing market policies, immigration policies). From 1972 to 1990 only those respondents who had mentioned the problem as important were asked the following question; the question wording showed only minor variations: "No matter what party you personally like best, which party/government would be able to handle this problem better?" First it was counted how often the SPD and how often the CDU/CSU were mentioned as more competent to handle a problem. Then the number of CDU/CSU problem-solving attributions was subtracted from the number of

SPD problem-solving attributions. For 1965 and 1969 -3 was recoded to -5 (strong CDU/CSU problem-solving capacity); -2 was recoded to -3, -1, 0 and $+1$ remained the same; $+2$ was recoded to $+3$; $+3$ was recoded to $+5$ (strong SPD problem solving capacity). For the other years, the scale goes from -5 (strong CDU/CSU problem-solving competence) to $+5$ (strong SPD problem-solving competence).

1998: "What, in your opinion, are the most important problems facing the nation today?" (For the two most important problems mentioned): "Which party do you think is able to handle this problem best?" First it was coded how often a CDU/CSU or a SPD problem-solving capacity was mentioned. Second, CDU/CSU problem-solving capacity was subtracted from SPD problem-solving capacity. Third -2 was recoded to -5 (strong problem-solving capacity CDU); -1 was recoded to -3; 0 remained 0; $+1$ was recoded to $+3$; $+2$ was recoded to $+5$ (strong problem-solving capacity SPD).

6

Prime Ministerial Contenders in Canada

RICHARD JOHNSTON

Are Canadian elections peculiarly vulnerable to leader effects? That they are is a contention dating back at least to André Siegfried's remarkable early study and seems to be a stylized fact of recent research.[1] It is not hard to outline a case as to why this might be so. But the case is not clearly about leaders' personalities. And the evidence for it is often weak, open to rival interpretations, or not on the main issue. This chapter tries to right the balance, at least for elections since 1988.[2]

It begins by outlining the specifically Canadian arguments for taking leadership seriously and the evidence said to back them. The arguments turn out to refer mainly to "indirect" effects in the sense used by Anthony King in Chapter 1. It treats leaders as if they are embodied preferences, so to speak. The actual evidence is largely silent on the content—personality or otherwise—of Canadians' leader judgments, at least so far as those judgments are linked to the vote. Likewise, most accounts control for competing explanations weakly, if at all. And none considers personality for its net, election-day effect.

Working through each argument also reveals that each is highly contingent. In general, they apply more to certain parties than others, more to big parties than to small ones, more to catch-all parties than to programmatic ones. They also seem to apply more to periods of flux and to new parties than to stable periods and old parties. Some of these contingencies may be contradictory, so sorting out their empirical implications for a small number of cases is not straightforward.

Filling the gaps requires an account of the personality factors worth taking seriously. It also requires a basic estimation strategy, which sets leader

---

[1] André Siegfried, *The Race Question in Canada* (Toronto: McClelland and Stewart, 1966). The original translation was published in 1907.

[2] Leader factors conceived generally have been objects of study for elections before 1988 and this chapter makes reference to studies employing earlier data. Only since 1988, however, has it been possible to consider leaders' personalities in a consistent and coherent way.

attributes into proper context. Finally, and based on this estimation strategy, comes the accounting for net aggregate effects.

If the focus is on perceptions of personality, it is natural to ask how manipulable these perceptions are. In particular, can perceptions be modified over the course of a campaign? If they can be, does this expand or contract their net effect at the end of the exercise, on election day? The appeal of personality to strategists might be that a positive view of their own leader or a negative view of the opponent, if cut through the entire electorate, creates an across-the-board advantage. The campaign should compound this advantage. But the voters most susceptible to such arguments may already support the party making the claim, so changing leader images may be more a conserving force than a disruptive one.

Finally, I supply an account of a special sort of "indirect" effect. In certain—probably rare—instances, perceptions of a leader's personality can be cashed in on perceptions of a policy option. If the policy is central to electoral contestation, associating it with a leader who stands out as exceptionally credible or as exceptionally lacking in credibility can affect the outcome. The leader's own traits can be a factor in policy persuasion.

Why Leaders Should Matter in Canada

Two features of Canadian parties and elections may make leaders peculiarly important. First, access to the top position in Canadian parties is more detached from the parliamentary body than is true in any other Westminster system. This raises the possibility that leaders will be judged independently of their parties, exactly as early proponents of extra-parliamentary selection intended. Second, on the question most central to Canadian politics—the place of Quebec and French Canada in the larger polity—parties contending for power commonly adopt centrist positions, and they tend not to divide sharply on other possible dimensions. This, arguably, creates a vacuum that leadership might fill.

Both arguments are subject to contingencies. Both are really about big parties, ones with serious prospects of forming the government. Smaller parties are not in the business of supplying prime ministerial contenders. And smaller parties may not be in the brokerage business, or if they try to be, their very smallness suggests that they regularly fail. Smaller parties may thus, by accident or design, have more clearly demarcated group bases. All of the above may be contingent on the stability of electoral patterns. Even a brokerage party has some base and some history. The relevance of base and history depends on whether the next election is fought on the same ground as previous ones. When the rules of engagement change, history becomes less of a guide and personality may come to the fore.

Institutional Features

Canada's traditional parties of government, the Liberal and Progressive Conservative parties, are classic examples of the cadre party.[3] Each grew out of the parliamentary politics of the 1840s and 1850s, and down to 1919 leader selection was a matter solely for the parliamentary party. In the aftermath of World War I and a crisis over military conscription, however, the parliamentary Liberal party found itself reduced to a Quebec-dominated rump. In 1919, when the party was forced to choose a successor to the late Sir Wilfrid Laurier, this rump hardly seemed the appropriate body to make the choice. Only a convention would do, not least because it could represent parts of the country absent from the party's parliamentary group. To minimize the appearance of ethno-regional discord, voting for leader was by secret ballot. The Liberals won the next election in 1921. Later in the 1920s the Conservatives found themselves in a somewhat similar predicament and adopted the same expedient, with the same effect in the following election. The parties drew the obvious conclusion and have used conventions ever since. New parties, typically with extra-parliamentary origins, have had little choice but to choose leaders by extra-parliamentary means.[4] Since 1990, the trend has been toward direct selection by parties' whole paid-up memberships.

The implication is that, somewhat uniquely among Westminster systems, Canadian parties choose leaders by an explicitly plebiscitary process. Many of the critical factors in the choice lie quite outside the constellation of power at the parliamentary center. The overt and highly mediated coalition-building typical of old U.S. presidential conventions is not realistically available where the ballot is secret. And the choice is not reversible by the parliamentary party. Early on, forces behind the scenes mitigated this plebiscitarianism, as selection of constituency delegates was not always autonomous and many delegates were simply *ex officio*.[5] But the plebiscitary trend was genuinely upward and many conventions, especially from 1957 on, were not readily controlled.

Party Convergence

It is commonplace that Canada's traditional parties are ones of brokerage.[6] This Canadian claim echoes a general one in the literature on party strategy.

---

[3] Maurice Duverger, *Les Partis politiques* (Paris: Armand Colin, 1951).

[4] This paragraph draws heavily on John C. Courtney, *The Selection of National Party Leaders in Canada* (Toronto: Macmillan, 1973).

[5] Courtney, *The Selection*.

[6] A classic early characterization is James R. Mallory, "The Structure of Canadian Politics," in *Canadian Politics* (Sackville, N.B.: Mount Allison University Publications, No. 4, 1947). The term recurs in Lawrence LeDuc, "Canada: The Politics of Stable Dealignment," in Russell J. Dalton, Scott C. Flanagan, and Paul Allen Beck, eds., *Electoral Change in the Advanced*

The standard claim in the rational choice literature is that two-party competition produces convergence on the electoral median.[7] That Canada has not been a real two-party system for decades does not matter to this argument. The critical thing is that serious contestants for office have never numbered more than two. But convergence on the main questions of politics is not always the norm in two-party systems, much less in multiparty ones. Historically minded students of party systems, such as Lipset and Rokkan, emphasize abiding links between parties and social groups, a pattern hard to square with policy convergence.[8] Indeed, such is the ubiquity of party divergence that some spatial models now turn the original conception of party strategy on its head.[9] To come back to Canada, Alan Cairns has argued that the country's electoral framework creates an abiding incentive for party divergence on sectional and language matters, and the article that makes this claim is probably the most celebrated single contribution to recent Canadian political science.[10]

But if claims for brokerage do not always fit the facts, they nonetheless express a real insight about electoral coalition-building in Canada. The examples Cairns cites reflect a recurring tendency for the Conservative Party to write Quebec off, which in turn licenses the Quebec Liberals to exaggerate Tory perfidy. So for extended periods the Conservatives would acquiesce in a structure of party competition that left them unable to form governments. This is because Quebec was the historic pivot for governments, in the following sense. Quebec seats came essentially *en bloc*. It was almost impossible to form a single-party majority without a majority of seats from that province. Without them, it was even hard to form a minority government. Minority governments that excluded Quebec were short-lived. Minority governments that included Quebec lived longer and often metamorphosed into full-blown majority governments. Conservatives who sought to build an effective governing coalition knew that they had to come to terms with Quebec, which in turn required them to mimic the Liberals.[11] And for almost all of this period the Liberal Party offered policies straddling the great divide. No matter that in earlier years the divide was as much religious as ethnic or linguistic. The party struggled to find the center even when the center seemed empty.

Industrial Democracies (Princeton, N.J.: Princeton University Press, 1984), and Harold D. Clarke, Jane Jenson, Lawrence LeDuc, and Jon H. Pammett, *Absent Mandate: Interpreting Change in Canadian Elections* (Toronto: Gage, 1991).

[7] The original source for this prediction is Anthony Downs, *An Economic Theory of Democracy* (New York: Holt Rinehart, 1957).

[8] Seymour M. Lipset and Stein Rokkan, *Party Systems and Voter Alignments: Cross-National Perspectives* (New York: The Free Press, 1967).

[9] See, for example, Stuart E. Macdonald, Ola Listhaug, and George Rabinowitz, "Issues and Party Support in Multiparty Systems," *American Political Science Review*, 85 (1991), 1107–31.

[10] Alan C. Cairns, "The Electoral System and the Party System in Canada, 1921–1965," *Canadian Journal of Political Science*, 1 (1968), 55–80.

[11] This is the argument in Richard Johnston, André Blais, Henry E. Brady, and Jean Crête, *Letting the People Decide: Dynamics of a Canadian Election* (Montreal: McGill–Queen's University Press, 1992), chap. 2.

In leader selection, Liberals took great care to stagemanage successions, and it was quite common for the party to choose a new leader seemingly from outside the pre-existing power structure, precisely to broaden its appeal. Also, the party alternated French and English leaders, about which more will be said below. These two patterns describe the selection of every leader from Laurier to Trudeau, if not since.[12] But then so was leadership critical for the Conservative Party, even if it managed things less adroitly. Tory leader selection was often a prime site for contestation over the proper approach to Quebec and French Canada, although it rarely featured a francophone or a Quebecker as a candidate. From the mid 1960s on, the party responded to the logic of the preceding paragraph by dragging itself, convention upon convention, toward the Liberal position on language issues and on the place of Quebec. The breakthrough was to choose Brian Mulroney as leader in 1983, who delivered the Quebec majority in 1984. So Mulroney's arrival and success confirmed the brokerage intuition. From 1984 on, voters were unable to see any difference between the major parties on the "national" question.[13]

Party Size

All the foregoing is really about big parties, contestants for power. Smaller parties may try to use leader selection to expand their base. Struggles for leadership commonly turn at least on the ideological position of the candidates, with electability being the strongest card that a centrist can play in an otherwise ideologically motivated exercise. But the electability card may be less effective precisely to the extent that ideology is important. Even if it is important, the party's remaining ideological baggage may suppress the impact of leadership. The party's very smallness may have the same effect: If the leader has no chance to be prime minister, why should voters make leadership a factor at all?

Electoral Flux

Periods of electoral instability seem ripe for leader effects, if only by default. Consider an argument by indirection. Where a party alignment is basically stable, voters should have had ample time, decades and more, to triangulate the basic stakes. Leader selection, even where it occasions conflict within parties, should be heavily under the control of abiding groups and lines of cleavage.

[12] The choice of John Turner in 1984 is ambiguous. On the one hand, he conformed to a Liberal type that predated Pierre Trudeau. On the other hand, he represented political forces quite different from Trudeau. In that sense, his selection was in keeping with the earlier ones. The choice of Jean Chrétien in 1990 certainly represented a departure from Turner's version of the party, but it was not so much a forward-looking move as a consolidation of the Trudeau-era definition of the party.

[13] On this see Johnston *et al.*, *Letting the People Decide*, chap. 3.

The party may choose the "wrong" leader from time to time, but successful parties should avoid this, and parties that do not are unlikely to contend for power, and so their choice will not matter much anyway.

In a period of flux, however, the institutional predictability of a stable alignment is, *ex hypothesi*, undercut. Ironically, voters are likely to know less about leaders of new movements than about more established figures. But, sometimes, new movements are led by old figures. And even when the leader is truly new to voters, they are still likely to get a quicker fix on leaders than on followers, as opposed to when an old party chooses a new leader.

The 1990s are a critical decade for this argument. More to the point, 1993 is the critical year. The vote shifts from 1988 to 1993 were as dramatic as any in Canadian history. The Conservatives and the New Democratic Party (NDP) each lost two-thirds of their 1988 shares. In seats, these two parties were simply decimated. Much of the slack was taken up by two essentially new parties, Reform and the Bloc Québécois. Each, obviously, was led by someone relatively new to the job. Lucien Bouchard, the Bloc leader, was not new to federal politics, as the party was formed by the defection of sitting members, mainly from the Conservative Party. Bouchard seemed immensely important to voters in Quebec, the one province where the party ran candidates. The leader of Reform was a true outsider, Preston Manning.[14]

Manning's example reveals a difficulty with the argument. If leaders are particularly important in a period of flux, where flux means the rise of new parties rather than just swings between existing parties, the leader of the new party may be obscure. This may abridge his or her potential effect. Moreover, new parties rarely break through to power, and certainly none did in 1993. This too should mute the impact of the new leader. We have, then, an embarrassing surplus of possibilities, especially for 1993.

The Evidence in Hand

The body of evidence so far is modest. The older commentators relied on narrative, unsurprisingly. Data bearing directly on the matter arrived with the survey-based Canadian Election Studies (CES), starting in 1965. Much of our current sense of leaders' importance derives from work by Harold Clarke and his colleagues, CES co-investigators in the 1970s.[15] They describe leaders as the "superstars of Canadian politics".[16] The primary basis for this claim is respondents' self-reports, where many respondents claim to have chosen the leader more than the party. The one explicitly comparative study of leader factors to include Canada does find that impact

---

[14] Even Manning carried a political pedigree. His father had been premier of Alberta.

[15] Clarke *et al.*, *Absent Mandate*. The 1991 volume carries forward work from an earlier edition, as well as from their in-depth study of the 1974 election, *Political Choice in Canada* (Toronto: McGraw-Hill Ryerson, 1979).

[16] Clarke *et al.*, *Absent Mandate*, p. 89.

from leader judgments (represented by "feeling thermometers") is slightly greater in Canada than in the other four Anglo-American democracies, even as leader judgments themselves were more detached from party feeling.[17] There is no evidence, however, to suggest that Canadian leaders have become more important since the 1960s. Indeed the burden of evidence suggests the opposite.[18] That leader factors weigh more heavily for big parties is strongly hinted.[19]

On the personality content of leader judgments, very little has been said. Early studies focused on open-ended responses about leaders and reached contradictory conclusions about the relative power of issue and personality.[20] The earliest direct examination of voters' perceptions of leaders' personalities did not connect those factors to the vote.[21] When the connection was finally made, it was indirect.[22]

Estimates of net impact are of the most recent vintage, so tell us nothing about the years before 1988. Johnston and his colleagues presented net estimates, but their accounting was for change over the campaign, not for election day.[23] Only with the 1997 election do we get an accounting for leaders' net impact on the outcome.[24] But for neither election is there an accounting for the net effect of personality factors in particular.

---

[17] Brian Graetz and Ian McAllister, "Popular Evaluations of Party Leaders in the Anglo-American Democracies," in Harold D. Clarke and Moshe M. Czudnowski, eds., *Political Elites in Anglo-American Democracies* (DeKalb, Ill.: Northern Illinois University Press, 1987). The impact that Graetz and McAllister estimate for Canada is only slightly greater than that for Great Britain. My characterization of their finding is based on a calculation of combined direct and indirect effects in their Figure 1, p. 56. Graetz and McAllister analyzed data from 1979, when Pierre Trudeau led the Liberal Party, so they may have caught a year of especially powerful impact. That year does appear as a local maximum for leader impact on Liberal voting in Elisabeth Gidengil, André Blais, Richard Nadeau, and Neil Nevitte, "Are Party Leaders Becoming More Important to Vote Choice in Canada?" (paper presented to the Annual Meeting of the American Political Science Association, Washington, D.C., 2000).

[18] Gidengil *et al.*, "Party Leaders."

[19] Clarke *et al.*, *Absent Mandate*, say this much. Gidengil *et al.*, "Party Leaders," find that leaders are generally more important for Liberal and Conservative voting than for the NDP and that the impact of Conservative leaders shrank as the party did.

[20] Clarke *et al.*, *Absent Mandate*, emphasized the issue content, but Graetz and McAllister, "Popular Evaluations," looking at much the same data, were more impressed by the personal content.

[21] Steven D. Brown, Ronald D. Lambert, Barry J. Kay, and James E. Curtis, "In the Eye of the Beholder: Leader Images in Canada," *Canadian Journal of Political Science*, 21 (1988), 729–55.

[22] Johnston *et al.*, *Letting the People Decide*, chap. 6. Johnston and his colleagues relate overall leader assessment, indicated by "feeling thermometer" scores, to perceptions of competence and character. But their vote estimations employ leader thermometers, which also incorporate nonpersonality factors, so the impact of personality factors in particular is not assessed.

[23] Johnston *et al.*, *Letting the People Decide*.

[24] Neil Nevitte, André Blais, Elisabeth Gidengil, and Richard Nadeau, *Unsteady State: The 1997 Canadian Federal Election* (Toronto: Oxford University Press, 2000).

How Leaders Matter

Leaders as Embodied Preferences

The theoretical case in the preceding section may be compelling, but are its arguments really about leaders' personalities? At best, the case is about leader factors in general and not about personality in particular. In fact, the narrative that lies behind those arguments turns mainly on nonpersonality factors, to "indirect" effects in this book's nomenclature. At the most general level, the leader's very identity is a sociodemographic and regional signal, an embodiment of policy orientation. Party elites know this and commonly try to choose leaders accordingly.

One recurring issue is the prospective leader's province of residence. This can show up in any of three ways.

(1) The party may draw a larger vote from the leader's home province than it would otherwise. Evidence for a short-run "favorite-son" effect is most compelling for Quebec, so this just reinforces the Quebec-as-pivot logic identified in the previous section.[25]

(2) Choice of leader may signal, indeed may entrain, commitment to a hitherto neglected province or region. The three outstanding examples are Laurier, whose selection began the process of winning Quebec for the Liberals, John Diefenbaker, who gave the Conservatives credibility in the West, and Brian Mulroney, who reversed Laurier's handiwork. This is not quite the same as a favorite-son effect. Diefenbaker's westward reorientation of the Conservative vote, for instance, required several elections and manifested itself mainly as the party declined elsewhere. Even if Mulroney's long-run impact was mainly to weaken his party everywhere, the post-1993 Conservatives retained some credibility in Quebec and that credibility was the closest thing the party had to a trump card. On the same logic, Laurier's legacy to the Liberals was not simply blown away by Mulroney.

(3) This last point reflects the fact that since Laurier's accession in 1887 the Liberal Party has perfectly exemplified a third way in which the leader's background matters. All this time, the Liberals have alternated French and English leaders. Even if Quebec voters were more enthusiastic about French than about English leaders, they recognized that the Liberal Party took their province seriously, seriously enough to give a province with 25 percent of Canada's population 50 percent of the party's leaders.[26] Since

[25] Richard Nadeau and André Blais, "Explaining Election Outcomes in Canada," *Canadian Journal of Political Science*, 26 (1993), 775–90.

[26] The party has never made alternation a formal constitutional requirement, and many convention delegates do not affirm it as a value. But critically placed elites clearly do value alternation and have acted to enforce it. If it was the non-Quebec turn, no francophone Quebecker would run. If it was the Quebec-French turn, only one would come forward and the party elite would rally around him. The current leader and prime minister, Jean Chrétien, broke the rule by

1983, the Conservatives have also succeeded in alternation, although not to much good effect.

Only recently have parties considered other representative criteria than province and language. Since 1989, gender has clearly been in play. The New Democratic Party has had only female leaders since that year, first with the selection of Audrey McLaughlin, then of Alexa McDonough. Most spectacular, however, was Kim Campbell, Conservative leader and briefly prime minister in 1993. So the 1993 election featured two female leaders, and they clearly redirected the bases of the vote, even if neither was, on balance, a success.[27]

What this all adds up to is the necessity of including statistical controls for the group and policy bases of the party system. Such controls are required, of course, to remove what we can of partisanship by another name. But we also must try to cover particular affinities or aversions between leaders and groups. Accordingly, in all estimations below are included party identification (dummy variables for each party), age, union membership, religious identification (dummy variables for Catholics and non-religious), ethnicity (five dummy variables), gender, and two issue variables, the major economic issue for the year,[28] and the Quebec/French Canada indicator appropriate to the party.[29]

Leaders as Personalities

A further implication is that personality factors should be represented as directly as possible, given that general indicators of the esteem in which a leader is held are likely to include much that has nothing to do with personality. Fortunately, notwithstanding the diversity of measures and starting points, studies of personality factors seem broadly convergent. Personality considerations seem to fall into two domains: *character*, the leader's integrity and empathy; and *competence*, the leader's intellectual and inspirational attributes.

running to succeed Pierre Trudeau in 1984. Senior Quebec party members opposed his candidacy and it failed. (The fact that this forced the party to choose an English leader over a French one did not help the optics of the 1984 election, when the Conservative leader was a Quebecker, Brian Mulroney.) Alternation continued with Chrétien's ultimate selection in 1990.

[27] Elisabeth Gidengil and Joanna Everitt, "Gender, Media Coverage and the Dynamics of Leader Evaluations: The Case of the 1993 Election," in Henry E. Brady and Richard Johnston, eds., *Capturing Campaign Effects* (Ann Arbor: University of Michigan Press, forthcoming); Brenda O'Neill, "The Relevance of Leader Gender to Voting in the 1993 Canadian National Election," *International Journal of Canadian Studies*, 17 (1998), 105–30.

[28] For 1988, relations between Canada and the United States; for 1993, support/opposition to the welfare state; and for 1997, willingness to be taxed. For more detail on measurement, see the Appendix.

[29] For every party except the Bloc, the measure taps how much the respondent is willing to do for French Canada/Quebec (varies by year). For the Bloc, the indicator is support for a sovereign Quebec. For more detail, see the Appendix to this chapter.

Whether each domain needs to be broken down further is a matter for dispute. What does seem clear is that each is best kept separate from the other. In the earliest work, integrity and empathy seemed statistically indistinguishable, in contrast to competence (mainly intellectual traits) and leadership (mainly inspirational ones), which did deserve to be distinguished.[30] Some analysts simply leave their trait list disaggregated.[31] The two-factor—"competence" and "character"—representation does seem to be gaining ground, however. It now seems to be the industry standard for Canada,[32] and the Canadian treatment converges remarkably with recent work on the British electorate.[33] In point of fact, a general assessment of leaders/candidates runs through all of the traits.[34] Distinctions in the domain rest as much on the face content of the trait items as on psychometric considerations. Also, as will be evident in a moment, average ratings of leaders are not systematically high or low for all traits for a given leader, as respondents clearly distinguish competence from character. In this chapter's analysis, additionally, a practical consideration forces us to keep the number of elements in play down to two. Trait lists are not identical from year to year, and the best way to keep track is to pool items into the two broad dimensions.

Figure 6.1 arrays leaders on the two dimensions for the 1988, 1993, and 1997 elections. The progression from top to bottom—three parties becoming five—reflects the fragmentation of the system that began in 1993. Each leader's score on each dimension appears as a deviation from the "grand mean" on that dimension across all that year's leaders.[35] Some leaders clearly stand out from the others, and one leader, Brian Mulroney, presents a sharply contradictory face.

- In 1988, Liberal leader John Turner and the NDP's Ed Broadbent anchored the extremes. Turner's special problem was widespread doubts about his competence, although he also had a character problem. Ed Broadbent was especially appealing for his character. The contradictory case was Brian Mulroney, seen as clearly a competent Conservative leader

[30] Donald R. Kinder, "Presidential Character Revisited," in Richard R. Lau and David O. Sears, eds., *Political Cognition* (Hillsdale, N.J.: Erlbaum, 1986).

[31] Notably Warren E. Miller and J. Merrill Shanks, *The New American Voter* (Cambridge, Mass.: Harvard University Press, 1996), who use the NES list first described in Kinder, "Presidential Character," and Clive Bean and Anthony Mughan, "Leadership Effects in Parliamentary Elections in Australia and Britain," *American Political Science Review*, 83 (1989), 1165–79, whose independently derived list strikingly resembles the U.S. one.

[32] Johnston *et al.*, *Letting the People Decide*, chap. 6.

[33] Marianne C. Stewart and Harold D. Clarke, "The (Un)importance of Party Leaders: Leader Images and Party Choice in the 1987 British Election," *Journal of Politics*, 54 (1992), 447–70.

[34] See, for instance, Kinder, "Presidential Character," Table 10.3, and Stewart and Clarke, "Party Leaders," Table 2. In each year presented below for Canada, trait items administered in a given year were subjected to exploratory factor analysis and all items for each leader loaded on the first component and, almost without exception, only on that factor.

[35] For more detail on index construction, see the Appendix.

but wanting in character. Not surprisingly, given these problems, the Liberal and Conservative campaigns worked hard at trying to reinforce perceptions of the other party's leader and to modify perceptions of their own. I return to this matter below.

• In 1993, three of five leaders drew remarkably similar assessments. The two who stood out did so only on competence. NDP leader Audrey McLaughlin

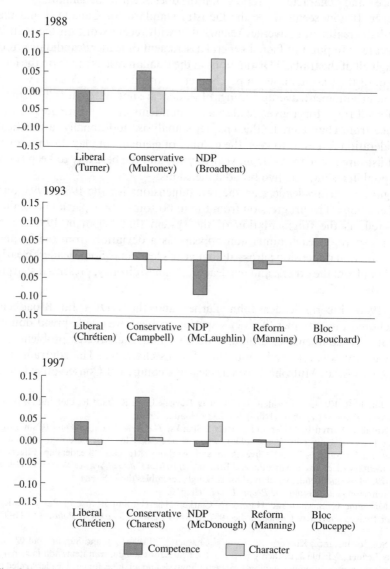

Fig. 6.1 The relative merits of Canadian leaders, 1988, 1993, and 1997

Note: Entry is each leader's mean rating relative to the mean rating of all leaders on the trait.

was perceived as little endowed with the stuff of leadership. Bloc Québécois leader Lucien Bouchard, in contrast, enjoyed remarkable credibility.[36]
• In 1997, the extremes were two new leaders, the Conservatives' Jean Charest and the Bloc's Gilles Duceppe. Again, the dimension that stands out is competence.

The ground for marked personality effects already seems weak. Of the thirteen leaders, six hardly seem to stand out (three in each of 1993 and 1997). Of the seven who do stand out, five are leaders of parties with no realistic chance of forming the government. Ed Broadbent (NDP, 1988) was poised to help get his party close to official opposition status, however. The same could be said of Lucien Bouchard (Bloc, 1993) and the opposite of Gilles Duceppe (Bloc, 1997). Audrey McLaughlin (NDP, 1993) could not help her party when it most needed it. Jean Charest (Conservative, 1997) *could* help his party in an hour of need. This leaves two cases of potential prime ministers, both in 1988: John Turner, who could only hurt his Liberals, and Brian Mulroney, who could have either effect, depending on which, if any, facet of his personality was primed.

Impact I: Individual Differences

The first step in gauging impact is to estimate how leader perceptions move individual votes. Table 6.1 presents coefficients of impact by leader, trait, and year. The impact of competence and character, then, is assessed against the background of the system's sociodemographic base and current issues. Estimation is by Ordinary Least Squares (OLS) regression.[37]

The first thing to emerge is that character counts more than competence. Averaged across all leaders and years, the impact of character judgments (0.23) is about half again larger than that of competence perceptions (0.15). Some of this may reflect the peculiar circumstances of 1988, when two leaders had clear character problems and in which the trustworthiness of one, Brian Mulroney, was particularly at issue in voters' coming to judgment on that election's huge

---

[36] In both 1993 and 1997, Reform leaders were not assessed by Quebec respondents and Bloc leaders were assessed only by Quebeckers. Neither party ran candidates where the other did, and so assessments of the other leader were simply irrelevant. Thus comparisons between Bloc and Reform leaders are never made, and comparison between either leader and Liberal, Conservative, and NDP leaders requires special attention to arithmetic.

[37] Strictly speaking, OLS is inappropriate where the dependent variable is dichotomous. I employ it because of the transparent interpretability of the coefficients. Estimation by logit yields the same pattern across all years and leaders as far as statistical significance is concerned. The logits suggest that some of the variation in OLS coefficient magnitudes is an artifact of distributions on the dependent variable. NDP OLS coefficients, in particular, are biased toward zero because of the party's relatively small size in the 1990s. This bias is in accord with this book's emphasis on factual impact, supplemented by historically specific counterfactuals. In net-effect analyses below, where control variables and baselines are set at historically realistic values, grinding leader differences through OLS coefficients and then through logit ones yields roughly the same counterfactual outcomes.

Table 6.1. The impact of Canadian leaders' perceived traits, 1988, 1993, and 1997

Year/ Party leader	Competence		Character		
	β	s.e.(β)	β	s.e.(β)	(N)
1988					
Liberal	0.157	0.060**	0.229	0.059***	(1,876)
Conservative	0.048	0.052	0.307	0.047***	(1,872)
NDP	0.122	0.060*	0.179	0.057**	(1,877)
1993					
Liberal	0.231	0.042***	0.238	0.043***	(2,585)
Conservative	0.112	0.032***	0.175	0.038***	(2,586)
NDP	0.037	0.029	0.074	0.028**	(2,589)
Reform	0.355	0.052***	0.507	0.057***	(1,914)
Bloc	0.041	0.081	0.364	0.084***	(544)
1997					
Liberal	0.231	0.037***	0.256	0.038***	(2,160)
Conservative	0.201	0.039***	0.013	0.061	(2,082)
NDP	0.163	0.041***	0.186	0.042***	(2,036)
Reform	0.152	0.038***	0.397	0.042***	(1,550)
Bloc	0.044	0.060	0.075	0.074	(532)

*$p < 0.05$; **$p < 0.01$; ***$p < 0.001$.
Note: Estimation by OLS. Coefficients extracted from comprehensive model. For details see text.

central issue, commercial union between Canada and the United States.[38] The difference is also quite marked in 1993, however. Only in 1997 do the two kinds of assessment carry roughly equal weight; it may be significant that leader traits carry the least weight overall this year. It seems premature to construct a generalization out of this finding.[39]

Both conditioning factors clearly operate. The bigger a party, the greater the impact of its leader's personality. And the election that brought the most change, the 1993 event, also featured the sharpest leader effects. These two patterns work somewhat at odds, however, as 1993 left all parties but the Liberals distant from power. Thus, the overall relationship between party size and personality impact is weak.[40] Partly this reflects the large Bloc and Reform coefficients for 1993. The decline of both coefficients in 1997 seems to validate both conditions. The 1997 election largely replicated the 1993 one, which reminds us that it was not the 1990s in general but the 1993 election in particular that brought great change. So by 1997 the electoral pattern was clear once again, and the special impact of Bloc and Reform leadership receded. And what 1993 brought was fragmentation of the party system, leaving only the Liberal Party

[38] For more on this intersection of leader and issue judgments, see Johnston *et al.*, *Letting the People Decide*, and below.

[39] Miller and Shanks, *New American Voter*, also find this pattern, but the same cannot be said for Bean and Mughan, "Leadership Effects." Stewart and Clarke, "Party Leaders," just find weak effects all round.

[40] Across the thirteen estimations the correlation between party size, whether indicated by vote share or by seat share, and average leader trait coefficient is 0.36. It has already been noted, however, that some of this may be an artifact, a floor effect.

with realistic access to power. The shift should make leader considerations *less* relevant than ever. It is tempting, then, to read 1997 as paradigmatic, the true indication of the new order of things. The 1993 election stands out as the moment of flux, when leadership is peculiarly salient.

Impact II: Net Effects

Table 6.1 describes hypothetical effects, the difference in the probability of choosing a party made by a shift of one unit on the scale of personality perception. As coded, a unit shift means going all the way from one perceptual extreme to the other, from saying that the word or phrase does not fit the leader at all to saying that it fits very well. For the comparison of two randomly selected individuals for a given year, the coefficient exaggerates likely differences. More critical still is the very fact that individuals actually do differ between themselves. The ultimate question is: What is the *net* effect of variation once offsetting differences between individuals are canceled? The answer to this question involves taking the evidence from Figure 6.1, which shows the balance of perception by leader and trait dimension, and grinding it through the machinery of Table 6.1. The result is Figure 6.2, which shows for each leader and year, the net effect of each trait dimension and the combined effect of the two.[41] The exercise implicit in the figure is to compare each actual leader to a notional one whose ratings are at the sample mean.

Such effects stand out most clearly for 1988. The Liberal and Conservative parties both suffered for their leadership and the NDP benefited. In each case, the effect was in the neighborhood of two percentage points.[42] Now consider what happens when we take one leader and substitute another leader for him. If we replace either Turner or Mulroney with the NDP's Ed Broadbent, we predict a net gain for the Liberals or Conservatives, respectively, of nearly 4 points.[43] The political significance of a 2–4 point shift depends on context. The most intriguing exercise is to imagine Broadbent moving into the Liberal leadership. This would move the Liberals up from 32 percent to 36 percent of the popular vote. If this came entirely at the expense of the Conservatives, the latter party's share would drop from 43 to 39 percent, right on the brink of losing its parliamentary majority.[44] Given the stakes in 1988, a Conservative

---

[41] This exercise is closely akin to that in Bean and Mughan, "Leadership Effects." Below, I walk through thought experiments explicitly modeled on theirs. Conceptually, where Table 6.1 describes "hypothetical" effects, Figure 6.2 presents "level" effects. The distinction is described with special lucidity in Christopher H. Achen, *Interpreting and Using Regression* (Thousand Oaks, Calif.: Sage, 1982).

[42] This is roughly the impact found by Bean and Mughan, "Leadership Effects."

[43] Again, this is very close to the value that Bean and Mughan calculate for the Hawke–Howard comparison.

[44] These Liberal and Conservative shares, given the seat–vote relationship then in force, would give the Conservatives slightly over 50 percent of seats in the House. See Johnston *et al.*, *Letting the People Decide*, Figure 1-1.

Johnston

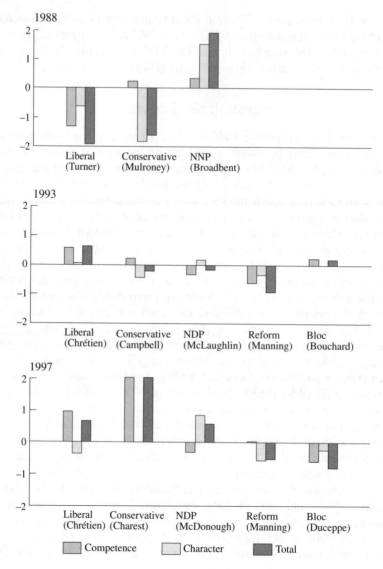

Fig. 6.2 Net impact of Canadian leader traits, 1988, 1993, and 1997

Note: Impact in percentage points of vote.

minority government would have fallen quickly and the Canada/U.S. Free Trade Agreement, precursor to NAFTA, would not have been implemented. But this is a generous estimate of the leader effect and it presupposes a straight exchange of votes between the Liberals and the Conservatives. To the extent that Liberal gains came at the NDP's expense, the impact on the Conservative seat share would be nullified.

For no other year are net effects remotely comparable. Especially weak is the pattern for 1993. The strongest indication is that Jean Chrétien helped his Liberals, but only by a tiny amount. They were likely to win a comfortable majority anyway. Preston Manning may have hindered his party's rise, but that rise was still spectacular without Manning's personal help. Had they won the additional percentage he seems to have cost them, they might have harvested a few more seats and so nudged the Bloc Québécois aside as the official opposition. The critical thing about 1993, indicated by Figure 6.1, is that few leaders stood out and those who did had very little net effect on their party's fortunes.

The 1997 pattern basically offers more of the same. The Conservative and Bloc leaders were more clearly polarized than any leaders had been in 1993. Their respective positions did seem to tell for their parties. The modest negative impact of Gilles Duceppe on his Bloc may have contributed to that party's reverse and consequent loss of official opposition status. Also contributing to that reverse was the Conservative Party's modest recovery, an important fraction of which came in Quebec. And Jean Charest materially contributed to that recovery. Figure 6.2 suggests that the Conservatives would have won 2 percent less of the vote had Charest not stood out from the pack. The party's total gain over 1993 was 3 points.[45]

For all that these estimates rest on inescapably shaky measures and specifications, they are probably about right. On the matter of specification, I could have elaborated each year's equation further, and doing so would probably have reduced the *ceteris paribus* effect imputed to leaders' personalities. I chose not to do so to maximize comparability across years. Offsetting this underspecification is the fact that personality perceptions are measured with considerable error, which should reduce the estimate of their effect.[46] Taking this all together, the estimates in Table 6.1 ought to be in the ballpark.

In the grand scheme of things, those estimates imply that personality is *not* the mainspring of Canadian electoral choice, but is a factor at the margin. Where margins are close, personality is worth dwelling on. In 1993 and 1997, the closest margins did not involve the formation of the government but of the opposition. In the short run, who forms the opposition may be relatively inconsequential, but it can matter greatly for the long run. In 1988, there is a hint that a stronger Liberal leader might have placed the Conservative majority in doubt, but he would have to have been much, much stronger. Over much of Canada's electoral history, the gap between the popular vote shares of the two front-running parties has been too great for the modest permutations implied in Figure 6.2 to matter.

[45] This is almost exactly the estimate in Nevitte *et al.*, *Unsteady State*.

[46] In a multivariate setup, measurement error does not automatically reduce the value of each individual coefficient. Even a badly measured variable, if it is better measured than the others, can absorb effect that does not properly belong to it. My sense, however, is that, of all the variables in the estimations, the personality measures are the weakest.

Campaign Dynamics of Leader Perceptions

Yet leadership seems to be a major focus of campaigns in Canada. This was clear in the first campaign study in 1988, and that year does not seem unique.[47] One reason may be that personality perceptions, though modest in their net effect are still more manipulable than other factors. The general presumption is that campaigns rarely persuade voters on substantive matters of policy. The best they can do is prime certain issues at the expense of others.[48] Perceptions of leaders, especially if the leader is new on the scene, may be more labile.

Figure 6.3 suggests that perceptual movement is possible, at least for some leaders some of the time.[49] For simplicity's sake, leader perceptions are presented summarily, as mean values on a 100-point scale, modeled on the U.S. NES "feeling thermometer." I declined to use the thermometer in earlier analyses because it carries too much nonpersonality freight. Even with party identification and the like controlled, it is still infused with the party, group, and policy judgments that are not this volume's central concern. But its dynamic variation over the campaign does depend heavily on the person of the leader.[50] And in each election one leader seems to stand out as figure against ground.

In 1988, that person was John Turner. If at the start his ratings relative to the others were desperately poor,[51] with three weeks to go he drew even with both rivals. He did fall back, but at the end he was closer to his rivals than to his own starting point. For 1993, the striking figure was Conservative leader Kim Campbell. She stood much the highest at the start, but with five weeks to go she swiftly lost ground, then slid still more. Her chief rival, Jean Chrétien, gained ground slowly, with a total gain almost as large as her total drop. In 1997, the clearest movement involved Campbell's successor, Jean Charest. He began with ratings close to those for Jean Chrétien, but pulled away steadily. This evidence suggests that a campaign focus on leadership, by analysts or by party strategists, is not misplaced.

[47] For 1988, see Johnston *et al.*, *Letting the People Decide*, especially chap. 6.

[48] But see the discussion in the next section.

[49] Tracking in Figures 6.3 and 6.4 exploits the fact that the day of interview in recent Canadian Election Studies is itself a random event, just as is initial selection to the sample. Thus, days can be compared graphically without controls for respondents' accessibility. Because daily samples are small, the data must be smoothed and the sampling variance burned off, as it were. Smoothing in these figures is accomplished by "loess" (locally-weighted least squares). See William S. Cleveland, *The Elements of Graphing Data*, 2nd edn. (Summit, N.J.: Hobart, 1994), for an accessible introduction to the technique.

[50] Johnston *et al.*, *Letting the People Decide*, chap. 6.

[51] That Brian Mulroney, clearly less highly regarded as a person than Ed Broadbent, enjoyed a thermometer rating to match Broadbent's testifies to the infusion of these ratings with non-personality covariance. Mulroney benefited from association with a party that was much more popular than the NDP.

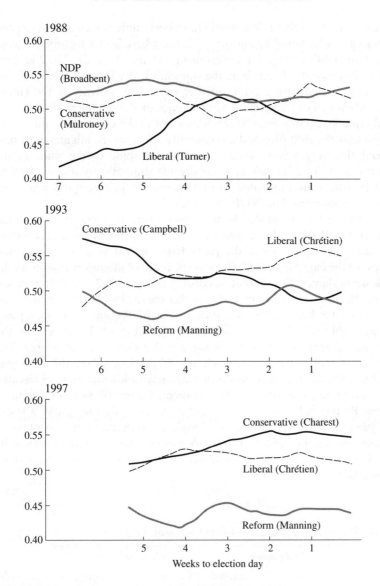

Fig. 6.3 Impact of the campaign, Canada, 1988, 1993, and 1997
Note: Daily mean ratings smoothed by loess (bandwidth = 0.3 for 1988, 1993; 0.5 for 1997).

But it is important to keep this movement in context. In two of three instances, 1988 and 1993, the net effect of the campaign was to *reduce* the net election-day effect of leader factors. Only in 1997 did the campaign magnify differences, but as Figure 6.2 indicated, this was a sideshow. The 1988 reduction is particularly striking. Had the pattern of the early campaign been that of election day, the Liberal loss would have been more severe than suggested by Figure 6.2. This could be another instance where leader factors mattered more for opposition than for government. At the start, the NDP seemed poised to displace the Liberals as the opposition. By the end, although the NDP was endowed with a rather greater numerical presence in the House than it had ever enjoyed before, it was still back on the sidelines. This is to say not only that leadership became less important at the end than at the beginning, but that the shift also had a conserving effect on the alignment of parties. And this very fact probably accounts for some of the shift, as the reevaluation of John Turner proceeded most dramatically among Liberal identifiers, who were motivated to find reasons to like him and who were much more numerous than NDP identifiers.[52]

The story for 1993 is subtler. Kim Campbell was the focus of much of the campaign. On the eve of the campaign, she was seen as the Conservative trump card, poised to rescue the party from several years of dismal poll readings. In the campaign itself, she was the focus of attention, mainly as she went down in flames. For all that, according to Figure 6.2, the difference she made on election day was small. Does this mean that she never mattered much, even when her personal standing was high? The answer is no, a point made by Table 6.2. Table 6.2 replicates the setup of Table 6.1 for the Conservatives, this time for vote intention rather than the vote proper. The estimation is replicated for three phases of the campaign, the days just before her collapse, the three weeks immediately following, and the last two weeks. Before and just after the key moment, Campbell was as relevant as Chrétien. By the end, however, now that it was clear that her party was out of the running and that she was no longer a prime ministerial contender, judgments on her no longer seemed to matter. Note that the coefficients for the last campaign phase in Table 6.2 below resemble those for the post-election estimation in Table 6.1.

Table 6.2. The declining relevance of Kim Campbell, 1993

	Competence		Character		
	β	s.e.(β)	β	s.e.(β)	(N)
10–20 Sept.	0.257	0.072***	0.265	0.086**	(669)
21 Sept.–13 Oct.	0.111	0.045*	0.344	0.054***	(1,579)
14–24 Oct.	0.165	0.057**	0.151	0.065*	(813)

*$p < 0.05$; **$p < 0.01$; ***$p < 0.001$.
Note: Estimation by OLS. Coefficients extracted from comprehensive model. For details, see text.

[52] Johnston *et al.*, *Letting the People Decide*, chaps. 6 and 8.

A Caution: Leaders and Issues

Buried in the 1988 data is a special kind of indirect effect, which leads us to understate one way in which personality perception was important to that election. Its key issue, as mentioned, was a proposal for commercial union between Canada and the United States. Canadians historically recoiled from such proposals, with business and labor united in opposition and all dealings with the United States vulnerable to being styled as threats to Canada's historic British connection. By 1988, however, the British connection was just that, historic, and the business community now supported closer ties with the United States. But the agreement that embodied the commercial union was complex, hardly transparent in its overall implications. One potentially effective way to drive a wedge between the broad middle of voters and the agreement was to discredit the deal by association with the man ultimately responsible for striking it, Prime Minister Brian Mulroney. The potential for damage is indicated in Figure 6.1, where Mulroney's character problem is one of the key features. Especially prominent on the character scale was the word "trustworthy," Mulroney's weak suit. Opponents of the trade agreement routinely referred to it as the "Mulroney Trade Deal," and deluged voters with advertisements claiming that the Mulroney ("Lyin' Brian") style was to say one thing and mean another. To the extent that this campaign was effective, judgments on the prime minister might also be built into judgments on the agreement, a key direct factor in the vote.

Figure 6.4 shows that this was so, by showing the campaign time path of support for the agreement, conditional on an experimental randomization. The survey question asks about support or opposition to "the Free Trade Agreement reached . . . with the United States [the previous] October." The key experimental variable was the identity of the negotiator, of exactly who had reached the agreement with the United States. Half the sample was asked about an agreement reached between *Canada* and the United States. The other half was asked about an agreement reached by the *Mulroney government*. Otherwise, all that distinguished these groups was a random number. Only respondents who did not identify with the Conservative Party are included in Figure 6.4.

What the figure reveals is that over the first half of the campaign, the identity of the negotiator was absolutely critical. Until early in the middle week, respondents in the "Canada" condition were roughly 10 points more likely than respondents in the "Mulroney" condition to support the agreement. Clearly this consideration was not the only one at work, as support was slipping in both groups all through the period in which the experiment exerted its greatest effect. And what does its effect mean? Obviously, that so modest an induction can make such a difference to support for so consequential a document indicates the correctness of its opponents' tactical insight. But it also indicates that that insight was not fully realized until later in the campaign. It still mattered whether or not our survey supplied the consideration, a

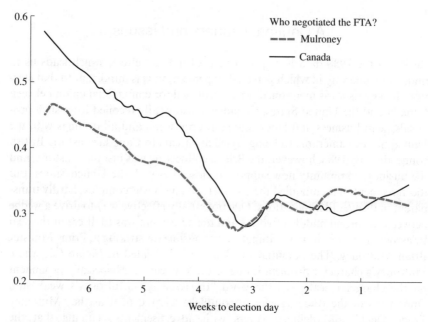

Fig. 6.4 Leadership and issue judgment: support for the Free Trade Agreement, 1988
Note: Daily mean ratings smoothed by loess (bandwidth = 0.3).

reminder of the prime minister's role. If the anti-Mulroney campaign really had moved voters, they would have internalized this consideration, and our giving or witholding it would not have mattered. The middle week supplied the missing link, saw the opposition point driven home, notably in the English-language leaders' debate. (This debate is also reflected in judgments on John Turner; see Figure 6.3.) At this point, the "Canada" line collapsed into the "Mulroney" one. The campaign was now supplying the consideration; it no longer mattered that we continued to withhold it from the "Canada" group. Thereafter, the treatments made no difference, but support slipped no further, indeed recovered slightly.

In the end, the prime minister's character vulnerability was not fatal, not to the agreement, not to his reelection. But it did put both projects at risk, and salvaging the position required a vigorous counterattack. Some of the recovery involved arguments on the merit of the agreement. But a recurring theme of Conservative stump speeches and advertisements in the late campaign was a mirror image of the Liberal attacks that nearly brought the agreement and the Tories down. The Conservative assault has been called the "Bombing the Bridges" campaign, to smash John Turner's credibility as an interpreter of the agreement and so disable the overall critique.[53]

[53] Graham Fraser, *Playing for Keeps: The Making of the Prime Minister, 1988* (Toronto: McClelland and Stewart, 1989), chap. 12, especially pp. 321–2.

More generally, the 1988 campaign alerts us to a role for personality that is no less important for being rare. When a novel but complex issue arises, voters look to the political class for cues. Politicians they dislike can be as critical as ones they basically like.[54] Personal characteristics may be especially telling when a political figure tries to convert credibility into support for a position at odds with the party's traditional commitments. This Mulroney was doing, for his party had been the traditional opponent, in the name of the British connection, of closer relations between Canada and the United States. And the agreement between Canada and the United States typifies the most wrenching question of our time, continental or global economic integration. It was the precursor for NAFTA, of course. And the election, although not formally a referendum, was referendum-like. As such it resembles questions raised by the consolidation of the European Union, notably the common currency. The credibility of the individuals making the cases for and against could be critical. Where, we should ask, do those judgments of credibility originate?

Conclusions and Some Speculation

Canadian voters do take leaders' personalities into account when coming to electoral decisions. Leaders' perceived competence for the job, a compound of leadership and intelligence, and their character, combining integrity and empathy, affect vote choice, at least at the margin. Voters seem able to distinguish the competence and character dimensions, at least in the sense that a leader who is above average on one dimension can be below average on the other. In the elections studied here, character seemed to be the more important consideration. Other things being equal, both considerations were more important the closer the party was to forming the government. Personality considerations also seem telling if the party has just burst on the scene, such that there are few other bases for judging the party. These two sentences are somewhat offsetting, as new parties are rarely close to forming the government. It is striking that, for the two new parties on the Canadian scene, leader factors were more important in the year of breakthrough, 1993, than in the year of consolidation, 1997.

All of the foregoing applies to individual differences, to the electorate in cross-section. Most of the variation across individuals is offsetting, even when the major sources of individual difference—partisan affiliation, sociodemographic group membership, and region—are controlled. Net effects, the translation of the electorate-wide balance of judgment on a leader into systematic advantage or disadvantage for his or her party, are much smaller.

[54] Arthur Lupia, "Busy Voters, Agenda Control, and the Power of Information," *American Political Science Review*, 86 (1992), 390–404.

At their maximum, in 1988 when contrasts among leaders were sharp, the impact of leadership was on the scale observed elsewhere.[55] But not even the hard-fought 1988 election was all that close.

This chapter documents an instance where character mattered in a manner that was no less remarkable for being indirect. Judgment on the major issue of 1988, commercial union between Canada and the United States, was affected by Prime Minister Brian Mulroney's reputation as untrustworthy. To this extent, focusing on his perceived character, holding voters' positions on that issue constant, understates his importance. His unasked-for role in voters' judgments on a new but profoundly important issue exemplifies a general process in electoral politics, the use of salient politicians as cue-givers by voters in coming to judgment on policy. But asking voters to judge policy directly is the very definition of a referendum. The 1988 election was, in fact, more like a referendum than any other in Canadian history, apart from the 1891 and 1911 elections, also fought on commercial union between Canada and the United States, and the 1917 one, on conscription. At least in each of those cases, voters' own identification with or repulsion from the British Empire provided the pivotal cue. In 1988, the guideposts were fewer. It seems reasonable for voters to ask about both the character and the competence of both advocates and opponents of an important measure when so much is on the line. Most elections are simply not like this. Their issue content is more likely to be understood on partisan lines, and party should largely override personality.

At least it should for most Canadian elections. As this chapter was being written, Pierre Trudeau died. It seems likely that, had we the means, we would find that judgments on his personality counted for more than judgments on his successors. Indeed, there are indirect but strong indications of this on the published record.[56] But this is only to say that once there were "giants in the earth."

No longer: any remaining doubt that the giants have disappeared from Canadian politics was banished by the 2000 election. Three leaders—Chrétien for the Liberals, McDonough for the NDP, and Duceppe for the Bloc—were the same as in 1997. There is no reason to think than any of these stands out from the pack any more than in the earlier year. Jean Charest was replaced by Joe Clark, a former Tory leader and prime minister, and Clark probably stood out even less than Charest did. This leaves Stockwell Day, the new leader of a new/old party, the Alliance, lineal descendent of Reform. The Alliance was intended to facilitate a nationwide appeal, in particular to make it easy for Tory voters to abandon the ancestral party federally without seeming to support a party with another name.[57] And the new leader seemed to possess

[55] The closest parallel seems to be Bean and Mughan, "Leadership Effects," for Australia.

[56] See especially Gidengil *et al.*, "Party Leaders."

[57] The official name of the new entity, the Canadian Conservative and Reform Alliance, was constructively ambiguous. Several provincial Tories were conspicuously present at the creation.

considerable energy and panache, so the hope was that, on the general logic of personality perception, his appeal would transcend party. The Alliance did pull a larger share than Reform had, even as the Conservative share fell. But the Alliance gamble was also seen to fail, as the new party's seat gains were not commensurate with its vote gains. Alliance gains and Tory losses occurred in different provinces. The Alliance mainly consolidated its Western base, while the Conservatives retreated from Quebec, Jean Charest's province. In short, the dynamics have the wrong geography to be attributable to personality. Instead they carry implications about policy and sectional appeal. There does seem to be some suggestion that the stalling of the Reform advance was attributable to the Liberals' success in imposing a negative definition on Stockwell Day. But that definition seems to have been as much about policy, about Day's social conservatism in particular, as about his personality.[58]

Appendix

Personality Traits

The basic form of the leader trait battery is:

Now, we'd like to know about your impressions of the party leaders. I am going to read a list of words or phrases people use to describe political figures. After each one, I would like you to tell me how much the word or phrase fits your impressions . . . How much would you say [word or phrase] fits your impression of [leader]: A GREAT DEAL, SOMEWHAT, A LITTLE, or NOT AT ALL?

The table shows the traits that were investigated in each year. Each item was rescaled to the 0,1 range with positive values indicating greater desirability. The index is the simple sum of the item scores for the dimension, with the index value also rescaled to the 0,1 range.

Table 6.A.1. Personality traits investigated for Canada, 1988, 1993, and 1997

Dimension	1988	1993	1997
Competence			
	Intelligent	Intelligent	
	Knowledgeable		
	Provides strong leadership	. . . leadership	. . . leadership
	Man of vision		In touch with the times
Character			
	Trustworthy	Trustworthy	Trustworthy
	Moral		
	Compassionate	Compassionate	Compassionate
	Really cares about people	Arrogant	Arrogant

[58] Since the election, doubts about his personality have also surfaced, inside his party as well as outside. But we should be wary of reading postelection patterns back into the campaign.

Issue Measures

French Canada/Quebec, 1988, 1993, 1997:

Some people think that too much is being done [to promote the French language in Canada/for Quebec]. Others feel that not enough is being done [to promote French/for Quebec]. How much do you think should be done [to promote French/for Quebec]? MUCH MORE, SOMEWHAT MORE, ABOUT THE SAME AS NOW, SOMEWHAT LESS, MUCH LESS, or haven't you thought much about it?[59]

Sovereignty for Quebec:

Are you very favorable, somewhat favorable, somewhat opposed, or very opposed to Quebec sovereignty?

Canada/U.S. Relations (1988):

Some people believe that Canada should have closer ties with the United States. Others feel that Canada should distance itself from the United States. How about you? Do you think that Canada should be: MUCH CLOSER to the United States, SOMEWHAT CLOSER, ABOUT THE SAME AS NOW, SOMEWHAT MORE DISTANT, MUCH MORE DISTANT, or haven't you thought much about this?

Welfare State (1993), a five-item index:[60]

On the deficit, which comes closer to your own view?

> One: We must reduce the deficit even if that means cutting programmes.
> *or*
> Two: Governments must maintain programmes even if that means continuing to run a deficit.

If you had to, would you cut spending in the following areas A LOT, SOME, or NOT AT ALL.

> —Welfare?
> —Health Care?
> —Unemployment Insurance?

Which comes closer to your own view:

> One: If people had to pay a fee each time they go to [a doctor/a hospital] there would be less waste in the health care system.
> *or*
> Two: If people had to pay a fee, [low income/some] people would not be able to get the health care they need.

Taxes (1997):

We face tough choices. Cutting taxes means cutting social social programmes and improving social programmes means increasing taxes. if you had to choose, would

---

[59] "French" in 1988; randomization between "French" and "Quebec" in 1993; "Quebec" in 1997.

[60] For more detail on the index, see Richard Johnston, André Blais, Henry E. Brady, Elisabeth Gidengil, and Neil Nevitte, "The 1993 Canadian Election: Realignment, Dealignment, or Something Else?" (paper presented to the Annual Meeting of the American Political Science Association, San Francisco, 1996).

you cut taxes, increase taxes, or keep taxes as they are? [CUT A LOT, SOMEWHAT, OR A LITTLE?/INCREASED A LOT, SOMEWHAT, OR A LITTLE?]

Acknowledgments

This chapter was written with the support and indulgence of the Annenberg School for Communication, University of Pennsylvania, and its Dean, Kathleen Hall Jamieson, who knows a thing or two about leadership. The data for the chapter come from recent Canadian Election Studies, for two of which, 1988 and 1993, the author was principal investigator. Getting to this point would not have been possible without the help, counsel, and hard work of André Blais, co-investigator on the 1988 and 1993 studies and principal investigator on the 1997 one, and Henry Brady, Jean Crête, Elisabeth Gidengil, Richard Nadeau, and Neil Nevitte, co-investigators on various combinations of these studies. Anthony King's comments on an earlier draft materially improved the chapter. None of these individuals or institutions bears any responsibility for errors of style or interpretation.

7

The Leadership Factor in the Russian Presidential Election of 1996

TIMOTHY J. COLTON

Supplementing the club of established democracies with the Russian case fruitfully expands the scope of this book. As Anthony King observes in Chapter 1, and as specialists on the former Soviet Union tend to agree,[1] there are good reasons to suppose that electoral politics will be more leadership-driven in a democratizing or semi-democratic nation than in older democratic polities possessing entrenched party systems and coherent issue agendas. The Russian Federation's watershed election of June–July 1996, in which its founding president, Boris Yeltsin, staged a stirring comeback to defeat the neo-Communist opposition and earn a second term in office, offers an excellent opportunity to put this proposition to the test. As we shall see, perceptions of the personal characteristics of the presidential candidates did exert substantial effects on the choices of the Russian electorate in 1996. Thorough examination discloses them and the underlying dynamic of transitional politics to be highly complex. The leadership card in post-Communist elections should be neither overlooked nor overstated. Most of all, it should not be oversimplified.

The New Russia and the 1996 Election

The competitive elections instituted by Mikhail Gorbachev in the late 1980s as a rejuvenating tonic for the Soviet system were destined instead to be a poison pill, ushering in the destabilization and sudden collapse of the old regime. Loosening of the Kremlin leadership's grip on high office allowed its nemesis, Boris Yeltsin, to become a member of the Soviet parliament in 1989

---

[1] See, for example, Richard Sakwa, *Russian Politics and Society*, 2nd edn. (London: Routledge, 1996), p. 115; and Jerry F. Hough, "The Failure of Party Formation and the Future of Russian Democracy," in Timothy J. Colton and Jerry F. Hough, eds., *Growing Pains: Russian Democracy and the Election of 1993* (Washington, D.C.: Brookings Institution, 1998), p. 688.

and a member and then speaker of the Russian parliament in 1990. Yeltsin capitalized on the opening to attack Gorbachev, discredit the Communist Party of the Soviet Union, and air his ideas for radical political and economic reforms. On June 12, 1991, he won Russia's inaugural presidential election in a landslide. It was Yeltsin's presidential mandate that gave him the authority to stare down the hardline *putsch* of August 1991 and, before the year was out, to emerge from the crisis of Soviet power as undisputed head of the Russian successor state. The first national election in post-Soviet times, and the first Russian election since before 1917 to be fought by multiple political parties, was for seats in the two houses of parliament in December 1993.[2] A second parliamentary election, to the lower house (the State Duma) only, was held in December 1995. On both occasions, virulent critics of Yeltsin and his administration seized the high ground. The erratically nationalist LDPR (Liberal-Democratic Party of Russia) topped the polls in the party-list vote in 1993 and the KPRF (Communist Party of the Russian Federation) followed suit in 1995. NDR (Our Home Is Russia), the pro-Yeltsin bloc led by Prime Minister Viktor Chernomyrdin, had to settle for one-tenth of the party-list vote in the 1995 election.

The long-awaited presidential election scheduled for mid 1996 had a prelude uproarious even by the standards of a polity buffeted by regime change. The vicissitudes of half a decade of fitful economic reforms and of the guerrilla war in the North Caucasus republic of Chechnya, where civilian casualties mounted and tens of thousands of Russian troops had been bogged down since December 1994, had sapped the popularity of the president, plunging ratings of public confidence in him into the single digits. His physical and mental condition had deteriorated apace. As was now a routine occurrence, Yeltsin was in seclusion and under tight medical supervision for the bulk of the disastrous Duma campaign. The Duma results prompted him to conclude, rightly or wrongly, that no progressive politician except him had a chance to grab the presidential prize in 1996.[3] Nevertheless, Yeltsin delayed for months an irrevocable decision about his own participation and, as Russians eventually learned, about whether there would be an election at all. His official entry into the race, announced to fanfare in his home region of Sverdlovsk on February 15, did not dispel the uncertainty. The group of

---

[2] That election coincided with a referendum that ratified a draft constitution proposed by Yeltsin. The constitution contained the legal underpinnings of the new parliament. Without ratification, the election would have been moot. For analysis, see Colton and Hough, *Growing Pains*.

[3] Without doubt, Yeltsin's opinion about the unelectability of the two practical alternatives to him among pro-reform politicians—his prime minister, Viktor Chernomyrdin, and the leader of the Yabloko party, Grigorii Yavlinskii—was self-serving. He had no difficulty imposing his will on Chernomyrdin, who had little hope of prevailing in a presidential campaign unless he waged it as Yeltsin's designated heir or, better still, as acting president (as Vladimir Putin was to do in 2000). Yavlinskii could not be so easily deterred and wound up running and finishing fourth in 1996.

insiders installed at the helm of his reelection campaign, captained by First Deputy Prime Minister Oleg Soskovets and the chief of the Kremlin guard, Aleksandr Korzhakov, had no stomach for their assignment. Horrified at the prospect of losing out to the Communists, they lobbied for calling off the election, disbanding the Duma and the KPRF, and proclaiming a state of emergency. A panicky Yeltsin, as he confirms in the latest volume of his memoirs, had his aides pen decrees ordering a police crackdown and a two-year postponement of the vote. He relented and tore up the drafts only on March 23, 1996, less than three months in advance of election day. He was shamed into the retreat, he says, by his daughter Tatyana Dyachenko and her ally Anatolii Chubais, the architect of the privatization of Russian industry, whom he named to replaced Soskovets as his senior campaign manager.[4]

Once invested in the campaign, Yeltsin never looked back, although the political atmosphere continued to be edgy and he and his adversaries traded accusations of betraying Mother Russia and inciting civil strife. Yeltsin bested the field with 35.8 percent of the vote in the preliminary round of the election on June 16 and carried the two-candidate finale on July 3, with 54.4 percent. As anticipated, the biggest threat to the incumbent was Gennadii Zyuganov, the chairman of the central committee of the KPRF, who garnered 32.5 percent of the votes in the first round and 40.7 percent in the runoff. Three other candidates surpassed 5 percent in the first round— Aleksandr Lebed (14.7 percent), Grigorii Yavlinskii (7.5 percent), and Vladimir Zhirinovskii (5.8 percent)—while the five remaining aspirants, reminiscent of the fringe candidates and spoilers who find a niche in every U.S. presidential election, were confined to less than 1 percent each. Some 1.6 percent of the voters cast their ballots against all the candidates in the first lap, a permissible option under Russian law; 4.9 percent rejected both finalists in the second.[5]

Political parties, staples of the Russian scene since Gorbachev had legalized them at the start of the 1990s, were serious yet nowhere near dominating players in the election of 1996. Unlike the Duma, where the rules of the game staked out half of the seats for lists of candidates filed by parties and quasi-parties, in the presidential election independents and partisan nominees vied on an equal footing.[6] Three of the ten declared candidates—Yeltsin, Lebed,

---

[4] See Boris Yeltsin, *Prezidentskii marafon* (Moscow: ACT, 2000), pp. 22–33. The pretext for the decrees was going to be a Duma resolution passed on March 15. The Duma, with Communist deputies leading the way, condemned the Belovezhskaya Pushcha accord of December 1991 which dissolved the USSR and established the Commonwealth of Independent States. The tale of the struggle over the election was earlier told from the point of view of the advocates of cancellation in Aleksandr Korzhakov, *Boris Yeltsin: Ot rassveta do zakata* (Moscow: Interbuk, 1997), where there is reference to high-level meetings on a possible cancellation occurring in April.

[5] The percentages of the popular vote given here are of the valid votes cast, excluding spoiled ballots. Total valid ballots cast were 74,515,019 in the first round and 73,910,698 in the runoff.

[6] To be eligible, all candidates, whether partisan or independent, had to collect the signatures of one million citizens, drawn from at least fifteen units of the Russian Federation.

and Gorbachev, the deposed Soviet president—opted to run as independents. Yeltsin had the ardent endorsement of NDR and Lebed the blessing of KRO (the Congress of Russian Communities), whose ticket he had co-headed in 1995; neither wished to be captive to the narrow constituencies of those parties. Zyuganov of the KPRF, Yavlinskii of the liberal Yabloko movement, and Zhirinovskii of the LDPR wore the colors of parties that had run in the preceding year's parliamentary election and had hurdled the 5 percent threshold for entry into the Duma.[7] Four candidates, all of them to finish with less than 1 percent, represented esoteric parties and factions that had sat out the Duma election.[8]

It would not be outlandish to suggest that the personalities of the candidates loomed larger in the electoral calculations of Russians in 1996 than they would in a consolidated Western democracy. Arguably, the alternative beacons for guiding voter choice shone faintly at the time. The parties were of recent vintage and organizationally shaky; governmental institutions were in turmoil; the discourse of national politics was tentative and fluid; the very boundaries of the country were newly drawn and porous. The images projected by individual Russian politicians might be conjectured, by contrast, to have been more sharply etched and so more legible to ordinary people. One could further guess that such images would have resonated with cultural predispositions in a land ruled until 1917 by autocratic tsars and, for most of the twentieth century, by CPSU general secretaries who wrapped themselves in personality cults and to all intents and purposes wielded monarchical power.[9]

The cast of characters in the 1996 election presented an intriguing medley of human types. Yeltsin and Gorbachev were veterans of the hegemonic CPSU apparatus who had traveled dramatically different roads away from it during the *perestroika* period. Yeltsin, with his knack for rousing gestures and his legendary foibles—most blatantly a weakness for alcohol which had sparked embarrassing diplomatic incidents—was incomparably the more colorful of the two. But the fallen Gorbachev, the man who had halted the Cold War, was also a figure of historic stature. Zyuganov, formerly a CPSU propaganda specialist

---

[7] Strictly speaking, Zyuganov was nominated by an umbrella organization, the Bloc of Popular-Patriotic Forces of Russia, but the bloc was under KPRF control.

[8] An eleventh candidate, Aman-Geldy Tuleyev, the governor of a Siberian province, withdrew the week before the first round and received several hundred write-in votes.

[9] Robert C. Tucker, "Post-Soviet Leadership and Change," in Timothy J. Colton and Robert C. Tucker, eds., *Patterns in Post-Soviet Leadership* (Boulder, Colo.: Westview, 1995), p. 6. On personalized power and personality cults under tsarist and Soviet rule, see Michael Cherniavsky, *Tsar and People: Studies in Russian Myths* (New Haven, Conn.: Yale University Press, 1961); Robert C. Tucker, *The Soviet Political Mind: Stalinism and Post-Stalin Change* (New York: Norton, 1972); and Christel Lane, *The Rites of Rulers* (Cambridge: Cambridge University Press, 1981). The most durable personality cult in the USSR commemorated the first leader of the Soviet regime, Vladimir Lenin. "Every visitor to the Soviet Union," Lane wrote almost sixty years after Lenin's death, "is aware of the fact that the visual image and the words of Lenin accompany Soviet citizens from the cradle to the grave and that one cannot move about in public places without noticing the omnipresence of Lenin" (Lane, *The Rites of Rulers*, p. 210).

in Orël province and at party headquarters, epitomized the gray *apparatchik* who had kept faith with state socialism; he brandished a ponderous rhetorical manner to match. The most flamboyant of the presidential hopefuls was Zhirinovskii. A Moscow lawyer until he initiated the LDPR in 1990, Zhirinovskii ripened into a consummate publicity-hound and rabble-rouser, delighting in his own notoriety. Lebed was a professional military officer from the Soviet army's elite airborne branch who had retired from the service as a two-star general in 1995 to throw his hat in the political ring. He was most renowned for commanding the Russian Fourteenth Army in Moldova, the newly independent state wedged between Ukraine and Romania, where during the communal hostilities that erupted in 1992 he brokered a truce between Slavs and Romanian-speakers. Lebed's gruffness, masculine and soldierly bearing, and his combat record in Afghanistan and Moldova, chronicled in a best-selling autobiography,[10] endowed him with a distinctive profile. Yavlinskii, an economist by training (and, like Lebed, an amateur boxer in his youth), had come to the forefront in 1990 as one of the authors of the abortive 500 Days reform plan; since then he had been a parliamentarian and party organizer and a ubiquitous voice in the debates about the economy, human rights, and Chechnya. The other candidates, too, mostly sported unconventional biographies: Svyatoslav Fëdorov, a celebrated eye surgeon and the creator of a pioneering employee-owned health clinic; Yurii Vlasov, once a world-champion weightlifter and now a member of the Duma and mouthpiece for Russian chauvinist causes; and Vladimir Bryntsalov, a businessman who had made millions in the pharmaceuticals and vodka industries. Only the think-tank scholar Martin Shakkum, nominee of the tiny Party of Socioeconomic Reform, deserves to be categorized as totally obscure.

From the outset, publicity teams resorted unabashedly to the candidates' personas as selling aids. Television, radio, and newspaper clips, leaflets and posters—and, for the defender of the status quo, Yeltsin, sweetheart news coverage in state-owned and state-influenced media outlets—all were mobilized for the task. Commercials touting the *nouveau riche* Bryntsalov relied on flippant banter and slightly risqué sketches of him flirting with his expensively attired wife. For Vlasov, the hook was his glory days as a medal-winning athlete. Yavlinskii wooed voters with broadcast vignettes featuring babushkas in the countryside singing jingles about Yavlinskii that contained no political message whatsoever.[11] General Lebed's handlers blended televised shots of him in and out of mufti, mini-lectures on law and order, and witty asides with an anti-establishment bite: Lebed's giant build, baritone voice, and provincial looks added force and authenticity to these clever idioms.[12]

---

[10] Aleksandr Lebed, *Za derzhavu obidno . . .* (Moscow: Moskovskaya pravda, 1995); translated as *General Alexander Lebed: My Life and My Country* (Washington, D.C.: Regnery, 1997).

[11] Michael McFaul, *Russia's 1996 Presidential Election: The End of Polarized Politics* (Stanford, Calif.: Hoover Institution Press, 1997), p. 54.

[12] McFaul, *Russia's 1996 Presidential Election*, p. 53.

Even the peddlers of more ideological platforms pulled out the stops to humanize the outpourings of the candidates. A shirt-sleeved Zyuganov was filmed in the company of blue-collar workers, peasants, and pensioners—social groups he hoped to rally to his banner. To dull traditional anxieties that Communists would stifle religious freedom, he courted the votes of believers by appearing in photographs with Orthodox priests.[13] Yeltsin, his health temporarily on the mend, crisscrossed European Russia and Siberia with the Kremlin press corps and a squad of doctors in tow, shaking hands, kissing babies, disbursing petty favors to villagers, and gyrating on concert stages to the beat of local rock bands. In his memoir, he underscores the deft use of televised imagery in making his pitch. He recollects the glossy promotional series entitled "Vote With Your Heart":

Humble people were shown speaking on the television screen what they thought of me. Today it is difficult to imagine what an effect this had on the campaign. Interest in the president's personality rose. The people were surprised and started thinking. [They could see] how strong the contrast was between the image of the president that had developed and this summons. It was as if the voters had woken up. Sure, they could have wagered on Yavlinskii, Lebed, or Zhirinovskii. But were these candidates prepared to guarantee our welfare? Were they ready to protect people from our current social upheavals? Most likely not. And look at the new Yeltsin—he has come alive, he is up to something, so maybe we should bet on him again![14]

Personalization was not always calm and constructive. It took an especially incendiary tack in the Zyuganov campaign. Zyuganov's anti-Yeltsin propaganda, a biographer of Yeltsin writes, harped on contradictory themes, all of them exuding contempt for the president as an individual. Hundreds of anti-Yeltsin cartoons appeared daily in the popular democratic press. Yeltsin the candidate was depicted at once as a brazen liar, wily, brutal, and imperious—and as a sickly, drunken idiot, manipulated by his entourage.[15] With only the bland Zyuganov as a foil, Yeltsin strategists stuck mainly to swipes at the KPRF program and at what they portrayed as the party's intention to restore Soviet totalitarianism.[16]

Sizing up the Candidates

To say someone beamed such-and-such a signal at the electorate is not synonymous with saying the signal was received and internalized. On that subject,

---

[13] Stephen White, Richard Rose, and Ian McAllister, *How Russia Votes* (Chatham, N.J.: Chatham House, 1997), p. 257.

[14] Yeltsin, *Prezidentskii marafon*, p. 35.

[15] Leon Aron, *Yeltsin: A Revolutionary Life* (New York: St. Martin's Press, 2000), p. 609.

[16] The well-funded Yeltsin campaign actually did the most negative advertising in 1996. Of the respondents to our postelection survey (see Appendix) 30 percent reported encountering negative publicity materials. Of those, 84 percent said they saw anti-Zyuganov materials; 26 percent saw anti-Yeltsin materials.

the researcher cannot do without the testimony of the citizens themselves. What did Russians know and make of the pretenders to the presidency? While we cannot reprise how they reacted to particular cartoons, videos, or sound bites, we do have intelligence about their assessments of the candidates. A large-scale face-to-face survey of eligible voters with which I was associated, implemented in the weeks after the election (see the Appendix for details), posed candidate-centered questions of several kinds.

The first solicited comprehensive evaluations of all ten of the candidates. Respondents were asked to express their evaluations on a 101-degree feeling-thermometer with a midpoint of 50 degrees, patterned after the thermometer scale employed in the U.S. National Election Studies (NES).[17] Table 7.1 sets out the responses to this query. Most Russians in 1996, it is apparent, were well enough up to speed on the candidates to recognize their names and to offer net judgments of them. This is so notwithstanding the thronging field of contestants and the late exposure of a number of them to the national political audience. For each candidate on the first-round ballot slip, ranging in salience from the old hand Yeltsin at the upper end (who culled almost 27 million votes) to the novice Bryntsalov at the bottom end (with 127,000 votes), an average of nearly 90 percent of survey respondents recognized the politician and approximately three-quarters volunteered an evaluation of him on the feeling thermometer. For the five best-known candidates—Yeltsin,

Table 7.1. Citizen recognition and evaluation on a "feeling thermometer" of the ten Russian presidential candidates*

Candidate	Percent who recognize candidate	Percent who recognize and evaluate candidate	Mean feeling-thermometer rating (0 to 100)	Percent who give thermometer rating of 0
Boris Yeltsin	99	95	47	18
Gennadii Zyuganov	99	93	44	24
Aleksandr Lebed	98	91	56	7
Grigorii Yavlinskii	93	79	41	15
Vladimir Zhirinovskii	98	90	21	43
Svyatoslav Fëdorov	88	71	37	19
Mikhail Gorbachev	99	90	13	59
Martin Shakkum	61	41	14	59
Yurii Vlasov	64	43	17	48
Vladimir Bryntsalov	80	64	7	78
Average	88	76	30	37

*Total N = 2,472 weighted cases.

[17] Our thermometer has a scale from 0 to 100 degrees, where 0 degrees denotes that you very much dislike the given candidate, 50 degrees denotes that you like and dislike this candidate in equal measure, and 100 degrees that you like this candidate a great deal. The part of the scale from 0 to 50 degrees denotes that to a greater or lesser degree you dislike this candidate, and from 50 to 100 degrees it denotes that to a greater or lesser degree you like the candidate. Interviewers showed each respondent a picture of a thermometer with 0, 50, and 100 degrees marked.

Zyuganov, Lebed, Zhirinovskii, and Gorbachev—recognition levels were at 98 or 99 percent and evaluation levels hovered between 90 and 95 percent.

The approbation given the candidates ran a wide gamut. The average thermometer score for the best-regarded candidate in 1996 (Lebed, at 56 degrees) was eight times that imparted to the worst-regarded (Bryntsalov, at 7 degrees). Apart from the steep differences from candidate to candidate, the striking thing about column 3 is how low the troupe of candidates stood collectively in the public's esteem. Alone of the ten would-be presidents, the telegenic General Lebed made it over the 50-degree mark of indifference, and that by a scant 6 points. The mean thermometer rating dispensed was a miserly 30 degrees out of 100. Upwards of one-third of all evaluations came in at the worst possible grade—0 degrees (see column 4 of Table 7.1). Zero was the verdict rendered by more than 50 percent of our survey sample for three unlucky candidates (Gorbachev, Shakkum, and Bryntsalov) and by more than 40 percent for two others (Zhirinovskii and Vlasov).

If we juxtapose these scores to the results of the election, there is at first sight a certain rough justice to the comparison. The correlation (Pearson's r) between the mean score in Table 7.1's column 3 and the percentage of the aggregate vote harvested by the candidate in the qualifying round of the election is high ($0.71, p \leq 0.01$). There is no mistaking that the candidates afforded the lowest thermometer ratings in the postelection poll lagged in the vote tally on June 16 as well.

If we go on to line up respondents' thermometer scores with the voting choices they made as individuals, we detect a similar association. The scores conferred by respondents who actually voted for a given candidate are much loftier than those they give to the rest. The unweighted average across presidential candidates is 77 degrees on the thermometer for first-round supporters, or two-and-one-half times the sample mean (30 degrees) and triple the average score allotted to the candidates for whom a respondent did not vote (26 degrees).[18]

It is tempting to fasten on this association as proof of an iron link between candidate assessments and voting choice in 1996. But common sense and a reading of the comparative literature on political behavior hoist a pair of warning flags. One has to do with the breadth and vagueness of thermometer-type measures. In fixing the survey respondent's "like" and "dislike" of a candidate for public office, they may mix evaluations of the candidate *per se* with other attitudes that are for whatever reason intertwined with those sympathies. For example, a citizen's revelation that he likes Zyuganov could say

---

[18] Significant imbalances among the candidates linger for which I cannot account here. For nine of the ten candidates, the range of the thermometer scores ascribed to them by citizens who voted for the candidate was between 70 and 100 degrees (the exception was Shakkum, whose score was 52 points). For voters who voted for someone other than the candidate, the range was considerably wider—from a lowly 6 points (for Bryntsalov) to a high of 52 points (for Lebed).

as much about his opinion of the KPRF or the Soviet regime as of Zyuganov himself; likewise, a positive evaluation of Yeltsin might be shaded by admiration of the liberal political and economic reforms of the 1990s.

A second objection is that thermometer assessments can possibly be tainted by their cognitive proximity to the electoral choice. It is risky to peg the analysis on an association between two bits of information—how someone voted and her or his holistic feeling about the candidate voted for—which are gleaned in one and the same postelection interview. The hazard is of endogeneity, feedback from the act of voting onto attitudes that may have contributed to the citizen's decision.

Neither of these methodological hitches is crippling. So far as endogeneity is concerned, a glance back at Table 7.1 will certify that there is less than total equivalence between the blanket thermometer ratings and reported voting behavior. As mentioned above, the ranking of the average feeling-thermometer scores does split the minor from the major candidates. However, when it comes to the candidates who cleared 5 percent of the first-round popular vote— Yeltsin, Zyuganov, Lebed, Yavlinskii, and Zhirinovskii, who between them totaled 96.3 percent of the votes cast—the thermometer ranks them in the wrong order of finish. Had the feeling "temperatures" been nothing more than a reverse projection of citizens' political behavior, Boris Yeltsin, not Aleksandr Lebed, would have had the most stellar average score in our poll. Or, to state it from a different angle, had the thermometer scores been absolutely determinative of voting choice, the winner of the first round and in all probability of the entire election would have been Lebed, not Yeltsin. Lebed's average on the thermometer was nine points above Yeltsin's and twelve above Gennadii Zyuganov's, and yet Yeltsin amassed 21 percentage points more than the general in the vote on June 16 and Zyuganov 18 percentage points more.[19] Lower down on the list, it is noteworthy that the medical entrepreneur Svyatoslav Fëdorov gained a feeling-thermometer average of 37 degrees, within 10 degrees of Zyuganov and Yeltsin, but got all of 0.9 percent of the popular vote, scarcely eclipsing Gorbachev, Shakkum, Vlasov, and Bryntsalov.[20]

So far as the first criticism, the diffuseness of the thermometer scores, is concerned, an obvious remedy is to supersede them in analysis with better targeted assessments of the presidential candidates, bearing down on more specific aspects of their public personas. Fortunately, we wrote into the 1996 Russian survey questions that mitigate some of the shortcomings of the thermometer instrument. The inspiration was the battery of items, included in the American NES since 1980, which hinge on a construct of the ideal

---

[19] To put it yet another way, Yeltsin received about 568,000 popular votes for every degree he scored on average on the feeling thermometer. Zyuganov received about 550,000 votes for every degree, and Lebed about 196,000.

[20] This made Fëdorov's vote yield per average degree on the thermometer an abysmal 19,000 votes—about one-thirtieth the level of Yeltsin's.

president against which actual candidates might be measured.[21] By breaking candidate assessments down by discrete dimensions of character, this device to be both more accurate and also less vulnerable to being compromised by informants' voting preferences.

In the 1996 post election interview, the questionnaire inquired how Russians thought candidates stood up with respect to five desirable character attributes: intelligence ("an intelligent and knowledgeable person"); strength ("a strong leader"); integrity ("a decent and trustworthy person"); vision ("has his own vision of the country's future"); and empathy ("really cares about people like you"). Attitudes toward the candidates were put on a 4-point scale, with values for "No," "Probably no," "Probably yes," and "Yes." Interviewers asked the questions only about Yeltsin, Zyuganov, Lebed, Yavlinskii, and Zhirinovskii, the first five finishers in June 1996.

Table 7.2. Assessments of personality traits of five Russian presidential candidates*

Trait and assessment candidates	Yeltsin	Zyuganov	Lebed	Yavlinskii	Zhirinovskii	All candidates
Intelligence						
Percent able to answer	91	86	89	77	85	86
Mean score (scale 0 to 3)	1.89	2.20	2.48	2.43	1.49	2.10
Strength						
Percent able to answer	90	75	85	64	79	79
Mean score (scale 0 to 3)	1.51	1.77	2.46	1.41	1.25	1.68
Integrity						
Percent able to answer	80	73	82	62	72	74
Mean score (scale 0 to 3)	1.40	1.80	2.33	2.02	0.79	1.67
Vision						
Percent able to answer	87	81	81	70	80	80
Mean score (scale 0 to 3)	1.72	1.97	2.18	2.07	1.39	1.87
Empathy						
Percent able to answer	86	73	70	58	76	73
Mean score (scale 0 to 3)	1.04	1.55	1.94	1.53	0.67	1.35
All traits						
Percent able to answer	87	78	81	66	78	78
Mean score (scale 0 to 3)	1.51	1.86	2.28	1.89	1.12	1.73

*Total N = 2,472 weighted cases.

Table 7.2 maps citizen assessments of the personal traits of the star candidates. Ability to answer the trait-specific questions was rather less prevalent than it had been for the global thermometer ratings (nonresponses were on average 22 percent vs. an average of 10 percent unable to recognize and place the same five politicians on the thermometer). The assessments again cover an expansive spectrum. They are, on the whole, palpably less derogatory than the thermometer results. Translating the verbal responses into an equal-interval

[21] Warren E. Miller and J. Merrill Shanks, *The New American Voter* (Cambridge, Mass.: Harvard University Press, 1996), p. 416.

numerical scale from 0 to 3, the average assessment crops up at 1.73, or considerably above the midpoint of 1.50, whereas the average thermometer score for the same five candidates was 42 degrees, or well below the break-even point of 50 degrees. Only one of the principal candidates—Zhirinovskii, with a mean score of 1.12—has an average rating across the five attributes of below 1.5. Lebed as usual engenders the most flattering ratings, trailed by Yavlinskii, Zyuganov, and then President Yeltsin, with Zhirinovskii bringing up the rear. The fluctuation in the citizen-assigned scores across the trait items is less pronounced than it is across candidates, but again a definite *gestalt* can be spied. Russians in 1996 thought best of the presidential nominees' intelligence and worst of their empathy with people like themselves. Empathy, its average assessment 1.35, is the lone character trait for which the average evaluation dips under the midpoint.

Russians' stances on the distinct personality characteristics of politicians cannot be appreciated in isolation from one another. On the contrary, the evaluations are enmeshed in an elaborate lacework of associations. Trait-by-trait (see the upper panel of Table 7.3), there are compelling linkages among the ratings granted to each particular politician: the average inter-item correlation was 0.59 for the five spotlighted candidates in 1996. A citizen who was sure that Boris Yeltsin, say, was a decent and trustworthy leader was markedly more apt than the average respondent to go on to award Yeltsin high points for intelligence, strength, vision, and empathy. Presumably, the myriad associations across trait ratings echo a latent attitudinal factor—a kind of master evaluation of the named politician which finds an outlet, in amalgam with more particularized attitudes, in the evaluation of the specific traits. Over and above this commonality, the lower panel of Table 7.3 also demonstrates associations, albeit slender ones, among citizens' assessments of particular character traits across the field of politicians. Here, for instance, an individual who believed Yeltsin to be honest and trustworthy would be mildly more inclined than his peers to think generously of the integrity of all five candidates assayed. This finding hints at another subliminal factor, relating to the attractiveness of politicians in general. One duo—Yeltsin and Zyuganov, the gladiators at center ring—buck this generalization, in that the inter-item correlations are all negative, not positive. If we remove the Yeltsin–Zyuganov dyads, the average correlations for all five character traits increases, and the global average climbs from 0.15 to 0.19.

Added discussion along these lines would be in order if the goal were to probe grassroots estimations of politicians as such. But our objective is to harness the data about such sentiments to the explanation of voting. And here the finer-grained assessments of character traits encapsulated in Tables 7.2 and 7.3 raise some of the same questions as the feeling-thermometer indicators. They are superior in precision to the thermometer scores and hopefully not as susceptible to endogeneity bias. But, on the face of it, they get us no closer to decoding Russians' voting behavior. Truth is, the lineup

Table 7.3. Average inter-item correlations for leadership evaluations in Russia*

Candidate or character trait	Average correlation (Pearson's r)[†]
By candidate	
Yeltsin	0.65
Zyuganov	0.68
Lebed	0.55
Yavlinskii	0.54
Zhirinovskii	0.53
All candidates	0.59
By trait	
Intelligence	0.20
Strength	0.11
Integrity	0.08
Vision	0.22
Empathy	0.15
All traits	0.15

*Total N = 2,472 weighted cases.
[†] Missing values deleted pairwise.

of trait-based evaluations is *more at odds with the aggregate electoral results* than the ostensibly cruder thermometer ratings. In the vote standings after the first round, Yeltsin finished first, Zyuganov second, Lebed third, Yavlinskii fourth, and Zhirinovskii fifth. In survey respondents' assessments of the personality traits of these same candidates, the ordering, assigning all traits equal weight, is Lebed first, Yavlinskii second, Zyuganov a close third, Yeltsin fourth, and Zhirinovskii fifth. Yeltsin ranks a dreary fourth in appraisal of every one of the five personal characteristics. The discordance between the two rankings is a puzzle that only a more probing analysis can unravel.

Leadership Evaluations and the Vote

The most straightforward tactic for discovering the tie between leadership evaluations and civic behavior is to set one off against the other. Doing so for the 1996 Russian presidential vote and for the trait-specific candidate evaluations of individual survey respondents immediately unearths a correspondence of sorts. As an example, voters who answered a flat "No" to the query about Boris Yeltsin's integrity ultimately voted for the incumbent in the first round at a feeble rate of 6 percent, while for those who answered "Yes" the rate shot up to 72 percent. For the intelligence trait, first-round voting support of Yeltsin at the poles of the distribution was 5 percent and 57 percent; for strength of character, the ratios were 7 percent and 64 percent; for vision they were 6 percent and 61 percent; and for empathy they were 12 percent and

74 percent. On average, the gap in turnout for Yeltsin between those harboring the harshest and the most positive perception of him on a character attribute was 58 percentage points. A like tendency bears on all of the presidential candidates who accumulated more than 5 percent of the vote. The gulf in voting support separating unequivocal detractors ("No") from unequivocal devotees ("Yes") averaged 61 percentage points for Gennadii Zyuganov, 20 percentage points for Aleksandr Lebed, 23 points for Grigorii Yavlinskii, and 21 points for Vladimir Zhirinovskii. Beyond the general parallel, we are in the accustomed predicament of witnessing unexplained discrepancies among the candidates. Votes for the political heavyweights Yeltsin and Zyuganov seem to be much more sensitive to personality evaluations than for the eight lightweights knocked out in the qualifying round.

Taking Third Variables into Account

Any attempt to identify in rigorous fashion any syndrome of character-centric voting requires us to ask how much of the revealed association bespeaks a genuine relationship and how much is a mirage, a spurious relationship masking the deep-seated influence of other causal factors. As discussed above, amorphous feeling-thermometer scores may in some proportion reflect other attitudes; moving to trait-based indicators should lessen the problem yet will not necessarily lay it to rest. Moreover, other variables may be related to the behavioral outcome, and not only to assessments of candidates' characters. Omit those third variables from the exercise, and, insofar as they correlate significantly with leadership evaluations and with voting choice, any deductions made about the impact of leadership evaluations on the vote will be biased.

Commentary on mass politics in the post-Communist societies of Europe and Eurasia often implies that the menu of influences on their newly enfranchised citizenry is sparse. We have speculated about leadership evaluations being of exaggerated importance in Russians' voting decisions, by dint of the possible unimportance of rival considerations like partisan loyalties and issue preferences. But the relevance or irrelevance of such considerations to political action cannot be established *a priori*. It must be validated through painstaking empirical investigation, measurement, and estimation, informed but not dictated by theory. My own research on Russia's transitional electorate suggests that, far from operating in a vacuum, its members respond to a great many political inputs.[22] No study of leadership effects on voting will be sustainable, therefore, unless it acknowledges the possibility of multiple influences.

Table 7.4 illustrates the point. It crosses measures of a handful of attitudinal variables with character assessments of the four leading candidates, taking the

---

[22] I develop this argument at length in Timothy J. Colton, *Transitional Citizens: Voters and What Influences Them in the New Russia* (Cambridge, Mass.: Harvard University Press, 2000).

Table 7.4. Leadership evaluations and first-round voting choice, classified according to response to selected attitudinal questions

Attitudinal variable	Candidate			
	Yeltsin	Zyuganov	Lebed	Yavlinskii
Mean evaluation of candidate's integrity (scale of 0 to 3)*				
National economic trend in past year				
Much worse	0.79	2.14	2.09	1.92
Slightly worse	1.31	1.85	2.22	1.94
No change	1.64	1.64	2.46	2.12
Slightly or much better[†]	2.12	1.11	2.62	2.07
Partisanship				
NDR	2.33	1.25	2.61	1.98
KPRF	0.65	2.64	2.06	1.90
KRO	1.50	2.00	2.88	2.06
Yabloko	1.68	1.20	2.35	2.59
Nonpartisan	1.49	1.64	2.37	2.00
Best political system for Russia				
Unreformed Soviet system	0.77	2.41	2.11	1.87
Current political system	2.10	1.17	2.50	2.09
Western democracy	1.75	0.31	2.53	2.19
Approval of Yeltsin's performance as president				
Completely disapprove	0.29	2.30	1.83	1.83
Disapprove	0.62	2.20	2.18	1.87
Approve some, disapprove some	1.72	1.59	2.45	2.12
Approve	2.43	1.19	2.50	2.06
Completely approve	2.70	0.88	2.51	1.95
Percent who vote for the candidate in first round[‡]				
National economic trend in past year				
Much worse	16	50	19	8
Slightly worse	29	34	19	10
No change	42	23	20	9
Slightly or much better[†]	70	6	13	6
Partisanship				
NDR	88	1	10	0
KPRF	4	89	5	1
KRO	12	0	81	6
Yabloko	33	1	4	61
Nonpartisan	41	21	23	9
Partisan of KPRF				
Yes	4	89	5	10
No	41	22	20	10
Best political system for Russia				
Unreformed Soviet system	10	67	14	4
Current political system	67	4	16	9
Western democracy	48	8	20	15
Approval of Yeltsin's performance as president				
Completely disapprove	4	66	15	7
Disapprove	5	59	19	10
Approve some, disapprove some	43	19	22	10
Approve	81	3	7	6
Completely approve	96	0	2	0

*Total $N = 2,472$ weighted cases. Cell Ns vary by question.

[†] Categories collapsed because there are so few responses (eleven) in the "much better" category.

[‡] Participating voters only. Total $N = 2,013$ weighted cases. Cell Ns vary by question.

integrity trait as a case in point, and with respondents' voting choices in June 1996. (For economy's sake, I disregard the fifth-finishing Vladimir Zhirinovskii here and in the subsequent discussion. He did not differ a lot from his fellow nationalist, Aleksandr Lebed, in programmatic orientation, and had very few supporters in our survey sample.)[23]

For Yeltsin and Zyuganov, there are solid associations in both spheres. Respondents who believed in 1996 that the national economy was healing, who were partisans of the pro-Kremlin NDR movement, who preferred the current political system to the Soviet regime, or, notably, who spoke well of Yeltsin's performance in his first term were by hefty margins more liable than others to cede Yeltsin high marks and Zyuganov low marks for integrity. The flip side of the coin is that persons for whom the Russian economy was going downhill, who were KPRF partisans, who were partial to a Soviet-type political system, or who frowned upon Yeltsin's conduct in office were much more inclined to say Yeltsin was dishonest and untrustworthy and to salute Zyuganov's qualities in that regard. As is vital to our concerns, the same sorts of association pertain on the voting front: optimism about economic trends, support for NDR, a preference for the current political order, and approval of Yeltsin's work as president comport with a first-round vote for Yeltsin; it is the converse for Zyuganov. For the third- and fourth-ranking candidates, Lebed and Yavlinskii, the relationships are murkier, and yet even here there are some regularities, notably for partisanship (in favor of KRO for Lebed, in favor of Yabloko for Yavlinskii) and for the nature of the political system.

Modeling the Phenomenon

When potent multilateral associations tie in citizen assessments of a politician's character to other political attitudes and to the act of voting, it is inadmissible to leap to conclusions about electoral consequences that fail to take on board the potential role of those corollary attitudes. We know that in 1996 Russian electors who were convinced that Yeltsin was a conscientious and trustworthy leader were more apt than others to acquiesce in his reelection. But we also know that those same voters by and large adopted an upbeat view of the economy, did not have a partisan attachment with the KPRF, preferred the contemporary political regime to the Soviet dictatorship, and approved of Yeltsin's actions as president. That being so, the autonomous electoral effect of appraisals of Yeltsin's integrity can be disentangled only through multivariate analysis in which appropriate statistical controls for the confounding variables are put in place. To deal with the complexity and

---

[23] Exclusion of variables and variable categories specific to Zhirinovskii makes a next to imperceptible difference to the analysis of other candidates and is immaterial to the conclusions drawn. Fewer than 4 percent of our survey respondents who voted reported choosing him in the first round. Yeltsin, Zyuganov, Lebed, and Yavlinskii supporters came to 93 percent of the participating voters in our sample.

interconnectedness of the attitudes and behavior under scrutiny, the model utilized must have multiple layers or stages.

As in other work, I adapt to Russian conditions the multistage model of electoral behavior delineated in Warren E. Miller and J. Merrill Shanks' *The New American Voter*, the culmination of two generations of electoral research in the United States.[24] The causal sequence I assume to apply has a family resemblance to the sequence postulated in *The New American Voter* but also departs from it in ways that accommodate core realities of a post-Communist country, typified by messy and half-completed transformations of its political, economic, and social arrangements and practices. Following Miller and Shanks, I locate leadership evaluations well along in the causal flow and thus prone to be influenced by a plenitude of causally prior variables. I assume that the social characteristics of the Russian voter enter the chain of causality, climaxing in the vote, as its first link and so must be invoked as controls for the analysis of all subsequent stages; the citizen's perceptions of current economic and also political conditions in the country join the equation at a second stage; normative opinions on public issues and transitional partisanship, nascent attachments to political parties, come in conjointly at a third stage; retrospective assessments of the performance of incumbent office-holders (president and prime minister) at the fourth stage; evaluations of the personalities of candidates, the crux of this chapter, at the fifth stage; and prospective evaluations of the candidates' eventual actions in elected office at the sixth and final stage.[25]

The estimation of influences on the vote in Russia is hugely more complicated than in a Western setting. The difficulties begin with proper specification of the dependent and independent variables. In most mature democracies that directly elect their head of state, calibrating the outcome poses no great dilemma: either there are two or three candidates, typically all party nominees, or, if there are more, they can conveniently be arrayed along a well-understood continuum such as a left–right scale.[26] Russian voters have been

---

[24] See especially Colton, *Transitional Citizens*. Leadership evaluations are discussed in chap. 6 of that book.

[25] The most perplexing question regarding this sequence is about the relationship between partisanship and leadership evaluations. It is more troubling than usual in the analysis of Russian parliamentary elections, where parties are more central to the process, but even there I would stand by the model as the best we can do at our present state of knowledge. It is impossible to adjust the causal sequence *ad hoc* from one party or leader to the next, since effects on the behavioral outcome must be estimated in a single overarching model. See the discussion in Timothy J. Colton, "Parties, Leaders, and Voters in the Parliamentary Election," in Vicki L. Hesli and William M. Reisinger, eds., *Elections, Parties and the Future of Russia* (Cambridge: Cambridge University Press, forthcoming). In our 1996 postelection survey, 31 percent of Russian voters qualified by my standards as "transitional partisans," that is, they identified one party or quasi-party as "my party" or said there was a party which better than the others reflected their "interests, views, and concerns." More than two-thirds of the electorate must be considered nonpartisan at the time, which would be inordinately high in most Western democracies.

[26] This is nimbly done for French presidential elections in Roy Pierce, *Choosing the Chief: Presidential Elections in France and the United States* (Ann Arbor: University of Michigan Press, 1995).

confronted by a welter of candidates who defy classification on any consensual scale. Hence the necessity of constituting the dependent variable as discrete, nonordered categories. For the analysis I report here, the categories represent a first-round vote for Yeltsin, for Zyuganov, for Lebed, for Yavlinskii, or, as a fifth possibility, for any other candidate or against all the candidates; in the runoff, the categories represent a vote cast for Yeltsin, for Zyuganov, or against both. In terms of independent variables, analysis of citizen perceptions of candidates' character traits is snarled by the sheer profusion of candidates in a Russian election. To check singly for the electoral import in June–July 1996 of each of the personal attributes about which we know something would eat up twenty degrees of statistical freedom—five attributes × four candidates. Not wanting to overload the model, and mindful of the correlations among scores for particular traits, I have combined the information about the perceived characteristics of every candidate into a composite four-point index. It is coded as the mean of the scores the respondent assigned each candidate for intelligence, strength, integrity, vision, and empathy, rounded off to the nearest integer.

Estimating Leadership Effects

Table 7.5 lays out some results of a multistage statistical analysis of the 1996 vote for the four top candidates for president. The estimation was generated by multinomial logit, a maximum-likelihood method well suited to analyzing the determinants of categoric dependent variables that are nonorderable and discrete.[27] The raw regression coefficients are of no substantive interest and are hypersensitive to specification of the contrast category. The parameters listed are estimated first differences in the predicted probability of the respective voting outcomes prevailing that I have obtained, along with confidence intervals, from a statistical simulation.[28] Each first-difference estimates the change in the predicted probability of the citizen voting for the candidate in question that is associated with a change in the independent variable from its minimum to its maximum value, holding the specified control variables constant at their medians. Independent variables in the model influence the dependent variable directly and indirectly, via other variables intermediate between them and the dependent variable. When, for any independent variable, the controls encompass all causal variables that are causally prior to and

[27] For succinct descriptions of multinomial logit, see J. Scott Long, *Regression Models for Categorical and Limited Dependent Variables* (Thousand Oaks, Calif.: Sage, 1997), chap. 6, and G. S. Maddala, *Limited-Dependent and Qualitative Variables in Econometrics* (Cambridge: Cambridge University Press, 1986), chap. 2. Sample means (weighted for household size—see the Appendix) have been substituted for missing values on the attitudinal variables.

[28] One thousand simulations were done for each estimation, using Michael Tomz, Jason Wittenberg, and Gary King, "CLARIFY: Software for Interpreting Statistical Results, Version 1.2.2" (Cambridge, Mass.: Harvard University, March 3, 2000—at http://king.harvard.edu). CLARIFY is used in conjunction with the STATA package.

simultaneous with the quantities of interest, I refer to the measure of effect, again borrowing from Miller and Shanks, as the "total effect" of the independent variable, "an approximation of the overall extent to which differences between voters on that variable were in fact responsible for 'producing' differences between them in their vote."[29]

The statistics in the first row of Table 7.5 recapitulate the bivariate relationship between the explanatory variable (the summary leadership evaluation) and the behavioral outcome (the probability of voting for the candidate named in the column heading). Parameters in consecutive rows of the table estimate the independent variable's impact as variables in the various stages of the model are introduced into the logit estimation one bloc at a time. The total effects occupy the row in bold typeface, second from the bottom. Residual effects, measuring the personality effects that survive once all variables in the model have been assimilated, are in the last row of the table. Table 7.5 records only those effects on the vote that spring directly from the category of the dependent variable to which the column is dedicated. Column 1, for instance, estimates the influence of evaluations of Yeltsin's character on

Table 7.5. Elaboration of the impact of evaluations of the leadership qualities of the candidates on the Russian presidential vote[†]

Variables progressively incorporated in regression	First round[‡]				Runoff[§]	
	Yel.	Zyug.	Leb.	Yav.	Yel.	Zyug.
Bivariate—summary evaluation of the given candidate only	0.69**	0.69**	0.20**	0.26**	0.82**	0.78**
Multivariate—summary evaluation of the candidate, controlling progressively for:						
Social characteristics	0.73**	0.58**	0.21**	0.23**	0.83**	0.74**
Also current conditions	0.62**	0.61**	0.25**	0.26**	0.76**	0.78**
Also partisanship (but not issue opinions)	0.60**	0.45**	0.28**	0.23**	0.71**	0.68**
Also issue opinions (but not partisanship)	0.60**	0.46**	0.26**	0.28**	0.66**	0.58**
Also partisanship and issue opinions	0.58**	0.35**	0.28**	0.24**	0.62**	0.50**
Also retrospective evaluations of incumbents	0.43**	0.27**	0.25**	0.20**	0.30**	0.33**
Also other candidates[¶]	**0.49**	**0.28**	**0.28**	**0.19**	**0.36**[‖]	**0.32**[‖]
Also prospective evaluations of candidates	0.38**	0.21**	0.16**	0.10*	0.22**[‖]	0.24**[‖]

** $p \leq 0.01$
* $p \leq 0.05$
† Differences in predicted probabilities.
‡ Sample $N = 1,990$.
§ Sample $N = 1,937$.
¶ Bold typeface shows the total effect of leadership qualities.
‖ Two finalists only.

[29] Miller and Shanks, *The New American Voter*, p. 196. Miller and Shanks used linear regression to estimate their total effects, a statistical method that would be out of place in the study of Russian voting.

the first-round vote for Yeltsin; effects on the Yeltsin vote of opinions of Zyuganov, Lebed, and Yavlinskii were computed but are not recited here.[30]

The key estimates of influence in Table 7.5 are the total effects, controlling for the confounding influences of causally antecedent or concurrent determinants. All things being equal, the analysis verifies that the citizen who adhered to the most favorable net evaluation of a presidential candidate's personal qualities was more apt to vote for that candidate in the first round in 1996. The effects of character assessments are *sizable* and they are *asymmetrical*. They ranged in round one from 0.16 (16 percentage points) in the instance of Grigorii Yavlinskii to 0.49 (49 percentage points) for Boris Yeltsin. Gennadii Zyuganov and Aleksandr Lebed both exhibit total effects of 0.28 (28 percentage points), just below the middle of the domain bounded by Lebed and Yavlinskii. In the winner-takes-all second round, the magnitude of the total effect declines by about one-quarter for Yeltsin (from 0.49 to 0.36) and rises a modicum for Zyuganov (from 0.28 to 0.32).

Differences Across Candidates

Clearly, then, public impressions of the candidates' personal characteristics mattered in the molding of the support base of all four of the candidates. Equally clearly, they mattered more for some candidates than for others. The president's self-congratulatory claim in his memoirs that the image of "the new Yeltsin" spun by his campaign advisors "woke up" the electorate turns out to be not so bad a précis of the reality. Yeltsin truly was the prime beneficiary of the personalization of the 1996 Russian campaign. Unlike a simple twinning of candidate appraisals and voting choice, we have our hands here on measures of independent effects, purged of the effects of third variables that happen to be associated with candidate evaluations and the vote. To the extent that candidate evaluations are derivatives of other variables, the inclusion of those variables as controls in the model should have eliminated the confounding effects. We can rest assured, for example, that the revealed association between evaluations of Zyuganov and the likelihood of voting for him is not just an offshoot of KPRF partisanship or of disapproval of Yeltsin's accomplishments as president.

Row-wise comparisons in Table 7.5 round out the picture. Among other things, they show character assessments of Yeltsin and Zyuganov exerting exactly equal effects on the first-round vote when the analysis takes a bivariate form. As other variables fold sequentially into a multivariate analysis, the observed impact of character evaluations on the vote for Zyuganov drops about twice as fast as with the Yeltsin vote, so that by the total-effect stage it is considerably smaller than for Yeltsin. For Yavlinskii, the bivariate starting

---

[30] Typically, these effects are negatively signed and smaller in magnitude than the effects for the candidate to whom the column is dedicated.

point is much lower than it is for Yeltsin or Zyuganov, but the decline in apparent impact is less abrupt. For Lebed, we have a curious twist: in the bivariate estimation, the influence of character assessments ranks lowest of any of the four candidates, but by the all-important total-effect stage it has swelled modestly to the point where it is dead even with the effect observed for Zyuganov. In the runoff round between Yeltsin and Zyuganov, there are no egregious differences, as we run an eye down Table 7.5, in the starting and end points of the estimates.

The row-to-row differences in Table 7.5 let us make inferences about causal pathways to the vote. The larger the difference in the predicted probability of voting for a candidate from one row to the next, the more we can impute differences in voting behavior to divisions on the bloc of explanatory variables that is injected into the estimation at that stage. The row-wise disparities, and taken together the disparities between the first (bivariate) and the seventh (total-effects) row, indicate the degree to which assessments of the candidates' personal qualities mediate between other variables and Russians' voting decisions in 1996.

For Yeltsin, the most precipitous decline in predicted probabilities in both the first round and the runoff materializes when retrospective evaluations of his presidential record and of the Russian government are incorporated into the model. What this means is that candidate evaluations in 1996 were transmitting the background effects of evaluations of incumbents more than those of any other variables. For Zyuganov, partisanship and issue opinions figure more prominently in the story, but the main thing is how massive the cumulative decline in the apparent influence of evaluations of leadership qualities is for the runner-up in the election. More than any of his opponents, citizen assessments of Zyuganov's character are freighted with *other* meaning. Once these anterior influences—for perceptions of current conditions, partisanship, issue opinions, and evaluations of incumbents—are filtered out of the estimation, our measure of the total effect of the personality factor on the Zyuganov vote comes out just around the average for the foursome of candidates. For Lebed, as we have said, the momentum is gently in the opposite direction. Evaluations of his leadership qualities were *not* systematic proxies for other attitudes, as they were in part for Yeltsin, Zyuganov, and Yavlinskii. That is why controlling for cognate variables does not deflate estimates of the electoral effect of evaluations of Lebed's personality. General Lebed is from this angle the closest thing to a purely personalist candidate in 1996—the man on horseback who promised the nation only himself.

The candidates can be differentiated along one more axis. Recall that our omnibus indicator of the candidate's character, like the trait-specific measures from which it stems, has four values. The total effects register the difference brought about by hiking the character evaluation from its very lowest level ("No") to its very highest level ("Yes"). They do not specify which particular

Table 7.6. Decomposition of total effects of evaluations of the leadership qualities of the candidates on the Russian presidential vote[†]

Change in value of summary evaluation	First round[‡]				Runoff[§]	
	Yel.	Zyug.	Leb.	Yav.	Yel.	Zyug.
"No" to "Probably no"	0.13**	0.02**	0.03**	0.00**	0.18**	0.01**
"Probably no" to "Probably yes"	0.17**	0.06**	0.08**	0.02**	0.12**	0.07**
"Probably yes" to "Yes"	0.18**	0.20**	0.17**	0.16**	0.07**	0.24**

**p ≤ 0.01
[†]Differences in predicted probabilities.
[‡]Sample $N = 1,990$.
[§]Sample $N = 1,937$. Considers the personal qualities of the two finalists only.

step or steps within the amplitude of the character measure, if any, are most pertinent to the voting choice. As can be seen in Table 7.6, these step effects are anything but homogeneous.

Two divergent configurations are manifest. In the first, evinced by Zyuganov, Lebed, and Yavlinskii, there is a tidy progression from a very small effect for the first increment through to a large effect at the last step. Voters were not much aroused by poor or mediocre assessments of these candidates. It pretty well took the exuberance connoted by an absolute "Yes" to coax a citizen to vote for any of the three. For Yeltsin, though, the cognitive mechanism was very dissimilar. In the first round, the effect of a shift from the iciest average rating of the president's personal qualities ("No") to the next rating up (the still chilly "Probably no") far outstrips what we discern for the other candidates. The same holds for the ensuing shift in attitude (from "Probably no" to the warm "Probably yes"). At the last stage, the values for Yeltsin (for the shift from "Probably yes" to the very warm "Yes") are about on a par with Zyuganov, Lebed, and Yavlinskii. In the runoff, Yeltsin and Zyuganov could not have cast more different shadows. For Zyuganov, as in the first round, the only displacement in attitude that begets a large difference in the likelihood of voting for him (0.24 out of the total effect of 0.32) is the switch from "Probably yes" to "Yes." For Yeltsin, half of the total effect (0.18 out of 0.36) originates in the shift from "No" to "Probably no" and another third (0.12 out of 0.36) in the shift from "Probably no" to "Probably yes."

All of which is to say that in 1996 Russian voters set the character bar lower for the winner, Boris Yeltsin, than they did for his challengers. Unqualifiedly friendly feelings were needed to spur a vote for the other candidates; for the sitting president, a notch or two above outright animosity was frequently good enough. This information puts in perspective the much-ballyhooed miracle of Yeltsin's political comeback. So far as we can say that his political resurrection was manufactured through the media-promoted inflation of his personal reputation, the crucial achievement was in dampening rancor toward him, not in instilling affection or enthusiasm.

Differences Across Voters

Throughout this chapter we have spoken sweepingly about the median Russian voter. As a final pass at the problem, let us leave the median voter behind and ask if personalistic considerations contributed more to the decisions of certain voters than they did to others. Of special interest to ascertain would be if the effect that perceptions of the candidate's character have on behavior is modulated by the citizen's prior political orientation. Would the electoral choices of people already amenable to one of the candidates in the race be less governed by their assessments of the candidate's character than those of the average citizen? Or might the relationship be the reverse, so that citizens who otherwise leaned toward a candidate would be influenced more, not less, by the personality factor? The first hypothesis posits personal magnetism as a substitute for nonpersonal sources of electoral preference; the second sees it as a complement to them.

We can glimpse the possibilities by referring to one concrete attitude we know was correlated with voting preference in 1996—approval of Boris Yeltsin's performance in his first term as president. In general, the more Russians approved of the incumbent's record, the more probable it was that they would vote to reelect him to a second term. The simulation described in Table 7.7 shows how those approving or disapproving opinions in turn conditioned the way character evaluations of the candidates made themselves felt. With some caveats, the data point persuasively to a *complementary* relationship.

The total-effect parameters for all four leading candidates in the first round and for Zyuganov in the second round vary systematically with the level of approval of the president's record. For Zyuganov in the first round, for example, the total effect of the evaluation of his character on the chances of voting for him grows steadily from 0.08 for citizens who fully approve of Yeltsin's performance in office (and who *ceteris paribus* would have preferred to vote for Yeltsin) to 0.46 among those who completely disapprove

Table 7.7. Total effects of evaluations of the leadership qualities of the candidates on the Russian presidential vote, by approval of Yeltsin's performance as president[†]

Approval of Yeltsin's performance as president	First round[‡]				Runoff[§]	
	Yel.	Zyug.	Leb.	Yav.	Yel.	Zyug.
Completely disapprove	0.22**	0.46**	0.38**	0.24**	0.44**	0.69**
Disapprove	0.37**	0.39**	0.35**	0.23**	0.50**	0.53**
Approve some, disapprove some	0.49**	0.28**	0.28**	0.19**	0.36**	0.31**
Approve	0.49**	0.16**	0.19**	0.14**	0.19**	0.14**
Completely approve	0.38**	0.08**	0.11**	0.08**	0.08**	0.06**

**p ≤0.01.
[†] Differences in predicted probabilities.
[‡] Sample N = 1,990.
[§] Sample N = 1,937. Considers the personal qualities of the two finalists only.

of Yeltsin's performance (whose inclination for extraneous reasons would have been to vote for Zyuganov). In the second round, the range for Zyuganov is almost identical—from 0.08 to 0.44. Lebed and Yavlinskii exhibit the same relationship in diluted form, with a range from 0.11 to 0.38 for Lebed and from 0.08 to 0.24 for Yavlinskii. In other words, for the foremost challengers to Yeltsin, electoral responsiveness to the citizen's estimation of the candidate's personal qualities is anywhere from three to nearly six times more among persons who are extremely critical of the president's record than among those who are extremely satisfied with it.

For Yeltsin in the first round the logic is the same, only this time with the estimated effect of character assessments going up as the citizen's evaluation of Yeltsin's performance improves, in keeping with the predilections of the electorate. Notice the slump in the total effect on the Yeltsin vote in the last two rows of column 1. That diminution brings out the major qualification that has to be lodged here: namely, that the estimated effects of leadership evaluations—and indeed in principle of any explanatory variable—will taper off if and when the predicted probability of the base category for the estimation attains high values (it will asymptotically approach a predicted probability of 1). With all the control variables held constant at their median values, with attitude toward Yeltsin's presidential performance set at "Approve," and with evaluation of Yeltsin's leadership qualities set at its minimal level, the probability of the citizen voting for Yeltsin in the first round would have been 0.53. The maximum change a shift in the evaluation of Yeltsin's qualities to its maximum level could have induced would accordingly have been 0.47 (1 minus 0.53). The 0.38 value in the bottom cell of column 1 falls somewhat short of that limit. In the second round, this syndrome besets the Yeltsin vote with a vengeance. The total effect of leadership evaluations on the vote for the incumbent peaks at 0.50, in the "Disapprove" category. By the time we are in the "Approve some, disapprove some" zone, the predicted probability of voting for the president even for the citizen with the most negative possible assessment of his personal qualities has soared to 0.56. At successive stages, that value reaches 0.78 and 0.91, leaving precious little latitude within which character assessments can play a causal role.[31]

Conclusions

Exhausted by his last campaign, Boris Yeltsin was stricken by a near-fatal heart attack on the night of June 25–26, 1996, the week after the first round of the election. The severity of his illness kept secret from them, the voters

---

[31] A similar asymptotic effect can be brought out experimentally for other categories of the dependent variable, most readily by simultaneously altering the values of more than one independent variable.

trooped to the polls in the runoff, on July 3, to give him his coveted triumph over Gennadii Zyuganov.[32] Submitting to heart bypass surgery that autumn, Yeltsin never returned to form. His second term as president was sullied by frequent hospital stays, palace intrigues, and cabinet shuffles, and in 1998 by a collapse of the ruble and default on Russia's foreign debt. Yeltsin resigned on December 31, 1999, a half-year before expiry of his mandate. He turned the reins over to a handpicked successor, Vladimir Putin, who exploited a second war over Chechnya to swiftly build a reputation as a worthy leader for the new century.

In the 1996 election, the first to be waged in transitional Russia since the rupture with Soviet Communism, images of the personal traits of the candidates were a common thread in the public campaign. Election advertising was often highly personalized in style and content, even for those candidates, like Yeltsin and Zyuganov, who made value-laden, ideological appeals to the people. These seeds fell on fertile soil in the private world of the citizen. Russian voters were well informed about the candidates and quite capable of expressing discriminating opinions about them in survey interviews. A scale constructed from appraisals of each candidate's intelligence, honesty, integrity, vision, and empathy proves to be a strong predictor of electoral preference in the first and second rounds of the vote.

The behavioral effects of personality assessments we have estimated and interpreted in the framework of an intricate motivational process involving a multitude of explanatory variables. Controlling for causally antecedent and concurrent variables, the chances of a citizen voting for any one candidate rose, in round numbers, by between 20 and 50 percentage points if he or she held the most favorable possible impression of that politician's character, as opposed to the least favorable. The relevance of leadership evaluations varied from one candidate to the next and from one citizen to the next. Yeltsin got more of a boost from character assessments than the opposition, mostly because Russians gauged him by a uniquely indulgent yardstick. Perceived personal qualities had their heaviest influence on the calculus of decision when they augmented other considerations that already prejudiced a voter in a candidate's favor. Their impact was lightest when they had to work against the grain of such considerations.

The individual-level analysis of the vote does not, however, single out the personality component as having decisively determined the outcome of the election saga. It is hard to conceive of any candidate for a major governmental office being as unloved as Yeltsin was in 1996 and still getting within hailing distance of a win. The only credible counterfactual scenarios for the election involve Yeltsin radiating a better, not a worse, popular image—in which event his edge over Zyuganov, Lebed, and the also-rans would have

---

[32] Ignoring his doctors' advice, Yeltsin limped into a polling station to vote for himself on the morning of July 3. Film was immediately broadcast on national television.

been greater than it was factually, not less. Yeltsin, it is fair to say, won reelection in spite of his personality, not because of it. Had his personal qualities been swapped with those of his most crowd-pleasing rival, Aleksandr Lebed, his lead at the finish line would have been even longer than it was.

Nothing in the experience of 1996 indicates that personalized campaigning and, inasmuch as we saw it with Yeltsin and his foes, personalized voting will subside in Russian mass politics any time soon. If anything, the electronic marketing of candidate images stands to gain in professionalism and sophistication. Putin's one-round victory in March 2000 showed once again the advantages of incumbency and, this time, administered a lesson in how governmental control of news programming and the skillful engineering of newsworthy events themselves could, when tethered to an attractive candidate, sway the electorate. The growth of alternative foci for civic choice—such as partisan identification and more coherent debates over economic and social issues—will alter the context within which political personalities seek to market themselves and their wares. But, rather than squeezing out personalized images, the evolving transitional environment may well bestow on them more opportunities to flourish and, in combination with reinforcing attitudes, to shape citizen conduct.

Appendix

An account of the face-to-face panel survey on which the analysis rests is available in Timothy J. Colton, *Transitional Citizens: Voters and What Influences Them in the New Russia* (Cambridge, Mass.: Harvard University Press, 2000), Appendix A. The survey was designed and executed by the author, by William Zimmerman of the University of Michigan, and by Russian colleagues in the Demoscope group at the Institute of Sociology of the Academy of Sciences, headed by Polina Kozyreva and Mikhail Kosolapov, in association with Michael Swafford. Funding was provided by the Carnegie Corporation of New York and the John D. and Catherine T. MacArthur Foundation.

The survey had three waves—one before the State Duma election of December 17, 1995, a second after it, and a third after the runoff round of the presidential election, held on July 3, 1996. The attitudinal measures utilized here were collected in the third wave; the demographic data used in the statistical analysis was mostly plucked in the first wave. Three-quarters of the third-wave interviews were completed by August 1 and the rest by mid-September. Of the 2,841 panelists interviewed in the first wave, 2,776 were reinterviewed in the second wave and 2,456 in the third. These are high reinterview rates by Western standards, but such results were attainable in Russia in the 1990s when interviewers were properly trained and supervised.

Respondents were selected in a multistage area-probability sample of the voting-age population, with sampling units in thirty-three regions of the Russian Federation. Substitutions in the field for designated members of the panel were prohibited. To correct for the over-representation of individuals in small households brought about by the sampling procedure, all univariate and bivariate statistics are weighted by the number of adults in the dwelling unit. The weights are not invoked in the multivariate analysis.

Full descriptions of the variables used in the regression analysis may be found in Colton, *Transitional Citizens*. The model of the 1996 presidential vote comprises fourteen sociodemographic indicators, four assessments of current economic and political conditions, eight dummy variables for partisanship, ten issue opinions, and two evaluations of incumbents. For the first round of the presidential election, the model also incorporates evaluations of the personal characteristics of the four leading candidates and prospective evaluations of their likely performance in office. For the runoff round, this information is included for the two finalists only.

8

Conclusions and Implications

ANTHONY KING

It is time to remind the reader what this book has—and has not—been about. It has not been about political leadership in general or about the relationship between political leadership and individual political leaders' personalities. In particular, it has not been about the electoral impact that party leaders and presidential candidates may well have as a result of their impact on their parties or governments. It has therefore had little to say about such phenomena as François Mitterrand's success in establishing the Socialists as the dominant party on the French left in the 1970s, or about Margaret Thatcher's ideological reorientation of the British Conservative Party in the 1980s, or about Bill Clinton's impact on the Democratic Party in the United States in the 1990s. All of these developments were of crucial significance. All made possible electoral outcomes that would almost certainly otherwise not have occurred. All owed much to the personalities of the three individuals referred to. But they are not what this book has been about.

Rather, our focus has been on the impact that leaders' personalities and other personal traits may have from time to time, not on their parties or governments but on individual voters' willingness to vote for them and consequently on the outcomes of the elections that they contest. The line of argument usually runs: (1) voters have likes and dislikes of leaders and candidates; (2) on the basis of those likes and dislikes, voters form overall evaluations of leaders and candidates; (3) voters' overall evaluations of leaders and candidates have a considerable bearing—perhaps a decisive bearing—on how they actually vote. The line of argument then usually continues: (4) because voters' overall evaluations of leaders and candidates have a considerable bearing on the votes of individuals, they also, therefore, often have a bearing on the outcomes of whole elections.

It should be obvious that no one disputes the truth of proposition (1). Most voters, of course, have likes and dislikes of the leaders and candidates whom the main political parties present them with. To be sure, a very few eligible voters are completely closed off from the entire political process and scarcely know the names of their national leaders, let alone have strong (or even weak) views about them. But the great majority of citizens in established democracies do know the names of the leaders of the major political parties and do have views about them. It was a very rare American who had no views about Bill Clinton in the 1990s or who had no views about George W. Bush in the early 2000s. It was, likewise, a very rare Briton who had no views about Tony Blair or his various Conservative opponents from 1994 onward. If casual observation were not thought sufficient to establish this point, then testimony is readily available from mountains of academic survey data and data from the commercial opinion polls. Almost without exception, top political leaders are seriously famous people.

Nor does anyone dispute the truth of proposition (2). People not only have likes and dislikes of political leaders: They use those likes and dislikes to form overall judgments of them. Those judgments may be simple and positive: "I think Bush is a great leader." They may be simple and negative: "Gore is too much of an egg-head to be effective." Or they may contain both positive and negative elements, with either the positive or the negative preponderant: "I wish Bush were brighter, but in the end he really does speak for people like me." Survey data again testify to the prevalence of such overall evaluations; and both political scientists and psychologists have devoted much effort—with some success—to trying to sort out the cognitive and affective processes that go into the formation of these evaluations.

But it is at stages (3) and (4) of the argument that dubiety enters in—or, rather, should enter in—because it does not follow from the fact that people have likes and dislikes of political leaders, and on the basis of those likes and dislikes form overall evaluations of them, that those evaluations will necessarily have a decisive influence on how they vote. They may, or they may not. Moreover, as we have repeatedly insisted, even if they do influence the voting behavior of individuals, they may, or they may not, have that influence on a suffcient scale and with sufficient lopsidedness to determine the overall outcome of any particular election. These points need to be emphasized, if only because considerable numbers of academic researchers take the truth of propositions (3) and (4) for granted and, on that (unquestioned) basis, proceed to devote much time and energy to exploring the psychodynamics associated with propositions (1) and (2). Our purpose in this volume has been, instead, to refuse to take propositions (3) or (4) as read but to try to decide whether, and under what circumstances, each of them is true or not.

As must be evident from the preceding chapters, this testing of propositions (3) and (4) took place without prejudice. There was no intention to confirm or disconfirm the truth of either of them. The intention was merely to subject both of them to the most rigorous empirical tests that could be devised. Our expectation, in so far as we had one, was that sometimes leaders and candidates would prove to have been decisive and that sometimes they would not. If that proved to be the case, the issue would then be one of determining what kinds of circumstances affected the scale, or lack of it, of party leaders' and candidates' personal influence.

It goes without saying that, at one level, the focus of this book has been quite narrow. If it had been a book about Winston Churchill, it would have said nothing about Churchill's wartime leadership, nothing about his decision under pressure to hold a general election before the end of World War II in 1945 and nothing at all about the reforms that his colleagues instituted in the Conservative Party following its 1945 defeat. Its focus would have been exclusively on Churchill's personal appeal to the voters in the three elections he fought as Conservative leader: on his reputation as a great wartime leader, on his inimitable rhetoric, on his famous cigars, and on his V-for-victory sign. Similarly, the treatment of Bill Clinton in the preceding pages has by no stretch of the imagination constituted an in-the-round survey of Clinton's presidency or even of Clinton the New Democrat and skilled (or was he?) political campaigner. Much, we happily acknowledge, has been omitted here.

Yet the narrow focus of this book seems to us to be justified. The fact is that most citizens, most journalists, and, so it would seem, most academic political scientists believe that leaders' and candidates' personalities and personal traits are enormously important in democratic elections and that very often they turn out to be decisive. They believe—although they might not put it quite like this—that whether people see Al Gore as a Volvo or a Maserati affects whether millions of Americans vote Democratic or Republican and that whether William Hague and his wife, Ffion, do or do not manage to have a baby affects whether millions of Britons are or are not prepared to vote Conservative. Most people do not advance a self-consciously "personalist" theory of elections and election outcomes. Rather, they take personalism for granted. Moreover, belief in the personalist theory, as we remarked in Chapter 1, affects whom the parties choose as their leaders and candidates, how those leaders and candidates campaign, and how, if they win, they go on to govern. In other words, the subject of this book may be narrow, but it is hardly trivial.

But is the personalist theory true? Each of the contributors to this volume has sought to answer that question for one specific country with respect to the years or decades during which good data have been available for providing an answer. Each of the contributors' chapters speaks for itself.

However, in the spirit of adventure, and eschewing the usual academic caution, Table 8.1 sets out the editor's best estimate of which elections over the past four decades in each of our six countries have, and have not, been decided by voters' comparative evaluations of the main political parties' leaders, chancellor-candidates, and presidential candidates. The estimates are based on all the available academic literature, not just on the chapters in this volume. And they are the editor's own; the other contributors to this volume are in no way implicated. Specialists on each country are free to contest, on the basis of the best evidence available to them, any or all of the estimates offered. Indeed, they are cordially invited to do so.

Table 8.1. Estimates of whether or not leaders' personalities and other personal characteristics determined election outcomes

	United States	Great Britain	France	Germany	Canada	Russia
1960	No					
1961				No		
1962					(No data)	
1963					(No data)	
1964	No	Yes				
1965			Yes	No	*Possibly*	
1966		No				
1967						
1968	No				Yes	
1969			*Probably*	No		
1970		*No*				
1971						
1972	No			*Probably*	No	
1973						
1974		Yes (Feb)/No (Oct)	*Possibly*		*Possibly*	
1975						
1976	No			No		
1977						
1978						
1979		No			No	
1980	No			No	No	
1981			No			
1982						
1983		No		No		
1984	No				No	
1985						
1986						
1987		No		No		
1988	No		No		No	
1989						
1990				No		
1991						
1992	No	*Probably*				
1993					No	
1994				No		
1995			*Possibly*			
1996	No					No
1997		No			No	
1998				*Possibly*		
1999						
2000	*Probably*					*Possibly*
2001		No			No	

Note that the emphasis in Table 8.1 is not on whether individuals' votes were swayed in either small or large numbers (in many cases, perhaps most, they were) but on whether such vote-swaying as took place influenced the overall outcome of that election, in the sense of influencing which party or candidate actually won. The estimates take into account voters' overall evaluations of, and preferences for, the principal leaders and candidates in comparison to one another. And they are based on an implicit counterfactual.

They compare each actual election outcome with what the outcome of that election would have been if the leaders and candidates of the main parties had been, in terms of their personalities and other personal characteristics, complete blanks: that is, if they had not existed at all as distinct human beings and if voters had been required, therefore, to make their decisions on the basis of solely impersonal criteria. Putting the same point another way, the table is based on the counterfactual notion that the main parties' leaders and candidates were, in personality and trait terms, clones, unable to be distinguished one from another.

Still in the spirit of adventure, the estimates in the table try as far as possible to eschew over-cautious responses. In other words, they would rather be wrong than safe. The question is: At this particular election in this particular country, were the principal candidates' personalities and other personal traits decisive? And in the great majority of cases, as can be seen, the answer given is either a blunt "Yes" or a blunt "No." Only in a few cases, where there must be a large element of doubt, have the cautious words "Probably" and "Possibly" been allowed to intrude. The period covered is 1960–2001. The elections covered are presidential elections in the United States, France, and, more recently, Russia, and national parliamentary elections in Great Britain, Germany (West Germany till reunification), and Canada.

What do the estimates in the table suggest? Before we address that question directly, comments on a few detailed points are probably in order. With respect to the United States, some non-American readers may be startled to see it categorically denied, in the left-hand column, that personal factors determined the outcome of the 1960 presidential election—the election in which John F. Kennedy narrowly defeated Richard M. Nixon. Surely, it may be protested, Kennedy owed his victory precisely to his youth, charm, and elegance compared with Nixon's five-o'clock shadow and generally shiftly demeanor? The answer is: No, he did not. Kennedy won because he was the Democratic Party's candidate in a year when the Democrats were almost certainly going to regain the White House anyway, not least because a substantial plurality of American voters were Democratic party identifiers. If anything, Kennedy as an individual was a handicap to his party. As a Catholic, he cost the Democrats substantial numbers of votes, mostly among southern Protestants.

With respect to Great Britain, some non-British readers may similarly be startled to see it denied, equally categorically, that Margaret Thatcher's personal qualities made a decisive contribution to the Conservative Party's victories in 1979, 1983, and 1987. Surely people at those elections voted in their millions for the Iron Lady, the woman of steely conviction, the United Kingdom's veritable queen-empress? The answer, again, is: No, they did not. In 1979, when Thatcher was still leader of the opposition, her personal standing trailed behind that of the incumbent prime minister, James Callaghan. In 1983 and 1987, she was, indeed, held in higher personal esteem than either of her successive Labour rivals—Michael Foot in 1983 and Neil Kinnock in 1987—but, given the then state of the British Labour Party, the Conservatives would have won those elections under almost anyone. Thatcher's personal ascendancy over her rivals contributed, at most, to the sheer scale of her party's victories. In connection with Great Britain, the double entry for 1974 should probably also be explained. Because, following the general election of February 1974, no party controlled a majority of seats in the House of Commons, another election was held in October of the same year.

It is harder to say anything definite about a number of France's presidential elections. In the first place, there have been so few of them (only six since 1960 compared with eleven presidential elections in the United States and eleven general elections in Britain); and, in the second place, the history of academic survey research has been much patchier in France than in most of the countries we have covered (with no ongoing national election study on the model of those in the United States, Britain, and Germany). This second factor is the main explanation for the fact that there are more tentative judgments in the French column than in any other. What does seem to be clear is that the formidable presence of Charles de Gaulle made all the difference in the 1965 election.

The single most striking detail with regard to Germany is the coincidence of Helmut Kohl's electoral success—or, more precisely, the CDU/CSU's electoral success under his leadership—with Kohl's personal unpopularity. A plurality of Germans voted for his party, but they neither liked him nor greatly respected him. As with Margaret Thatcher in Britain, he owed his apparent success, not to voters' fondness for him as a politician or human being but to the weakness of the opposition and (more in Germany than in Britain) to the strength of the nation's economy during his period in office. An economic downturn in the late 1990s, together with the emergence of a more formidable personal rival in Gerhard Schröder, precipitated his political demise.

As in the case of France, firm conclusions about the role of party leaders in federal elections in Canada are somewhat inhibited, at least until the mid 1960s, by the absence of systematic, longitudinal survey data. Hence the "No data" entries in the Canadian column, the second from the right. Nevertheless, it would appear on the face of it that, contrary to the conventional wisdom among Canadian political observers and political scientists, the only election whose outcome in recent times probably turned on the relative merits of the rival party leaders was that of 1968, when the evidence suggests that the personal appeal of the Liberal leader, Pierre Trudeau, may well have tipped the balance in the Liberals' favor.

With regard to Russia, it goes without saying that, as there are no established norms in that country, each of the two presidential elections held there so far has to be considered largely in its own terms. There being no central tendency, there can be no outliers. Even so, it is striking that in 1996 Boris

Yeltsin won despite the fact that Aleksandr Lebed, one of his several opponents, was personally far more highly esteemed (Yeltsin finished first in the preliminary round, Lebed third). Vladimir Putin appears to have owed his victory in 2000 partly to his own personal appeal but mainly to his status as the incumbent president and to his ability, as president, to exploit the Russian state apparatus, including the state-controlled and state-influenced media, to his own electoral advantage.

But these are details. The remarkable thing about the estimates in Table 8.1 is that, taken as a whole, they suggest that, far from being normal, it is quite unusual for leaders' and candidates' personalities and other personal traits to determine election outcomes—not rare, but unusual. In other words, if the estimates in the table are broadly correct, the almost universal belief that leaders' and candidates' personalities are almost invariably hugely important factors in determining the outcomes of elections is simply wrong. Leaders' and candidates' personal characteristics usually count for something— of course they do—but not for nearly as much as is generally supposed. A traditional piece of lore thus turns out to be folklore, unable to withstand scientific inquiry.

Approximately four dozen elections are covered in the table. Of these, it is possible to say in the cases of scarcely more than a handful that their outcomes definitely or probably turned on voters' differing perceptions of the personal qualities and traits of the principal party leaders and candidates. As can be seen, the "No"s in the table overwhelm the "Yes"s. In the great majority of cases, the winning party would have won anyway, even if its leader or candidate had been no more highly regarded than his or her principal opponent. In some cases, the winner was actually *less* highly regarded than his or her principal opponent. Winning parties and candidates win for all kinds of reasons. Only very occasionally do personal factors of the kind discussed endlessly in newspapers and focus groups, and around fashionable dinner tables in Georgetown, Westminster, and the Fifth Arrondissement, turn out, in fact, to be decisive.

Two other features of the table are worth noting. One is the close similarity between the estimates for the United States and those for Germany. The United States is a country led by a single, highly visible individual, the president. It is also supposed to be a country characterized by both weak party organizations and weak (and weakening) party ties among voters. By contrast, Germany is a country led by a single chancellor, certainly, but a chancellor who functions as the head of a parliamentary-style cabinet that is, moreover, almost invariably a coalition cabinet. Germany is also supposed to be a country characterized by strong party organizations and still strong (though somewhat weakened) party ties. Yet the personal characteristics of presidential candidates and chancellor-candidates seem to count for little in both countries—or at least usually seem to count for little. Clearly there is a paradox here, one in need of resolution.

The other feature of the table worth noting—one consistent with the findings for Germany emphasized in Chapter 5—is that there has been absolutely no discernible change through time. It is very widely believed that, with the advent in recent decades of television, opinion polls, focus groups, political consultants, and modern marketing techniques, politics in every country has become more personalized, both in the sense that parties and candidates campaign in a more leader-centered manner and in the sense that voters increasingly respond to the messages transmitted by election campaigns that are conducted in this manner. The estimates in Table 8.1 do not speak to the question of how parties and candidates campaign, but they do speak to the question of voters' responses, and they contain precious little evidence that voters are responding to campaigns in increasingly leader- or candidate-centered terms. On the contrary, there is somewhat more evidence of leader-centered voting—or at least of leader-centered voting's being decisive—in the 1960s and 1970s than in more recent decades.

Nevertheless, the table suggests that there *are* some elections in which the leaders' and candidates' personalities and other personal traits *have* proved decisive. What have been the distinguishing features of those elections?

In Chapter 1, it was hypothesized that, other things being equal, the impact of leaders would be at its greatest when large numbers of voters perceived large differences between the competing leaders' or candidates' leadership-related characteristics. Clearly other things are often far from equal. In 1983 in Great Britain, for example, large numbers of voters perceived very large differences between the leadership-related characteristics of the Conservative prime minister, Margaret Thatcher, and the Labour opposition leader, Michael Foot. Foot's perceived ineptitude undoubtedly cost the Labour Party votes; but, even so, his ineptitude and Thatcher's undoubted leadership qualities did not determine the outcome of that election. The Conservatives won and Labour lost principally because the British economy in 1983 was recovering rapidly from a deep recession and because the Labour Party's policies that year were such as positively to deter voters from voting Labour (one wag, a Labour member of Parliament, dubbed Labour's 1983 election manifesto "the longest suicide note in history").

That said, most of the elections whose outcomes have apparently been determined by voters' judgments of the leaders' personalities have also witnessed large discrepancies between the rival leaders' personal standings. In Britain, Labour's Harold Wilson easily trumped the Conservative Party's leaders in both 1964 and February 1974. In France in 1965, the personal qualities of Charles de Gaulle, wartime hero and savior of the nation, trumped by a wide margin those of the then unknown left-wing candidate, François Mitterrand. Much the same applies to Georges Pompidou versus Alain Poher in France in 1969, to Willy Brandt versus Rainer Barzel in Germany in 1972, to Pierre Trudeau versus Robert Stanfield in Canada in 1974 and to John Major versus Neil Kinnock in Britain in 1992. The obvious, but important, exception is George W. Bush versus Al Gore in the United States in 2000. As Larry Bartels shows in Chapter 2 of this volume, neither man in 2000 enjoyed anything remotely approaching a personal ascendancy over the other, but that election was so close in every respect that any factor, including any personality factor, that worked in George W. Bush's favor, could have made, probably did make, the crucial difference.

It scarcely needs repeating that, as was also hypothesized in Chapter 1, extremely close elections are much more likely than landslides and foregone conclusions to be decided by personality factors. Such elections are much more likely to be decided by *any* factor. Sheer closeness was clearly the critical element in George W. Bush's defeat of Al Gore (or, if one prefers, in Gore's defeat of Bush) in the United States in 2000; and the elections in Britain that were definitely or probably decided by personality factors after 1960—those of 1964, February 1974, and 1992—were three of the four closest elections fought during that period. The 1972 election in Germany was similarly the only election during the past four decades at which the margin of second votes separating the CDU/CSU and the SPD was less than a single percentage point. By contrast, the 1965 and 1969 presidential elections in France were not especially close, and the personality factor will have to have played an unusually prominent role if it is to have determined the outcome of either of those elections. The pattern in Canada is unusually complicated, with apparently only a loose relationship between the role of leaders' personalities in election outcomes and the closeness of those outcomes.

The other hypotheses advanced in Chapter 1 relate to the political parties themselves and to voters' ties to them. One possibility is that the importance of leaders' personalities and personal characteristics will be at its maximum when voters' emotional ties to the parties are at their weakest—that is, either when levels of party identification are low across the electorate and/or when those voters who do identify with a political party do so only weakly. The other possibility, consistent with the first, is that voters are more likely to cast their ballots on the basis of the leading candidates' personalities and other attributes if they are unable to discern any other grounds—whether of policy or performance—for making their electoral choice. To use the phrase previously used in Chapter 1, leaders' and candidates' personalities under those circumstances may function as a sort of "tie-break." These two possibilities, especially the first, have been touched on frequently in these pages, but we have not set out to pursue either of them systematically.

At this point, social scientists, including political scientists, typically—and, it must be said, rather lamely—call for "more research." On this occasion, however, there is no need to *call* for more research: The need for it—both for original investigations and for the reanalysis of existing data—is obvious, especially given the central importance of the subject. How could students of voting behavior, not to mention their graduate students, possibly resist such a challenge?

Before they respond to it, however, we need to introduce a number of additional elements of complexity. Identifying genuine leader effects is not easy. No one ever said it was. Perhaps that is why so few political scientists have attempted the feat (in addition, of course, to the fact, of course, that many of them appear to have thought they knew the answers already).

One additional complication, especially in those parliamentary systems that still employ the traditional Anglo-American simple-plurality electoral system, is the disjunction that may well exist between winning votes and winning seats in parliament. Throughout most of this book, we have been able to identify the winner at every election without great difficulty. One party gains more votes than any other. As a result, that party gains more parliamentary seats than any other. But of course votes may not translate so neatly into seats. We said earlier that Harold Wilson and the Labour Party "won" the February 1974 election; and they did indeed win in the sense of gaining more seats in parliament than any other party. But not only did they not gain a majority of seats, they did not gain as many votes as the Conservatives, who "lost." In Canada in 1979, the Liberals led the Progressive Conservatives by more than 4 percentage points in terms of the popular vote, but the Conservatives gained more than twenty seats more than the Liberals in the House of Commons. Any attempt to assess the role that personality factors have played in determining who won any given election needs to address beforehand the question of what "victory" means for these purposes.

An additional and more important complication concerns the disjunction that often exists in parliamentary systems between votes and seats, on the one hand, and the party or parties that subsequently form the government, on the other. We have already noted one instance in the case of Germany, where in 1969 the CDU/CSU led by Kurt-Georg Kiesinger won both more votes and more parliamentary seats than the SPD led by Willy Brandt but where the SPD went on to form the government in association with the minority Free Democrats. In that case, as would normally happen in Germany, although the SPD on its own was outvoted and gained fewer seats in the Bundestag than the CDU/CSU, the SPD and the Free Democrats together did win a plurality of votes and an absolute majority of seats. Countries in which there is a disjunction between vote-winning at elections and the process of government-formation following elections are common on the continent of Europe (Israel is another instance) and, once again, anyone interested in assessing the political impact of party leaders' personal characteristics needs to decide in advance what "victory" means in these kinds of contexts. Decisions can, of course, be made, but they need to be made explicit.

The final complication worth remarking on has already been referred to by Richard Johnston in Chapter 6. Throughout this book, except in Chapter 6, we have focused exclusively, in connection with every election, on which party or candidate came first and on which party or candidate came second. But, of course, as Johnston points out, voters' judgments of the various party leaders in a multiparty system could determine which of a pair of parties came second or third and which of a pair of parties came third or fourth—and whatever rank-ordering emerged could then, in turn, have important implications both for immediate government-formation and for the longer-term structure of the entire party system in the country in question. Even in a presidential system, if three or more candidates run in an election and the third-placed candidate gains a substantial vote, it is open to ask whether or not that person's vote tipped the balance between the first- and second-placed candidates; and it is always possible that the third-placed candidate owed his or her relative success to personality factors. Ross Perot in the United States in 1992 and Ralph Nader in 2000 are potential cases in point. That possibility is another that has not really been addressed here.

These complications aside, it is the core finding of this book that, at least in the six countries covered here, personality factors determine election outcomes far less often than is usually, indeed almost universally, supposed. If this finding is correct, and it probably is, then it has implications not only for further research but for the practice of politics in most, perhaps all, democratic countries. It means, to be blunt, that a lot of political consultants and image-makers, especially those who work at the national level, are wasting their own time and their employers' money. It means, more importantly, that political parties choosing leaders and candidates should ask themselves less often "How will he or she go down with the electorate?" and more often "How will this person's policies and general political outlook go down with the electorate?" The evidence from all of our countries suggests that issues of performance and issues of policy loom much larger in most voters' minds than do issues of personality—always, of course, subject to the caveat that the leader or candidate must be at least minimally presentable. Nothing said here should be taken as giving political parties a license to choose clowns, incompetents, or criminals.

One final point must certainly be made. A group of political scientists has, it seems, discovered that the personalities of leaders and candidates matter a lot less, and a lot less often, in elections than is usually supposed. But the same group of political scientists has also observed that sometimes, against the trend, leaders' personalities and other personal characteristics do matter: that they can on occasion affect election outcomes decisively. And, of course, it is crucially the case that real-world politicians and their advisors can never know for certain, in advance, which those against-the-trend elections will be. To say, in retrospect, that the outcome of a particular election did not turn on the rival candidates' personalities and personal characteristics is not the same thing as having said, in prospect, that it was definitely, for sure, not going to do so. Like historians, political scientists need to get it right only after the event; politicians and their advisors need to get it right ahead of time. It follows that the practical implication to be drawn from this book is not that political parties can afford to be careless about the people they choose as their leaders. It is, more narrowly, that they would be well advised to focus more on potential leaders' probable impact on their party or government—that is, on their indirect electoral effects—and less on their immediate "voter-appeal"—that is, on their direct electoral effects. Modern elections, despite what is often said and written about them, are only very seldom beauty contests; witness the large numbers of media-friendly, telegenic, and allegedly charismatic candidates who fall by the wayside, not least in primary elections in the United States. Modern elections remain overwhelmingly *political* contests, and political parties would do well to choose their leaders and candidates in light of that fact.

SELECT BIBLIOGRAPHY

Needless to say, large numbers of books and articles on voting behavior contain brief passages on the electoral effects of leaders' personalities and other personal characteristics. This bibliography includes only books, chapters, and articles that deal mainly or extensively with this subject (or, in some instances, with the related but separate subject of how voters evaluate candidates and leaders).

Robert P. Abelson, Donald R. Kinder, Mark D. Peters, and Susan T. Fiske, "Affective and Semantic Components in Political Person Perception," *Journal of Personality and Social Psychology*, 42 (1982), 619–30.

John Bartle, Ivor Crewe, and Anthony King, "Was It Blair Who Won It? Leadership Effects in the 1997 British General Election." Paper presented to the Annual Meeting of the American Political Science Association, Washington, D.C., August 28–31, 1997.

Clive S. Bean, "Political Leaders and Voter Perceptions: Images of Muldoon and Rowling at the 1975 and 1978 New Zealand General Elections," *Political Science*, 32 (1980), 55–75.

Clive Bean, "The Electoral Influence of Party Leader Images in Australia and New Zealand," *Comparative Political Studies*, 26 (1993), 111–32.

Clive Bean and Jonathan Kelley, "Partisan Stability and Short-term Change in the 1987 Federal Election: Evidence from the NSSS Panel Study," *Politics*, 23 (1988), 80–94.

Clive Bean and Anthony Mughan, "Leadership Effects in Parliamentary Elections in Australia and Britain," *American Political Science Review*, 83 (1989), 1165–79.

Richard A. Brody, "Candidate Evaluations and the Vote: Some Considerations Affecting the Application of Cognitive Psychology to Voting Behavior," in Richard R. Lau and David O. Sears, eds., *Political Cognition* (Hillsdale, N.J.: Lawrence Erlbaum Associates, 1986).

Richard A. Brody and Benjamin I. Page, "Indifference, Alienation and Rational Decisions: The Effects of Candidate Evaluations on Turnout and the Vote," *Public Choice*, 15 (1973), 1–17.

J. Andrew Brown, "The Major Effect: Changes in Party Leadership and Party Popularity," *Parliamentary Affairs*, 45 (1992), 545–64.

Steven D. Brown, Ronald D. Lambert, Barry J. Kay, and James E. Curtis, "In the Eye of the Beholder: Leader Images in Canada," *Canadian Journal of Political Science*, 21 (1988), 729–55.

David Butler and Donald Stokes, *Political Change in Britain: The Evolution of Electoral Choice*, 2nd edn. (London: Macmillan, 1974), chap. 17.

Harold D. Clarke, Jane Jenson, Lawrence LeDuc, and Jon H. Pammett, *Political Choice in Canada* (Toronto: McGraw-Hill, Ryerson, 1979).

Harold D. Clarke and Marianne C. Stewart, "Economic Evaluations, Prime Ministerial Approval and Governing Party Support: Rival Models Considered," *British Journal of Political Science*, 25 (1995), 145–70.

Harold D. Clarke, Karl Ho, and Marianne C. Stewart, "Major's Lesser (Not Minor) Effects: Prime Ministerial Approval and Governing Party Support in Britain since 1979," *Electoral Studies*, 19 (2000), 255–73.

Pamela J. Conover, "Political Cues and the Perception of Candidates," *American Politics Quarterly*, 9 (1981), 427–45.

Pamela Johnston Conover and Stanley Feldman, "The Role of Inference in the Perception of Political Candidates," in Richard R. Lau and David O. Sears, eds., *Political Cognition* (Hillsdale, N.J.: Lawrence Erlbaum Associates, 1986).

Ivor Crewe and Anthony King, "Are British Elections Becoming More 'Presidential'?" in M. Kent Jennings and Thomas E. Mann, eds., *Elections at Home and Abroad: Essays in Honor of Warren E. Miller* (Ann Arbor: University of Michigan Press, 1994).

Ivor Crewe and Anthony King, "Did Major Win? Did Kinnock Lose? Leadership Effects in the 1992 Election," in Anthony Heath, Roger Jowell, and John Curtice, eds., *Labour's Last Chance? The 1992 Election and Beyond* (Aldershot, Hants.: Dartmouth, 1994).

Roseanne Foti, S. Fraser, and R. Lord, "Effects of Leadership Labels and Prototypes on Perceptions of Political Leaders," *Journal of Applied Psychology*, 67 (1982), 326–33.

Michael M. Gant and Dwight F. Davis, "Negative Voter Support in Presidential Elections," *Western Political Quarterly*, 37 (1984), 272–90.

Michael M. Gant and Lee Sigelman, "Anti-Candidate Voting in Presidential Elections," *Polity*, 18 (1985), 329–39.

Brian Graetz and Ian McAllister, "Popular Evaluations of Party Leaders in the Anglo-American Democracies," in Harold D. Clarke and Moshe M. Czudnowski, eds., *Political Elites in Anglo-American Democracies* (DeKalb, Ill.: Northern Illinois University Press, 1987).

Brian Graetz and Ian McAllister, "Party Leaders and Election Outcomes in Britain, 1974–1983," *Comparative Political Studies*, 19 (1987), 484–507.

Richard Johnston, André Blais, Henry E. Brady, and Jean Crête, *Letting the People Decide: Dynamics of a Canadian Election* (Stanford, Calif.: Stanford University Press, 1992), chap. 7.

Philip Jones and John Hudson, "The Quality of Political Leadership: A Case Study of John Major," *British Journal of Political Science*, 26 (1996), 229–44.

Max Kaase, "Is There Personalization in Politics? Candidates and Voting Behavior in Germany," *International Political Science Review*, 15 (1994), 211–30.

Stanley Kelley, Jr., *Interpreting Elections* (Princeton, N.J.: Princeton University Press, 1983).

Stanley Kelley, Jr. and Thad W. Mirer, "The Simple Act of Voting," *American Political Science Review*, 68 (1974), 572–91.

Donald R. Kinder, "Presidential Character Revisited," in Richard R. Lau and David O. Sears, eds., *Political Cognition* (Hillsdale, N.J.: Lawrence Erlbaum Associates, 1986).

Donald R. Kinder, Mark D. Peters, Robert P. Abelson, and Susan T. Fiske, "Presidential Prototypes," *Political Behavior*, 2 (1980), 315–37.

Hans D. Klingemann and Charles Lewis Taylor, "Partisanship, Candidates and Issues," in Max Kaase and Klaus von Beyme, eds., *Elections and Parties*, German Political Studies, Vol. 3 (London: Sage, 1978).

Hans-Dieter Klingemann and Martin P. Wattenberg, "Decaying Versus Developing Party Systems: A Comparison of Party Images in the United States and West Germany," *British Journal of Political Science*, 22 (1992), 131–49.

Richard R. Lau, "Negativity in Political Perception," *Political Behavior*, 4 (1982), 353–77.

Richard R. Lau, "Political Schemata, Candidate Evaluations, and Voting Behavior," in Richard A. Lau and David D. Sears, eds., *Political Cognition* (Hillsdale, N.J.: Lawrence Erlbaum Associations, 1986).

Milton Lodge and Kathleen M. McGraw, eds., *Political Judgment: Structure and Process* (Ann Arbor: University of Michigan Press, 1995).

Matthew Mendelsohn, "The Media's Persuasive Effects: The Priming of Leadership in the 1988 Canadian Election," *Canadian Journal of Political Science*, 27 (1994), 81–97.

Arthur H. Miller and Warren E. Miller, "Ideology in the 1972 Election: Myth or Reality—A Rejoinder," *American Political Science Review*, 70 (1976), 832–49.

Arthur H. Miller, William M. Reisinger, and Vicki L. Hesli, "Leader Popularity and Party Development in Post-Soviet Russia," in Matthew Wyman, Stephen White, and Sarah Oates, eds., *Elections and Voters in Post-communist Russia* (Cheltenham: Edward Elgar, 1998).

Arthur H. Miller, Martin P. Wattenberg, and Oksana Malanchuk, "Schematic Assessment of Presidential Candidates," *American Political Science Review*, 80 (1986), 521–40.

Warren E. Miller and J. Merrill Shanks, "Policy Directions and Presidential Leadership: Alternative Interpretations of the 1980 Presidential Election," *British Journal of Political Science*, 12 (1982), 299–356.

Warren E. Miller and J. Merrill Shanks, *The New American Voter* (Cambridge, Mass.: Harvard University Press, 1996), chap. 15.

Anthony Mughan, "Party Leaders and Presidentialism in the 1992 Election: A Post-War Perspective," in David Denver, Pippa Norris, David Broughton, and Colin Rallings, eds., *British Elections and Parties Yearbook, 1993* (Hemel Hempstead, Herts.: Harvester Wheatsheaf, 1993).

Anthony Mughan, *Media and the Presidentialization of Parliamentary Elections* (Basingstoke, Hants.: Palgrave, 2000).

Richard Nadeau and André Blais, "Explaining Election Outcomes in Canada," *Canadian Journal of Political Science*, 26 (1993), 775–90.

Roy Pierce, *Choosing the Chief: Presidential Elections in France and the United States* (Ann Arbor: University of Michigan Press, 1995).

Wendy M. Rahn, John H. Aldrich, Eugene Borgida, and John L. Sullivan, "A Social-Cognitive Model of Candidate Appraisal," in John A. Ferejohn and James H. Kuklinski, eds., *Information and Democratic Processes* (Urbana, Ill.: University of Illinois Press, 1990).

Richard Rose and Ian McAllister, *The Loyalties of Voters: A Lifetime Learning Model* (London: Sage Publications, 1990).

Shawn W. Rosenberg, Lisa Bohan, Patrick McCafferty, and Kevin Harris, "The Image and the Vote: The Effect of Candidate Presentation on Voter Preference," *American Journal of Political Science*, 30 (1986), 108–27.

Jerrold G. Rusk and Herbert F. Weisberg, "Perceptions of Presidential Candidates: Implications for Electoral Change," *Midwest Journal of Political Science*, 16 (1972), 388–410.

David Sanders, "Forecasting the 1992 British General Election Outcome: The Performance of an 'Economic' Model," in David Denver, Pippa Norris, David Broughton, and Colin Rallings, eds., *British Elections and Parties Yearbook, 1993* (Hemel Hempstead, Herts.: Harvester Wheatsheaf, 1993).

J. Merrill Shanks and Warren E. Miller, "Policy Direction and Performance Evaluation: Complementary Explanations of the Reagan Elections," *British Journal of Political Science*, 20 (1990), 143–235.

J. Merrill Shanks and Warren E. Miller, "Partisanship, Policy and Performance: The Reagan Legacy in the 1988 Election," *British Journal of Political Science*, 21 (1991), 129–97.

Lee Sigelman and Michael M. Gant, "Anticandidate Voting in the 1984 Presidential Election," *Political Behavior* 11 (1989), 81–92.

David K. Stewart and R. K. Carty, "Does Changing the Party Leader Provide an Electoral Boost? A Study of Canadian Provincial Parties: 1960–1992," *Canadian Journal of Political Science*, 26 (1993), 313–30.

Marianne C. Stewart and Harold D. Clarke, "The (Un)Importance of Party Leaders: Leader Images and Party Choice in the 1987 British Election," *Journal of Politics*, 54 (1992), 447–70.

Donald E. Stokes, "Some Dynamic Elements of Contests for the Presidency," *American Political Science Review*, 60 (1966), 19–28.

John L. Sullivan, John H. Aldrich, Eugene Borgida, and Wendy Rahn, "Candidate Appraisal and Human Nature: Man and Superman in the 1984 Election," *Political Psychology*, 3 (1990), 459–84.

Angelika Vetter and Oscar W. Gabriel, "Candidate Evaluations and Party Choice in Germany, 1972–94: Do Candidates Matter?" in Christopher J. Anderson and Carsten Zelle, eds., *Stability and Change in German Elections: How Electorates Merge, Converge, or Collide* (Westport, Conn.: Praeger, 1998).

Martin P. Wattenberg, *The Rise of Candidate-Centered Politics: Presidential Elections of the 1980s* (Cambridge, Mass.: Harvard University Press, 1991).

Herbert F. Weisberg and Jerrold G. Rusk, "Dimensions of Candidate Evaluation," *American Political Science Review*, 64 (1970), 1167–85.

INDEX

All references to election dates unless otherwise indicated are to presidential elections in the United States, France, and Russia, to federal elections in Germany and Canada, and to general elections in Great Britain.